# Edexcel GCSE

# Business:

## Business Communications

### Student Book

Andrew Ashwin • Nicola Walker

PEARSON

# Acknowledgements

Pearson Education Limited
Edinburgh Gate
Harlow
Essex
CM 20 2JE
England
© Pearson Education 2009

The right of Nicola Walker and Andrew Ashwin to be identified as the authors of this work has been asserted by them in accordance with the Copyright, Designs and Patents Act 1988.

ISBN 978-1-84690-498-1

Graphics by Kevin O'Brien
Photography Andrew Allen
Edited by Dave Gray
Proof reading by Mike Kidson

First edition 2009
15 14 13 12
10 9 8 7 6 5 4

Page origination by Caroline Waring-Collins, Waring Collins Ltd, Swordfish Business Park, Burscough, Lancs, L40 8JW
Printed and bound by Scotprint, Haddington, Scotland

The publisher and author wish to thank the following for materials and photographs used in the production of this book.

BP for a screenshot of www.bp.com, granted with kind permission; CosmoGirl for a screenshot of www.cosmogirl.com, granted with kind permission; HSBC for the HSBC logo sign, granted with kind permission; Telefónica O2 UK for a screenshot of www.o2.co.uk, granted with kind permission; and Namesco Limited for a screenshot of www.names.co.uk, granted with kind permission, Waring Collins for a screenshot of www.waringcollins.com, Bized for a screenshot of www.bized.co.uk, Sainsbury's for a screenshot of www.sainsburys.co.uk and Coastdale Parks for a screenshot of www.coastdaleparks.co.uk.

The publisher and authors wish to thank the following for photographs used in the production of this book.

HORTON/Rax Features p 38, PhotoDisc p 72, Rex Features p 58, Shutterstock pp 6, 7, 8, 12, 13, 16, 19, 20, 23, 24, 27, 28, 29, 31, 34, 35, 36, 41, 42, 43, 46, 47, 49, 53, 54, 55, 57, 61, 63, 66, 67, 68, 76, 79, 80, 81, 83, 84, 89, 90. 95, 98, 99, 103, 104, 108, 109, 113, 114, 117, 118, 119, 124, 127, 130, 135, Stockbyte pp 25, 50, 100.

Every effort has been made to locate copyright owners of material used in this book. Any errors and omissions brought to the attention of the publisher are regretted and will be credited in any subsequent edition of this publication.

Thanks

I would like to thank Tim, Florence, Henry and Imogen for their patience and understanding throughout the whole process of writing this book. Particular thanks to Andrew for all his support, guidance and contributions. In addition I would like to thank Kermit for all his encouragement. Nicola Walker

I would like to thank all my colleagues at Biz/ed for supporting me in doing this project, specifically Andy Hargrave, Jill Jones, Stewart Perrygrove and John Yates. There are many people who worked on the development of the qualification on which this book is based. Their faith, support, encouragement and considerable hard work and skill were crucial in getting the qualification live. As a result thanks go to Susan Hoxley, Kelly Padwick, Beverley Anim-Antwi, Derek Richardson and Lizzie Firth. No book would be produced without the dedication of the authors who combine considerable work pressures with the task of producing the book and supporting materials, mostly in their own time. The fact that the production process has been relatively trouble free is largely due to their dedication, commitment, professionalism and support. Thanks go to Alain Anderton, Ian Gunn, Keith Hirst, Andrew Malcolm, Jonathan Shields and Nicola Walker for their contributions and effort. At Pearson, Dave Gray has been a much valued publisher - his skill in handling people, deadlines, vast quantities of text and queries, whilst retaining patience and humour, has been invaluable. It has been a privilege to work with you Dave - thank you. Finally, thanks go to my family, Sue, Alex and Johnny for their patience and love. Andrew Ashwin

This material has been published on behalf of Edexcel and offers high-quality support for the delivery of Edexcel qualifications. This does not mean that the material is essential to achieve any Edexcel qualification, nor does it mean that it is the only suitable material available to support any Edexcel qualification. Material from this publication will not be used verbatim in any examination or assessment set by Edexcel. Any resource lists produced by Edexcel shall include this and other appropriate resources. Copies of official specifications for all Edexcel qualifications may be found on the Edexcel website: www.edexcel.com.

# Contents: delivering the EDEXCEL GCSE Business (Business Communications) Specification Unit 4

## Welcome to the Edexcel GCSE Business Studies series

The Edexcel GCSE Business Studies Series has been produced to build students' business knowledge, understanding and skills, and to help them prepare for their GCSE assessment. The books include lots of engaging features to enthuse students and provide the range of support needed. The student books in the series are:

- **Introduction to Small Business** covering Units 1 and 2 (compulsory for the Full Course) and Unit 6 (for the Short Course)
- **Building a business** (Unit 3)
- **Business Communications** (Unit 4)
- **Introduction to Economic Understanding** (Unit 5)

## Business Communications

Unit 4: The new specification is firmly rooted in why a business communicates with its stakeholders, how it does it and the associated problems that arise. This book explains the reasons for communication and the methods and problems of communicating successfully. It encourages understanding of these issues with plenty of case studies and practical activities.

## How to use this book

Each Edexcel GCSE Business Studies unit is divided into topics. These books are written in the same easy-to-follow format, with each topic split into digestible chapters. You will find these features in each chapter:

**Topic overview** A case study sets the scene for each topic, accompanied by a series of questions. Your teacher might look at this as a starter activity to find out what you already know about the subject. You'll find a summary of the assessment for the topic.

**Content and objectives** Each chapter starts with a case study to put the content in a context, followed by the objectives for that chapter.

**Edexcel key terms** are highlighted and defined in each chapter.

**Test yourself question practice** in every chapter contains objective and multiple choice questions.

**Over to you question practice** in every chapter. A short case study is followed by questions written in exam paper style.

### examzone

A dedicated suite of revision resources to help you prepare as well as you can. We've broken down the six stages of revision to ensure you are prepared every step of the way.

**Zone in:** How to get into the perfect 'zone' for revision.

**Planning zone:** Tips and advice on how to effectively plan revision.

**Know zone:** The facts you need to know, memory tips and exam-style practice at the end of every topic.

**Don't panic zone:** Last-minute revision tips.

**Exam zone:** What to expect on the exam paper and the key terms used.

**Zone out:** What happens after the exams.

# ResultsPlus

These features use exam performance data to help you prepare as well as you can.

There are TWO different types of ResultsPlus features throughout this book:

## ResultsPlus
### Watch Out!

Remember that the Internet has advantages and disadvantages to a business. Do not just assume that having a web site is a 'good' thing for every business and that it will automatically bring benefits.

**Watch out!** These warn you about common mistakes and misconceptions that students often make.

## ResultsPlus
### Build Better Answers

1 (a) Identify one legal consideration that a business needs to take in creating a web site. (1)

(b) Explain one possible consequence to the business if it did not take notice of the legal consideration you have identified in 1 (a) above. (3)

Technique guide: This is effectively one question split into two parts. In the first you are being asked to recall some knowledge and in part two to offer an explanation to highlight how ignoring the law might affect a business.

Think: Think carefully about both parts of the question. Try to choose a legal issue that you can easily explain in part (b).

■ **Basic** Identifies one possible legal consideration but offers no further comment or explanation. (1)

● **Good** Identifies one legal consideration and offers some explanation on how it might affect a business if it ignored the law. For example, it could lead to legal action against the business or it might put some potential users/customers off the site. (2-3)

▲ **Excellent** Identifies one legal consideration and provides an explanation that makes at least three links regarding the impact on the business. For example, legal action could be taken, the business could be sued which in turn might cost the business large sums of money and even cause it to have to close down. (4)

**Build better answers** give an opportunity to answer exam-style questions. They include tips for what a basic or incorrect ■, good ▲ and excellent ● answer will contain.

(a) Amelia runs a business called Pretty Pictures. She sells highly stylised art work which is noted for its vibrant colours. She decided to set up a web site to show the range of pictures she has through a virtual gallery. She has tried to register a number of domain names but has settled on www.amelias-pretty-pictures.biz

(i) What is meant by the term 'domain name? (1)

(ii) Explain **one** possible problem that Amelia might have with the domain nameshe has chosen. (3)

Think: What is a domain name? What are the main principles in registering a domain name? Has Amelia stuck to these principles? What problems could arise for users trying to type in her domain name?

| Student answer | Examiner comment | Build a better answer |
|---|---|---|
| (i) A domain name is the address for a business web site. | ■ A basic answer which shows some understanding but does not state the key element of a domain name. | ▲ To really make sure the examiner knows that you understand the term, you must state the fact that a domain name provides the means by which users can identify with the web site. Use an example to illustrate - Pretty Pictures is the name of the business; this is what identifies it. |
| (ii) The domain name she has chosen includes the name of the business and as such customers can find her. The problem is that it is quite long though. | ● A good answer that pin-points the main problem - the length of the domain name. However, it stops short of giving a little more development to get the full 3 marks. | ▲ Develop the answer by showing how a long domain name makes it more likely that people will make mistakes typing it in and that the use of hyphens is also adding to the potential for people to get it wrong. A domain name needs to be as simple and short as possible - make this point in relation to Amelia's web site. |

**Build better answers** are featured in the Know Zone at the end of each topic. They include an exam-style question with a student answer, examiner comments and an improved answer so that you can see how to build a better response.

## Assessment

Information on external examinations is covered in the Examzone at the end of the book. This provides details on assessment for Unit 4 (see pages 136-137).

# Topic 4.1: Communication

## Topic overview
This topic looks at the communication model and details how good communication works. It will include the reasons why businesses communicate and how communications can often fail. The benefits to a business of having good communications are examined, as well as the costs to a business of failing to keep a close eye on its communications.

## Case study
The whole thing was getting very annoying. Kim had been trying to juggle several claims on her time all at once. The customer she was dealing with was becoming increasingly angry at the fact that the order for 250 PlayStation3 consoles had not been delivered. The customer was a major retail store and was relying on the delivery to meet its customer needs in the run up to Christmas.

On the other hand she had her boss breathing down her neck wanting to know if she had solved the problem. At the same time, she had been talking to the distribution department to find out what the hold up had been. She had sent e-mails but did not seem to be getting anywhere.

She finally spoke to Barry in the warehouse on the phone and asked why the delivery was delayed. 'What delivery?' he queried? This worried her. 'The delivery I have been e-mailing about' she said. 'Not received any e-mails here' said Barry. 'What about the paper requisition order sent to you from the sales team?' asked Kim. She waited while Barry shuffled through some papers. 'No requisition for PlayStation3 in our paperwork either' he replied.

Kim said 'thank you' and told Barry she would get back to him after she had investigated what happened. It was no wonder she had not received any e-mails from them relating to her query. She checked her 'messages sent' box – oh dear, she realised she had added in an extra '.' in the e-mail address and this is why they had not been sent. She then chased up the sales team who confirmed they had sent the paper requisition through to distribution some weeks before. On checking, Kim found out that there had been a computer glitch on the day they sent the paperwork through and it had not been processed. It was all becoming clearer.

She drafted a letter to the customer explaining the problems they had experienced and confirmed that the order would be processed immediately and delivered in two days time. She also telephoned her contact at the company to reassure them that they would be receiving the letter and the order and apologising for the problems. The contact was not overly impressed but thanked her for sorting it out. 'You need to get things sorted better in future if you want to keep our business' he said. 'Perhaps your organisation needs to take more notice of the mission statement on your web site which promises 'the best quality, the best prices, quickly'. Kim said she would communicate the observation with her boss and thanked him for his understanding.

1. **What types of communication have been used in the passage?**

2. **What were the main communication problems that Kim faced in dealing with this problem?**

3. **What people were affected by the problems that Kim was dealing with?**

4. **What lessons might Kim and the organisation learn from this episode?**

## What will I learn?

**What is Communication?** Communication is a two way process and involves two parties, the sender and the receiver. Communication is all about the interaction with the other party.

**Why do we communicate?** We need to communicate to ensure that people understand what we want or need. Successful communication ensures that information is being sent to the right people and feedback allows the business to progress.

**What is the process of communication?** Throughout the course of any day people within an organisation will communicate, how depends on who they are communicating with, what the message is and how quickly they want a response. The type of communication will affect the success of the communication being received and acted upon by the receiver

Consideration needs to be given as to which method of communication will be used and the suitability of it for the intended audience.

**What can prevent good communication?** There are times when things get in the way of successful communication, causing a barrier resulting in the message not getting through. The main barriers to communication will be covered.

**What happens when business communication is good?** Good communication leads to a number of advantages to a business including increased sales, more motivated staff, and a better image/reputation.

**What happens if business communication is poor?** Any business will strive to be successful. It has to communicate with people internally and externally. Failing to do this could be disastrous for a business. Poor communication could result in reduced productivity and efficiency within the organisation. Bad news travels quickly and the business will soon lose customers as word spreads about problems.

## How will I be assessed?

- Unit 4 is externally assessed.
- You will sit an exam of one and a half hours duration.
- There will be a mixture of multiple choice questions, short answer questions and extended writing questions.

# 1 The communication model

8

## Case Study

Riswana runs her own fashion design company and has a small number of people working for her. For her business to be a success she has to sell her designs. She needs to ensure she keeps up to date with the latest trends and new fashion ideas that evolve. She has to be able to communicate these ideas and designs to her clients. Time is precious so Riswana uses a variety of communication methods to inform her clients of when she has completed work or to inform them of her latest designs. To ensure that Riswana satisfies her clients' requirements it is essential that she receives feedback. This tells her they understand the message she has sent and provides them with the opportunity to make changes or requests. There have been occasions when her clients have not given feedback as they misunderstood the initial information sent, resulting in staff being pushed to meet deadlines with completion time very tight.

## Objectives

- To understand what communication is.
- To understand how the communication model works.
- To interpret the communication model.
- To explain the concept of how information is successfully passed on.
- To understand that communication is not always successful.

## edexcel ⠿ key terms

**Sender/Source** – the person or group who is sending the message or information

**Receiver/Recipient** – the person or group who receive the message or information

**Feedback** – what confirms to the sender that the communication has been successful

## What is communication?

Communication is the transfer of information between two parties, the **sender** and the **receiver**. It is important that feedback is given so the sender knows that the message has been received and understood. There are many ways in which businesses communicate. Each method requires a response or **feedback**.

Figure 1 shows this. The language used in this text message is not formal. Some people might not be able to understand it if they do not use 'text speak.' To be sure that the message has been received and understood, the sender will expect a reply. In this case the reply answers the two basic questions – how the receiver is fine and that they are coming out tonight.

Without feedback businesses would be unaware whether a message or information sent has been received and understood. Businesses rely heavily on communication and without it they would not be able to survive. Communication is part of everyday life and in all aspects of business, no matter how large or small the organisation is.

Communication is something that every business has to consider and carries out everyday. This can include advertising and recruiting employees, working within a team, communication between management and workers and with suppliers and customers. Without it businesses and any other organisation would simply not survive. The whole concept of communication is the exchange of information between the **sender** or **source** and the **receiver** or **recipient**. The overall aim for a business is to communicate effectively to achieve the company goals and to be successful.

**Figure 1 – Communication via text**

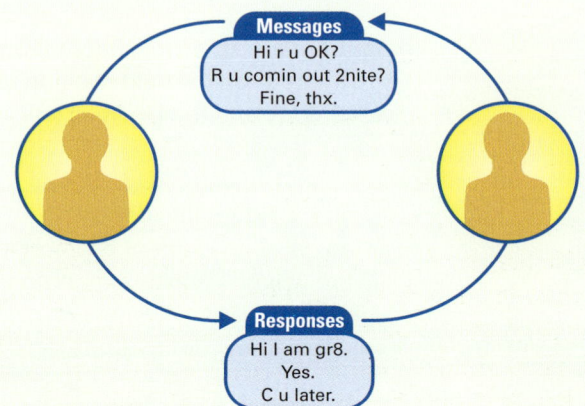

Messages
Hi r u OK?
R u comin out 2nite?
Fine, thx.

Responses
Hi I am gr8.
Yes.
C u later.

## The communication model

There are many ways to describe communication and it can be a complex process to describe. The communication model simplifies this process and demonstrates how communication works and what is required for successful communication.

This is how the model works. The **sender** is the source or person from an organisation who sends information. The information is sent to the **receiver**. The sender will only know if the communication has been received and understood successfully if **feedback** is provided. Feedback could be given verbally or by an action or a change in behaviour. This is true in every method of communication. The sender has control over the intended effect of the message being sent and has to select the most suitable method of communication to ensure that the message is interpreted correctly.

If there is some problem with the message sent by the sender the feedback or response from the intended audience will not be received. It is therefore essential that every organisation makes sure that the messages being sent are appropriate for the intended audience and sent using an appropriate method.

Lack of feedback might mean the information has not been received or understood and can affect the running and productivity of an organisation. Riswana needs to ensure she receives feedback from her clients in order for her business to be successful. If her clients do not understand a message or information sent or given to them it can delay progress with orders and affect the reputation of her business. For example, if she sends a message to a client asking them if they are happy with the design she has created, Riswana will expect to get a reply saying 'yes' or 'no'. If it is the latter then the client will need to communicate to Riswana what changes they want. If Riswana receives no response at all what is she to make of her message? Does she assume that the client is happy?

## How is information passed on?

Information informs. It can be in many different formats but still has the overall intention of informing people. The more detailed the information is, the more accurate the message will need to be.

Communication is not just about talking to people. Drivers in cars rely on road signs to inform them of where there are roadworks, a roundabout, speed limits and destinations. These signs communicate information. If drivers got lost regularly or drove into construction lorries in roadworks then the assumption would be that the signs were not doing their job properly.

Communication is not just about talking to people. It can be signs and advertisements.

In business organisations information or messages are being sent all the time using different communication **mediums**. If there is not adequate and appropriate feedback received then there can be a variety of problems that may arise. Riswana needs responses to her queries to enable her and her team to produce the designs required by her clients. If her message is not received then it can affect the length of time the business

Communication can be signs and advertisements

### Figure 2 – Feedback

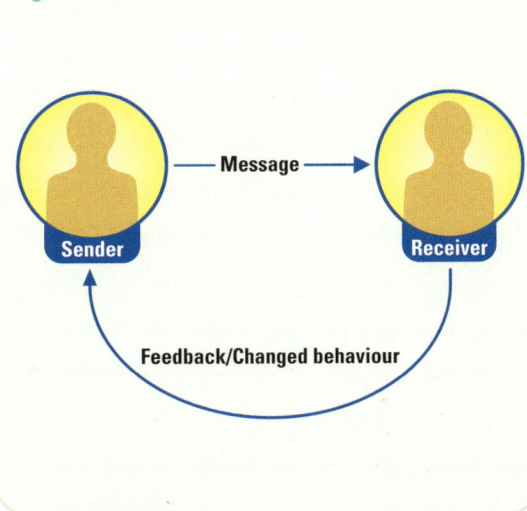

Sender → Message → Receiver

Feedback/Changed behaviour

edexcel ::: key terms

**Mediums** – the methods used to send the message or information, for example telephone, letter, email, fax, advert, and media such as TV and radio.

has to produce the designs and any sample material they may require. This may mean that her clients will not be satisfied and as a result may decide to use an alternative designer.

Communication comes in many forms and is all around us. An advertisement is a means of communicating information about new products, sales and product information. Flyers received through the post, posters advertising a concert, advertisements for clothes in magazines and in shop windows are all forms of communication between a business and its customers. These businesses will only know if their message has been successful if their products sell or tickets are bought. For example, a flyer comes through the door offering a 25% discount voucher on a new product. If the voucher is used then the business knows that the message/information sent has been successful. The feedback they receive is that people are buying the product.

One of the ways in which Riswana communicates with her clients is talking to them and showing them visual images of her designs. The information being given is both verbal and visual, which is suitable for the type of business that Riswana has. It enables her clients to give her instant feedback informing her of any changes they may wish to make and likewise provides Riswana with the opportunity to clarify exactly what the client's requirements are, to ensure she and her team produce the right product. The end result is that both parties are satisfied and the job will be done in the time available.

There are other ways in which Riswana can communicate with her clients and ensure that they receive information, for example email. Is this the right way for a fashion business to communicate with its clients? She will have to take into account the possible number of responses that might be needed to ensure that the final outcome is successful. It might take up a lot of time sending and responding to the messages and the use of technology may not appeal to some of her clients. Some may not have the facility to receive the information being sent. Not only would this consume a huge amount of time for both parties but it would not necessarily ensure that all the information had been sent, received or understood. It is therefore vital that Riswana communicates with her clients using the right medium or 'method' and is careful how she sends any information or messages.

## Success of communication

An important attribute to the success of any business is its communication strategy. Choosing the right method of communicating and one that suits the intended audience is important to any business organisation. The success of the communication will depend on whether the audience understands the communication received.

Riswana needed to inform her clients that she was increasing her prices. She had to ensure that she selected the most suitable method of communication; if she did not then she would risk losing their custom. She knew it would be impossible to see all her clients face to face before the start of the increase and felt that telephoning them was not an appropriate method to use. She thought it would be unprofessional and would not give her a record of them being informed. Riswana thought it was important that she had a record of the communication sent to all of her clients and made the decision to write to them all informing them of the increase in price rather than informing them verbally. She thought that this was a more professional approach and provided her with a guarantee that the message had been sent.

Riswana knew that she would not know if all her clients had received the letter until she had received some feedback from them, only then would she know if the message had been received and understood. This feedback might be through a telephone call, a letter, e-mail, fax or even through personal visit.

Her decision paid off. Most of her clients understood the reasons given for the price increase and continued to use Riswana's business.

Communication is not always successful. When an individual makes a phone call on a mobile phone where the network coverage is not strong the conversation can often break up. This interrupts the message being sent from the source to the receiver and therefore no relevant feedback can be given as the communication was incomplete.

For large organisations ensuring communication is successful can be the make or break of their survival in a competitive market. This was where Riswana had to make the right decision about contacting her clients. It was vital that she got the message across to her clients and that they understood it fully.

Television is a popular way to advertise and get messages across to different audiences. Many large organisations use this medium. It is an expensive way to communicate depending on the time of day the advert is shown but can be very effective. The advert has to be memorable and has to have something that makes people take notice of it. It has to have a message. Sometimes advertisers make the message deliberately obscure to make viewers think – this increases the likelihood that it will be remembered. Will the advert be understood by the audience it is aimed at? If these boxes can be ticked then the advert is more likely to be a success.

Magazine adverts for luxury cars include a nice surrounding or pleasant environment and a meaningful advertising

Vouchers communicate information to customers

headline - this will mean something to the reader (if they are interested in cars) and it should match the whole concept of owning and driving that car and the image that the company wants to get across. If this is how the reader feels when viewing the advert then the communication is a success.

## Summary

For communication to be successful for a business they must select the right method of communication and ensure that the message or information being sent by the source is received, understood and that feedback is given. For

Riswana's business receiving feedback is a key to the success of her company. There are times when communication is not successful, primarily this is due to the message not being understood or received together with a lack of feedback. Communicating using the right method is a key attribute to the success of the message being sent and the feedback that will be received. It is therefore vital for any organisation to ensure that the choice of medium suits the message or information being sent, is suitable for the intended audience and provides them with the opportunity to give feedback so the source knows that the message has been received and understood.

### ResultsPlus
**Build Better Answers**

Communication involves the exchange of information. How can this be measured as being successful? Select **one** answer.

A. The source sends a message to the receiver; the receiver gets it and waits.
B. The receiver sends the message and the source will receive the feedback.
C. A message has been sent and received with the receiver providing feedback to the source.
D. The source sends some information and a message and waits until the receiver gets it.

Answer C

Think: What actually does the receiver do when they get information or a message? Remember that the receiver must do something with the information or message to let the sources know that the information has been received and understood.

Then: Look at the options given and go through each one to identify whether the source sent the information or message? Has the receiver got the message and given feedback to the source? If this has happened then the source knows that the information or message has been received and understood. Therefore the exchange of information has been successful. After looking through each option, select which option has fulfilled these. Option C shows that the receiver has provided feedback to the source. This shows that the information or message has been successful. ■

Choose: After eliminating A, B and D, C is the option that gives a clear indication that the exchange of information has been successful. ▲

### Test yourself

1. Riswana sends a message to one of her clients. She is unsure if the message has been received and understood. Which of the following suggests that the communication has been successful? Select **one** answer.

   Riswana:
   A used the telephone to send the message
   B delivered the message personally
   C gets feedback from her clients
   D writes the message on a note pad

2. Which of the following represents the communication model? Select **one** answer.

   A Source - Receiver - Message - Feedback
   B Sender - Receiver - Feedback - Message
   C Source - Feedback - Message - Receiver
   D Source - Message - Receiver - Feedback

3. Which of the following best describes what communication is? Select **one** answer.

   A Transfer of information between one party, the sender, and the receiver
   B Transfer of information between two parties, the source and the receiver
   C Transfer of information between the receiver and the feedback
   D Transfer of information between the parties; the source, the receiver and feedback

### Over to you

A client of Riswana's has requested a meeting to see the latest evening wear designs Riswana has. They have left a message for Riswana with one of her staff with a list of dates they are available.

1 Using the communication model identify who is the client? (1)
2 Explain how the client will know that Riswana has received and understood the message. (3)

# 2 The purpose of communication

## Case Study

Hospital staff around the country provide a valuable service. The National Health Service (NHS) is a very large organisation, managing hospitals and local health trusts requires highly skilled managers. The whole population uses the NHS at some point in their lives and so have an interest in it. Everyone has a view about how the NHS should be run. The cost of wages for the NHS is around £70 billion a year so even small pay rises have a major effect on the cost of running the service. There is a relatively small number of managers in the NHS. Some managers get a pay rise of 38%. Medical staff including nurses, porters and other workers received only a 2% pay increase. The economic situation is such that workers felt this pay rise would not help them to maintain their standard of living. They and the trade unions were angry that managers had such a large pay rise but ordinary workers had to put up with only 2%.
The announcement by the NHS of the pay awards made the national press. On the face of it, this did not seem fair.

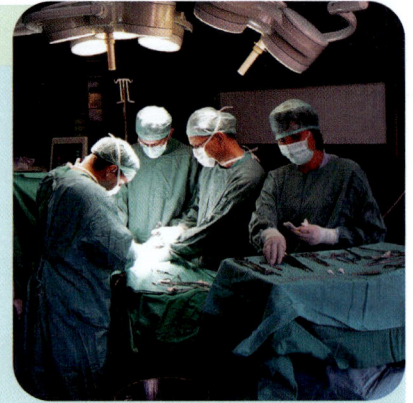

## Objectives

- To understand that communication is about the transfer of information from one party to another.
- To recognise that communication has to be directed to a variety of different audiences.
- To appreciate that different audiences have different requirements and expectations.
- To understand that as a result communication might cause conflict.

## edexcel key terms

**Audience** – who the communication is directed at.

## Communication is about the transfer of information

Communication is what keeps businesses going, without communication businesses would not know what the needs of their stakeholders are, for example:
- if a product or service is available;
- the thoughts of employees.

Business communication might involve people from within an organisation or between the business and other businesses, such as suppliers. The communication will occur when information is passed on from one party to another. How this information will be passed on will depend on the method used by the business. This could be by telephone, fax, email, letter and many more. The overall purpose is that the message or information being sent will be understood by the receiver. The business will look to see some evidence of feedback as a result. This may be through increased sales, attendance by shareholders at an annual general meeting (AGM), changed employee behaviour and so on. It is in the interest of the business that they transfer information on a regular basis to keep all necessary parties informed.

The NHS is a huge organisation. Within the NHS transfer of information occurs on a regular basis. Information is passed between different departments, different hospitals, medical staff, patients and families. Without this transfer of information it could affect the treatment of patients as the medical staff administering medication or care would not be aware of patients' needs.

## Communication is directed at different audiences

The information sent by a business will depend on who the intended **audience** is. An organisation might enquire about a new product that is due to be released that they want to stock on their shelves to sell. They will want to know how popular the manufacturers think it will be, and need to know how much it will cost them to buy to be able to calculate their added value and how many they can order at any one time.

When the Nintendo Wii was released in late 2007, stores were limited to the number they were allowed to order. It was essential that they ensured there was a sufficient number in store to satisfy customer demand. The business needed to communicate with their suppliers to see how many they could buy and then had to communicate with potential customers to inform them when the product would be available to purchase. The information customers wanted to know was when it was available in the shops to buy and what the selling price would be. Information that these audiences require, the suppliers and the customers, is different.

The NHS has many different people they communicate with. When you arrive at a hospital, be it by ambulance or not, a receptionist will ask for patient details and information about their injury or illness. Should they arrive by ambulance paramedics have to relay information to the medical staff about the patient telling them what has happened to them and what treatment they have had. The medical staff then have to communicate with patients, their families, doctors, porters and other medical staff to ensure that they receive the care and treatment needed for them to recover. The information required by each party will be different; the doctor will need to know about the medical condition of the patient so they can administer the correct treatment. Porters will need to know where to take the patient; this might be to the x-ray department, to theatre or to a different ward. Family will want to know what the diagnosis is, what treatment will be received and how long the family member will be in hospital for. Nurses will need to know what care the patient needs, what medication they require and how often they have to take it.

It is crucial to remember that the type of information given depends on the audience. Giving technical details of a condition to the patient's family may not be very helpful since it is unlikely that they would understand it. Giving information to NHS staff about pay might need to be handled with care to avoid misunderstanding of the reasons for decision making. A doctor in surgery might need to give very short, sharp and decisive instructions to colleagues in what could be a life-threatening situation.

## Different audiences have different requirements and expectations

Communication within the workplace and externally to an organisation involves passing information and instructions on. From the management's point of view they will hope it will increase the efficiency of the business and ensure that decisions are made to help the organisation operate efficiently. The likelihood of decisions being accepted by employees may depend on whether they have been involved in the decision-making in some way. This could include employees being consulted about changes that a business is looking to implement. Information passed on to stakeholders will be essential to ensure that they are kept up to date with the progress of a business. As businesses grow employees expect more from an organisation than just their wages so the need for communication between management and employees has increased.

Employees at the NHS were not happy about the pay rise they received and found it hard to comprehend how the managers had been awarded a larger percentage pay rise than them. No explanation was given to them and therefore they did not understand why their increase had been low in comparison. Had the employees been notified in advance about the pay rises and given valid reasons about the substantial difference this would have provided explanations. Such information might have pointed out that whilst the percentage difference seemed large the actual total sum might have been much smaller in comparison. Managers may not have had a reasonable pay rise for some years, their performance may have improved considerably and so this pay rise was justified. There might be many reasons but if all parties are not aware of the full information, the communication could be misinterpreted and **conflict** arise.

## Communication might cause conflict

The purpose of communication is far more than simply giving instructions to stakeholders. There must be a flow of communication between the business and its stakeholders. It is crucial that the communication is active and that both parties have the opportunity to provide feedback. A lack of communication can lead to misinterpretations, which in turn can lead to conflict between interested

**ResultsPlus Watch Out!**

Negotiation is not the same as consultation. Negotiation is an individual or group who will discuss or confer with others to agree terms or reach an agreement. Consultation involves more than one party which together reach a decision.

Communication between hospital staff is vital to ensure patients get the right treatment

**edexcel key terms**

**Conflict** – a clash between people; if employees and management disagree then it may cause conflict between the two sides.

parties. For example, a business may have a number of shareholders who have invested a lot of their savings and in return expect to see the business thrive and be successful, which will result in them being able to receive a return on their investment through their dividend. If the directors at the business decide that they will award themselves a large salary increase this will reduce the amount of money left for shareholders' dividends. The shareholders might disagree with the increase and be angry that part of their return has gone on increasing the salaries of the directors. This could lead to shareholders wanting to sell their shares in the business and if the majority follow suit then the reputation of the business will be at risk. This could lead to a fall in sales and possibly profits. It is in the interest of all parties to be informed of decisions. Communication is the link to all this.

The opinion of people will differ over the NHS pay increases depending on their perspective. NHS staff were not happy as they felt the pay increase would not make a difference to their standard of living. Trade unions became involved to support the workers with the press having it as a headlining article. However the managers thought it was a fair deal and were happy with the increase. The difference in opinion and the involvement of trade unions sparked conflict between different stakeholders. There had been limited consultation with staff and as a result they were unhappy about the decision.

The conflict between the different parties detracted away from the reasons as to why the difference was so great. Managers in the NHS are highly skilled and have a huge responsibility to ensure that the NHS operates as efficiently as it can and within their budget. The NHS employs over a million people, therefore to give them all a 2% increase will add a huge amount of money onto the NHS costs. There are far fewer managers than other staff such as nurses, doctors and porters. The cost of giving the managers a 38% increase will add less to the overall wage costs in comparison to the wage cost from the increase for other staff. Balancing the budget for the NHS is a task that many would shy away from. The increase managers receive may reflect the level of responsibility they have. What is important is how these points are communicated to all involved so that the different points of view can be considered. If the communication is handled badly then conflicts can arise.

Communication includes **negotiation** and **consultation**.

## edexcel ⠿ key terms

**Negotiation** – a process by which two or more parties engage in discussion to try and resolve a dispute and arrive at an agreed course of action.

**Consultation** – a process whereby one party may ask for the views or advice from other parties to help them arrive at a decision.

This could include:
- employees negotiating with management about personal objectives for the forthcoming year;
- departments negotiating with each other for resources;
- management negotiating with trade unions over pay and conditions.

With each one of these efficient communications will help to reduce conflict.

Within some organisations communication between management and employees may involve consultation; where management and employees are involved in decision making. Alternatively they could opt to do neither and simply state what the changes will be. Such a tactic is more likely to lead to conflict, however.

If the NHS chose to go down the route of negotiation or consultation it could lead to the time taken to make decisions increasing and delay the decision-making process. This could

## Test yourself

1. To communicate successfully a business needs to:

   A *make sure that a press release is always issued*
   B *consider the needs of the audience*
   C *make sure the audience is together in one place at the time of the communication*
   D *always use both oral and electronic means*

   Select **one** answer.

2. Katherine Guest, a nurse at a hospital, left a message with a consultant's secretary asking if she could contact her about the results of a patient's scan she had sent through to Katherine. She wanted some advice on how to relay the information to the patient and his family. Who is the intended audience of the communication? Select **one** answer.

   A *The consultant who needs to know what the results of the scan are*
   B *The nurse who needs advice on how to pass the message on*
   C *The patient and his family who need to know what the outcome of the scan is*
   D *The secretary who needs to know what information to pass on to the consultant*

3. Which of the following would be an important consideration for a business planning to make an announcement about plans for redundancies? Select **one** answer.

   A *Ensuring that all stakeholders are kept informed about the plans and the reasoning behind it*
   B *Only tell those staff who are going to be made redundant*
   C *Make sure that shareholders receive their dividend first before the redundancies are announced.*
   D *Ensure that all staff are given clear information about the reasons and the process*

be crucial to the operation and success of the organisation. However, what it could lead to is more understanding about the reasons for decisions. This could reduce conflict. Business organisations have to consider the balance between these things when thinking about communicating with stakeholders.

## Summary

The purpose of communication is about the transfer of information between different parties. Businesses must remember that it is important how they communicate. It is important that they appreciate that they will have to communicate with a variety of different audiences. The type of communication medium used and the nature of the communication will differ in each case. Within organisations the requirements of employees and managers, for example, may differ and the information they expect might be different. It is vital that these are considered when communicating. Should information not be passed on it can cause conflict between stakeholders. An organisation can either negotiate with stakeholders or enter into a consultation process to reach a decision.

## Over to you

Managers at Over2U, an independent education organisation, had seen a dramatic increase in the uptake of their support packs available for learners and their parents, designed to increase independent learning. Profits had increased from the previous year and the decision was made to reward the staff for their hard work by giving them a bonus. They were dedicated employees who provided excellent customer service. The staff worked hard and felt they had good working relationships with the management and that their hard work was valued. When it was announced that the management had made the decision to give all staff a bonus the staff were thrilled. Many had families and the bonus would help considerably. Staff were unaware of how much they would receive but thought that due to the growth and success of the company the bonus would reflect their hard work. Staff only found out the size of the bonus when they received their pay slips. Each worker received £100 but a member of the payroll staff revealed that managers had received £5,000. The workers felt very let down and that they had been treated unfairly. It was their opinion that they should have been consulted about the bonus particularly given that they thought they had a good working relationship with the management. Trust in the management quickly disappeared.

1. Identify **three** factors that led the staff to think that they would have received a larger bonus. (3)
2. Explain why the staff thought that the bonus management had given themselves was unacceptable in comparison to the bonus the staff had received (3)
3. Negotiating and consultation are two methods that could be used to decide on the size of a bonus. Would these methods have improved the communication over the bonus payments at Over2U? Justify your answer. (8)

**ResultsPlus**
**Build Better Answers**

A business has received its final accounts for the financial year and is preparing a report to communicate its performance. It has to provide this information to both shareholders and its staff. Discuss the differences in the way it would communicate this information to each. (8)

Technique guide: This is a question that is assessing your ability to recognise that different audiences require different means of communication for it to be successful. This will incorporate analysis and evaluative skills.

Think: What are the needs of the two audiences? Are they the same? How far do they differ? What type of information does each require?

Then: Make a decision about the different way in which each audience's need could be satisfied. Identify what ways might be used in each case.

Remember: It is vital that you demonstrate evaluation skills. This is about what the success of the communication in each case would depend upon. For example, the type of communication with workers depends on the size of the workforce and whether they are all in one place or scattered around!

Plan: Think through how you are going to structure your answer. Use the text and relate your answer to the business.

Write: Write out your answer and check the content against the question.

🟥 **Basic** Makes a simple reference to a difference with little or no support. For example, 'They could send a report to shareholders, but talk to workers'. (1-2)).

🟠 **Good** Provides at least one difference and offers some support to justify why the difference is appropriate. For example, 'Shareholders will require a detailed report of the accounts and so would need to be sent a formal report. Workers might not need as much detail so a summary letter could be sent to them. (3-5)

🔺 **Excellent** Provides at least one difference. Use of appropriate terms and concepts throughout the answer, demonstrating knowledge and application. Answer justifies why the difference is appropriate to the intended audience. For example, 'The shareholders of a business may number many thousands and be spread across the world. As a result they will need to provide the financial details as a report. This could be available as hard copy or online. It will contain detailed accounts of the business' performance because shareholders need such information to make decisions. Workers also need financial information but not in much detail. They need it to maintain focus and motivation. A newsletter or e-mail could be used to send the information. In smaller businesses staff could be given the information at a meeting. (6-8)

# 3 The process of communication

## Case Study

Workers at SatTel communications were shocked one morning when, on their way to work, they all received a text message on the mobile phones provided for them by the company telling them that the business had been forced to close and that their jobs no longer existed. Many workers knew that the business had been struggling but this had not been expected. The boss of SatTel, Josh Turner, was well known for being an autocratic manager. His style of running the business seemed at odds with the fact that it was supposed to be a communications business. The staff were outraged at the way they had been told they had lost their jobs and were even angrier when they arrived at the office to find they had to pick up their things and leave immediately. The local press lost no time in broadcasting how Josh broke the news to his staff in their evening edition.

## Objectives

- To understand the different methods that a sender might use to communicate information.
- To recognise that the method chosen affects how the message is received.
- To identify and explain advantages and disadvantages of different methods of communication.
- To appreciate that different businesses will use different methods of communication for different reasons.
- To appreciate that some businesses will use some methods of communication more frequently than others.
- To appreciate the role of feedback in recognising when a message has been understood.

edexcel key terms

**Medium** – the method used to communicate information or a message.

## What methods are used to communicate information?

There was a variety of ways that Josh could have used to tell his workers that they were redundant. The job is not one that any boss looks forward to but it is sometimes necessary. Staff in many businesses develop some loyalty to the business and they expect some respect and honesty in return. The method of communicating the redundancy that Josh had chosen could have been better. Given the nature of the message that he had to communicate there were other methods that could have been used. The method chosen to send a message is called the **medium**. Businesses use a variety of media to communicate information as shown in Table 1.

Josh could have used at least three different media to communicate the message to the staff that they had been made redundant.

- He could have called a meeting of all the staff to explain the situation the company was in. He could have explained what the effect would be on them of the closure - what redundancy packages they might expect to receive and when.
- He could have sent them all a letter explaining the situation.
- He could use text messages - the method he chose.

Almost every decision regarding communication in a business involves consideration about the medium to be used and how appropriate it is in making

Table 1 – Communication media

- Face-to-face - meetings, one-to-one meetings and presentations.
- Verbal/oral - through speaking.
- Electronic - e-mail, fax, video, telephone, TV, radio, podcast, the Internet etc.
- Visual - posters, notices, adverts.
- Written - letters, memos, scribbled notes etc.
- Sound.

sure that the message gets communicated successfully. In Josh's case, the message was certainly communicated but whether the communication was successful is another matter. Staff would have received and understood the message that their jobs had gone. However they are unlikely to have understood why their jobs had disappeared or what their situation was and what effect it would have on them. As a result only part of the message has really been communicated. The medium chosen by Josh left them feeling angry, frustrated and in need of further information.

The nature of the message is also something that needs to be taken into consideration when deciding on the appropriate medium. If the information to be communicated is technical or requires detailed explanation then written means are often appropriate. It gives the receiver the chance go back over the message several times

Table 2 – The advantages and disadvantages of different communication media

| Medium | Advantage | Disadvantage |
|---|---|---|
| Face-to-face/ Verbal/Oral | • Quick<br>• Personal<br>• Allows both parties to see and interpret body language<br>• Allows immediate response/feedback to be gained.<br>• Useful for both formal and informal situations (e.g. a formal presentation in a meeting or an informal chat over a coffee). | • Skill of the sender is important - presentations can be let down by a poor presenter.<br>• Response/feedback can be misinterpreted.<br>• Receiver does not have time to reflect and consider the message.<br>• Can be influenced by emotion which might act as a barrier. |
| Electronic | • Flexible - provides lots of different ways of communicating.<br>• Can save time and money.<br>• Can be a very fast way of communicating important messages. | • Can be abused by staff which costs time and money.<br>• Can sometimes be misinterpreted - e.g. the intention of the sender is not always clear in a text or e-mail message.<br>• Managing the hardware and software can be expensive and requires a high degree of skill. |
| Visual | • Can be very effective in catching the eye.<br>• Receiver can associate with visual images easier.<br>• Receiver can often find visual methods easier to remember.<br>• Is very flexible and can be used for a variety of purposes - through adverts, web sites, posters, leaflets, logos, photographs etc. | • Care has to be taken with design and use of colour.<br>• Sometimes limits the amount of information that can be given.<br>• Visual means of communication can be expensive to produce. |
| Written | • Provides a very formal way of presenting information.<br>• Allows complex and technical information to be communicated.<br>• Allows the receiver to take in the information at their leisure.<br>• Allows the receiver to go back and reflect on the message.<br>• Can be circulated through different means - post, e-mail, report, web site etc. | • Can be dependent on the quality of the language used.<br>• Assumes the receiver will spend time reading all the information (how many people read the small print on documents for example?).<br>• Some written information can be difficult to understand. |
| Sound | • Plays on the emotions - can be very effective in helping people remember things.<br>• Provides flexibility - lots of different ways of using sound. | • Can become obscured.<br>• Depends on the type of receiver, e.g. elderly people tend to interpret some sounds differently from younger people.<br>• Some sounds can be very annoying (the Crazy Frog) and the message can be lost. |

if need be to make sure that they understand it and to be able to reflect on the message. If the message requires a very quick response then a telephone call or a face-to-face chat may be more appropriate. If the message is aimed at communicating a new product launched by a business then a visual means may be the best way.

Sometimes several media can be used to communicate the same message. The annual report to shareholders of a public limited company is usually published as a hardcopy document but is also made available through the company web site in different formats including PDF (Portable Document Format). To help those with disabilities the company may also provide Braille or recorded versions for the blind.

The nature of the message also includes what message the communication is sending. If it is bad news then this may help to narrow down the range of appropriate media; if the news is good then different methods can be chosen. In Josh's case the news was bad and staff would have felt that they deserved more than a text message as the medium of delivery of that message. Most of the staff knew that there was nothing they could do about the closure of the business. What they wanted was to find out information to help them come to terms with what had happened and plan their future. They wanted a chance to meet Josh, to hear about why the business had closed, what redundancy terms they would get and so on.

## Advantages and disadvantages of different media

Before choosing the medium, a consideration of the advantages and disadvantages is necessary. Most communication methods have some good points and some bad points. The secret is to find the most appropriate way, one which minimises the bad points and maximises the good ones so that the message has the best chance of being understood by the receiver or the audience at which the message is targeted. Table 2 shows the advantages and disadvantages of different communication media.

## The use of different media

Some businesses will use different types of media more than others. For example, a large business with plenty of money may be able to use sophisticated and expensive ways of communicating. They might have extensive e-mail facilities, highly sophisticated web sites, spend money on promotional

campaigns that make use of radio and television, produce animations and video and so on. Smaller businesses may have to rely on a more limited range of media such as writing, the telephone or home made posters.

In some cases, businesses have deliberately set out to make use of one medium and try to avoid using others. Some low-cost airlines have advanced web sites that handle the vast majority of their communications. They try to encourage customers to use the web site to deal with queries as much as possible and do not have very large customer call centres and face-to-face opportunities. This helps them to keep costs lower which they then pass on to the consumer in the form of lower air fares.

Some firms, for example, legal firms, use a great deal of written and verbal forms of communication. It is important to their business that they build relationships with clients and the personal approach is often the best way to do this. Some very large firms use written means of communication with their stakeholders primarily because it is the most appropriate medium for communicating with large numbers of people who may be scattered across the country or even the world.

## The importance of feedback

The success of any communication depends on whether the receiver understands and can act on the message/information given by the sender. The sender can only know if the communication has been successful if there is positive feedback. The medium of communication used can have an effect on the success of the communication.

For example, assume a business wants to increase sales of its product. It decides that the appropriate medium is to launch a promotional campaign that uses visual images like posters and adverts. The communication will be designed to try and make customers more aware of the business and its products and be encouraged to go out and buy them. If as a result of the campaign sales of the product rise by 10% then the business may be able to consider whether the communication has been a success. If they targeted a rise in sales of 25% then the campaign may not have been as successful as they would have hoped. In reflecting on the campaign they might have had to consider what methods they used, whether these were the most appropriate and whether customers really understood the message.

In Josh's business, he adopted an autocratic method of running the business. This means that all decisions would have to come from him or at the very least go through him before being implemented. The use of this type of approach might mean that some staff would be reluctant to communicate problems to him for fear of how he might react. It may well be that problems had existed in the business for some time but because of the communication structures that exist, Josh was simply not getting the right feedback from his staff. He may have thought the business was doing fine but in actual fact it could have been declining over a period of time.

**ResultsPlus Watch Out!**

When tackling a question asking you to evaluate different methods of communication consider the audience that the message is aimed at, what response the sender wants, how quickly and what would be judged a successful outcome. This way you will be able to evaluate different methods more effectively.

## Test yourself

1. Which of the following is the best description of a medium of communication?
   A medium of communication is:

   A the range of methods a business uses to communicate with its stakeholders
   B the method used to send the message to the receiver
   C the way the receiver communicates the feedback to the sender
   D the different ways that the telephone can be used to transmit a message

   Select one answer.

2. Choosing the right medium is important in successful communication because:

   A the sender needs to make sure the receiver can see the message clearly
   B the receiver has to have some understanding of technology to access the message
   C it reduces the cost of production for a business sending messages to its shareholders
   D the nature of the message and how it is received by the sender will be affected by it

   Select one answer.

3. The following are all advantages of written communication except:

   A it assumes the receiver will read the information carefully
   B complex and technical information can be communicated
   C it allows the receiver to take in the information at their leisure
   D written media lets the receiver go back and reflect on the message

   Select one answer.

Mica is a part-time DJ and is putting together some jingles to help advertise her service.

Describe one disadvantage to Mica of using sound as a medium of communication. (3)

Think: What are the disadvantages of using sound as a medium? What could these disadvantages be in this context? Then: Think through how you are going to write your answer - you only have three marks to earn but you need to offer a developed answer to earn all three marks.

Write: Write out your answer.

**Basic** Gives one disadvantage but nothing else. (1).

**Good** Gives one disadvantage with some limited development. (2)

**Excellent** Gives one disadvantage, makes the link with the context clear and offers some development. (3)

## Over to you

Savera Khanum received a letter of complaint from a customer. Savera works as a service representative at a motor dealers. The customer came to the business for a standard service and had booked in several weeks before. He wanted a courtesy car but when he arrived at the garage there was no car available. It turns out that the person who took the initial call had entered the service into the order book but had not written down anything about the courtesy car. Now Savera had to find a way of dealing with a very angry customer who had complained that the whole of their day had been ruined by the 'incompetence of the staff' at the garage.

(a) Explain how Savera would have known that the communication between the customer and the garage had been unsuccessful. (3)
(b) Identify two possible communication media that Savera could use to respond to the angry customer. (2)
(c) In your opinion, which would be the best medium to use in this case? Justify your answer. (6)

# 4 Barriers to good communication

## Case Study

Brian Price runs a telesales company which sells gadgets online. Brian has invested £20,000 in a new e-commerce facility for the business which is designed to make the ordering and payment process easier for both his staff and, crucially, for customers. Brian used an Indian Company, DataSoft, to develop the software. The company was recommended to him by a friend and their estimate was much cheaper than other UK companies that Brian had contacted. All seemed to go smoothly despite the time difference between the UK and India which made it more difficult to contact Neesam, the project leader. However, in the first week when the software was being used, all sorts of problems arose that had not surfaced during testing. Customers were being charged twice for their orders, in some cases they did not receive their goods and staff kept experiencing crashing of their machines with the loss of information. Brian had contacted Neesam about the problems. Neesam had faxed him a document explaining how the system worked and how to correct the bugs that had crept in. Unfortunately, DataSoft could not do any further work on the system because the contract had ended and workers had been moved to other projects.

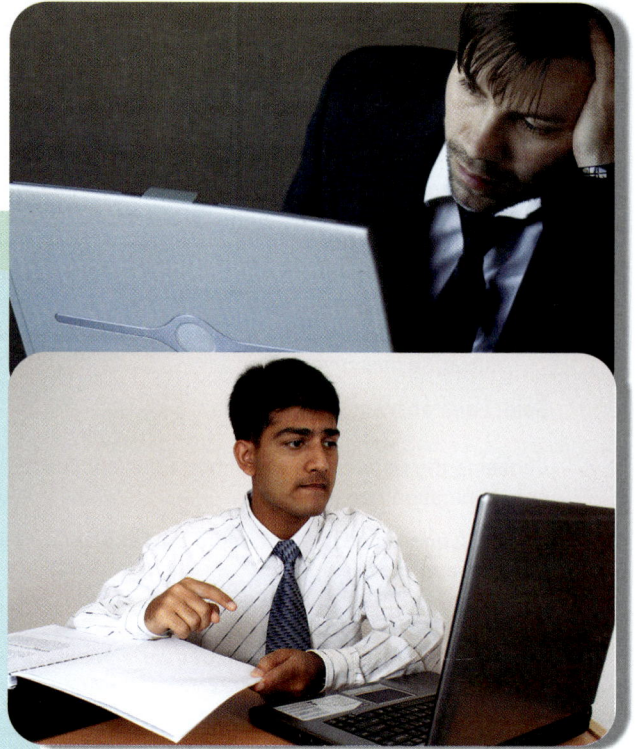

## Objectives

- To understand the main barriers which prevent successful communication.
- To understand the role played by the language used, content, emotions, knowledge of the receiver, position of the sender and the medium used in preventing successful communication.

## What is a barrier to communication?

We have seen so far that communication involves the sender and the receiver. Information passed from the sender to the receiver has to be understood for action to be taken. Positive feedback provides the means by which the sender knows that the message/information has been communicated successfully. In the case above there seem to have been all sorts of problems with communication which have only come to light when the software was first used. There seem to be problems for the staff, the customers are certainly experiencing problems and Brian and Neesam appear to have a different understanding of things.

When a message does not get through to the receiver it can result in several problems.

- There is no action taken by the receiver.
- The receiver misunderstands the message and acts in the wrong way.
- The receiver does not understand the message and simply ignores it.
- The receiver does not have the skills/knowledge/technique to be able to act on the message.
- The sender does get a response but it is not what they were looking for or expecting.

When any of these things happen there has been some sort of barrier to successful communication. The main barriers to communication are as follows.

**Language** If complex or inappropriate language is used the message may be obscured. In addition, the language may be something that the receiver simply does not understand, for example, if you do not speak Spanish you will not be able to understand a message in Spanish. Language can be a barrier to communication in spoken and written terms.

**Technical content** Some messages might contain detailed technical information. If the receiver does not have the technical knowledge then such a message might simply be beyond them.

**Inadequate feedback** Some messages may receive some feedback but not enough for the sender to decide whether the receiver has fully understood the message. The reason for the inadequate feedback could include missing parts to a letter, a disrupted phone call, text messages not being fully received, a lack of clarity in the reply and so on. When making presentations a speaker may look at his or her audience and might think that their message is getting through but in such a situation it is not always certain - despite the round of applause the speaker might get at the end of the presentation.

**Lack of understanding of what the receiver wants or needs** One of the key skills for any business person is to listen. By listening the sender can find out more easily what it is that the receiver might want. As a result the message can then be sent to make sure the receiver gets what they want. In many cases, people in businesses do not fully understand what their audience wants, needs or expects or simply ignores these needs.

**Emotional interference** Human beings are emotional creatures. When emotions get in the way the message can be obscured. Sending a letter to a customer when the individual is angry, shouting at an abusive customer, sending e-mails quickly without thinking and when angry, having to communicate to an audience when under stress and so on can all lead to the message not getting through properly and can create even more problems.

**The degree of knowledge and expertise of the sender and the receiver** The two parties to a message must be on the same wavelength for the message to be communicated successfully. If one person possesses knowledge that the other does not then the chances are that the communication will not be as successful as it could be. Such a situation increases the risk that a message can be misunderstood.

**The quality of the information sent** Understanding any message can depend on the quality of that message. If the message is confused or is difficult to interpret or decode then it may result in the receiver not understanding the message. This might also include making sure that the medium through which the message is sent is also of high quality.

**The use of an inappropriate medium** The medium used can make a big difference to whether the message is communicated successfully. If the medium is inappropriate it can lead to the message being misinterpreted or its intention being misunderstood. It can also make the receiver angry and not in the right frame of mind to accept the message. For example, there have been cases where employees have been told they have been made redundant by text message on their mobile phones. Using such a medium is unlikely to build any respect between sender and receiver.

**Lack of trust or honesty in the sender** Successful communication does rely to a large extent on the two parties to the communication trusting each other. If a person has lied in the past or gave information that is false or misleading then it is less likely that the receiver will take the message seriously again in the future.

**Cultural differences** There are many different **cultures** and what is acceptable in one may be unacceptable or even offensive in another. For example, in the UK,

edexcel ⠿ key terms

**Culture** – the beliefs and traditions of the people of a country or religion which sometimes mean similar messages/signals can be interpreted in different ways.

US and Europe direct eye contact is considered polite in conversation whereas in parts of Asia, including Japan and Thailand, too much eye contact is seen as being rude. In some countries, for example, in India and the Emirates, two men holding hands is seen as perfectly normal behaviour and a sign of friendship. In western countries it would be a sign of homosexual behaviour. The thumbs-up gesture is a sign of something positive in the west, but in some Asian and Islamic countries is seen as being rude.

**Poor listening skills** Part of the art of good communication is good listening skills on the part of both parties. If one or both do not listen to each other during the communication the chances of misinterpretation and misunderstanding are increased.

**The position or status of the sender** The view by the receiver of the status or position of the sender can make a difference to the communication. In a business, it may be that workers will listen to the boss of the firm more carefully and carry out their instructions than they might if being told by someone who they did not regard as being important. Letters sent by junior members of staff may not carry as much weight in the eyes of the receiver as one from a senior member of staff.

## The importance of good communication

Brian Price is learning the importance of making sure that barriers to communication are reduced to a minimum. The e-commerce sales facility was meant to make life easier but instead it is causing problems. Customers faced barriers to communication in that their orders were not being processed by Brian's company. The barrier to communication in this case could be the technology not working properly or the fact that consumers do not fully understand what they have to do. Some are being charged twice which might mean they are inputting the wrong information - again this could be the fault of the system or the instructions may not be clear enough.

Staff are also confused. They do not seem to understand the system they are working with. Brian had given them all training in the use of the system but had to privately admit that he did not really fully understand the information sent to him by Neesam and the team from DataSoft. It was hardly surprising he was not able to communicate the process fully to his staff. The staff felt frustrated by the system and Brian had become equally frustrated. He was very angry with himself at losing his temper with one member of staff who kept e-mailing him questions about the system. Everyone seemed to think he knew the answers and in his frustration he had found the member of staff and shouted at him for being 'difficult' in front of the other staff. This had not helped Brian to get his staff's support to help him out of the problems he had.

Then there were the problems with DataSoft. Brian had tried to phone Neesam but kept finding him out of the office.

He knew that it was difficult with the time difference but he had expected that Neesam and his team would have provided after sales support. On checking the contract he was still not sure - he was never very good with legal jargon. Brian had also read through the document Neesam had sent him, but he found it far too technical. It had been written by a software engineer who clearly assumed the reader would have the same knowledge as he or she did. In addition, the document had been translated from Hindi and the translator had done their best but may not have had as good a command of English as was necessary. There were some confusing parts to the document which really did not help.

All in all Brian had experienced a number of barriers to communication all in a very short space of time. The one good thing to come out of it was that he had realised that barriers to communication was not simply a case of a poorly worded letter or a telephone call that was breaking up - it could exist in lots of different forms and have some damaging effects on a wide range of the business's activities.

## Test yourself

1.  Which of the following could be a possible result of a message not being received properly? Select **one** answer.

    *A*  *A customer having to wait on the telephone*
    *B*  *An employee does something different from that intended by the sender*
    *C*  *A worker chooses to ignore a telephone call from a colleague*
    *D*  *The receiver responds positively to the message sent by the sender*

2.  Which of the following could be a possible barrier to communication? Select **one** answer.

    *A*  *Sending an e-mail to a colleague in anger*
    *B*  *Writing a letter to a customer*
    *C*  *Sending an e-mail instead of making a telephone call*
    *D*  *Choosing an appropriate medium to send a message*

3.  The chief executive officer of a large manufacturing firm decides to hold a series of focus groups with shop floor staff. A possible barrier to communication that might exist in such a situation might be the:

    *A*  *reliability of the workforce*
    *B*  *lack of direct communication between the CEO and the staff*
    *C*  *use of an appropriate meeting room*
    *D*  *position and status of the sender*

    Select **one** answer.

## Over to you

Claire worked as a customer service representative in a large call centre for a hotel reservation agency. Her job is to help customers book hotels and much of her work is for business customers looking for hotel accommodation. She had made a reservation for a customer at a hotel in Liverpool, but the customer had clearly not had the best experience. The customer phoned Claire and complained about the quality of the service he had received, He had turned up at the hotel but they did not seem to have a reservation in his name and it took a long time to get it sorted out. He had arrived late at night after a long day and did not want to go through such problems. Claire tried to apologise and explained that she could not understand what had happened. The customer was clearly not happy with her explanation and as the conversation continued he got more and more abusive. Claire finally snapped and told him in no uncertain terms where to go. Later that day she was called into her supervisor's office to explain her actions after the supervisor had received a complaint from the customer about her behaviour.

1. Identify **two** possible barriers to communication that have occurred in the passage. (2)
2. Identify one possible effect of the failure of communication in the passage. (1)
3. Explain how the effect that you have identified in (2) above might affect the business that Claire works for. (3)

## ResultsPlus
### Build Better Answers

The number of products at a flat pack furniture retailer being sent back to the store by customers had risen by 80% since a new instruction manual was included in the pack. Which **two** of the following are **most likely** to explain this rise? (2)

A  Customers do not like the product
B  The quality of the information in the manual
C  The new manual is printed on the wrong colour paper
D  The degree of knowledge of the customer in putting together the furniture
E  The new manual has made it easier to see the faults in the product

Answer B and D

Think: What are the main issues in the question - flat pack furniture needs clear instructions to help people put it together. The rise coincides with the new manual so it is likely that this is the cause. What could be causing the barrier to communication?

Then: Go through the options.

Review: Look at each option carefully. Try to dismiss the ones that are obviously wrong.

A is not right because customers presumably knew what the product looked like before buying it. The colour of the paper is unlikely to be a barrier to communication with regard to instructions so C can also be dismissed. This leaves B, D and E as options. A new manual is unlikely to highlight faults so this is also obviously wrong.

Decide: This leaves B and D. Make your decision as to the correct answers. Check to make sure you are happy with the answers. Both the quality of the information in the manual and the expertise of the customer who has to put the furniture together are likely to be barriers to communication so B and D are the most likely explanations.

# 5 The effects of good business communication

24

## Case Study

The British Cinema Group (BCG) owns a few small cinemas in the UK. Two years ago, managers spent time reflecting on sales figures and customer feedback forms and made a number of changes to the way the business ran as a result. They retrained their staff in customer service and put in place a new incentive scheme for staff to help support this training. They also created an advertising campaign, improved the quality of the information on the web site, and put in place measures to improve the appearance and cleanliness of their cinemas. They are now sitting down with the latest financial figures and new customer feedback forms to review the impact of the changes they had made.

## Objectives

- To understand the main ways in which businesses benefit from good communication.
- To understand the main benefits to businesses of good communication.

## How can good communications benefit a business?

The changes put in place by BCG were the result of feedback about the business. Sales figures tell a business something about what consumers think; if sales figures fall it could be because consumers are not happy with the product or the experience that they are receiving from the business. Of course, falling sales figures could be due to other factors as well, such as difficult economic circumstances or poor quality films. For BCG, the sales figures along with the results from the customer feedback forms will have sent a message about its business.

The management team was able to identify a number of factors from the feedback forms that might help explain part of the reason why sales had been falling. For the feedback forms to have any success as a means of communication, customers would have to see that the feedback they had given had been acted upon. The changes made by the business would have been a sign that this had in fact happened. Customer service, cleanliness and information about programmes were the main issues raised by customers. When they investigated further they found that the relationships between staff and some of their line managers was also a problem.

The management team hoped that the measures it had put in place would have led to improvements in the business performance. As in many cases with business, changes take time to implement and to have an effect. The team thought that two years was a good period of time after which to make some initial judgements about the success of the changes.

When considering the information they had collected from the new customer surveys and the financial data they were encouraged by what they read. It seemed that the measures they had put in place had been successful. The feedback forms were far more positive about the levels of customer service received and there was a large amount of responses that praised staff for their politeness, willingness to help, knowledge of the cinema and its facilities and their appearance. Sales had increased by 8% in the first year but by 22% in the second year. The management team were very pleased with these figures which were more than they had expected.

# Benefits of good communication

**Increased sales** One of the benefits of good communication to a business is increased sales. This might be as a result of a successful advertising campaign which has effectively engaged customers; it might be because promotional campaigns have been successful; it could be as a result of many years of building up **brand awareness**. In many cases, businesses are able to gain increases in sales through building reputation and trust. Brand awareness is part of that process.

**Building reputation** For BCG the challenge was to re-build its reputation which had suffered. This meant communicating trust, honesty, level of service and care right through the organisation. If a prospective customer telephoned the sales desk to buy tickets, that might represent the first impression that the customer had of the business. It was important to make sure that this communication was right. Getting the right attitude of staff to customers and other stakeholders was a major part of the training for the staff that BCG ran. The way a member of staff greeted a customer or supplier, for example, immediately communicates something to that person. BCG wanted their staff to communicate care, attention, consideration, politeness and knowledge. They wanted customers to feel that every time they visited the cinema they could be sure they would get a good customer service experience. This would encourage them to come back again and thus develop **customer loyalty** and increase sales.

The feedback forms gave some evidence that this had started to work. Responses agreed that staff were knowledgeable, that customers were greeted appropriately, that staff were polite and that they would recommend the cinema to friends and other people. 80% of customers who responded to the survey had said that if there was a choice between going to BCG's cinema and a rival then they would choose BCG - which might be one sign of customer loyalty. This information, however, also told BCG's management that there were still 20% who would not, so there was still plenty of work to be done.

**Motivation** One of the key areas for the management team was working with the staff to improve their **motivation**. When they began investigating the issues raised they found that there were problems with staff motivation, which was reflecting on the level of customer service they were offering. The retraining programme had focused on what **customer service** meant, why customers were so important to the business and the different skills that were required to improve customer service. The training programme had been on-going rather than just a one-off with a number of issues revisited several times. On one occasion staff had been taken away for a weekend at a hotel. They had spent Friday, Saturday and Sunday morning working on various programmes and training activities. In the afternoon and evening, staff had been able to use the hotel facilities which included spas, swimming pools, golf course and fitness and beauty centres. On the Saturday night, the whole team had been invited to a dinner where the management awarded a number of prizes for improvements in performance. The feedback from this was that staff felt valued and that they really enjoyed the opportunity to work and relax. The management believed that if they communicated respect and care to the staff this would lead to staff responding in kind and would also feed through to the way they dealt with customers.

**Improvements in efficiency** The management had seen some benefits to this in improvements in motivation. Staff absence and **staff turnover** had both fallen; punctuality had increased and efficiency had improved as a result. Staff had said that they were happier at work and looked forward to coming to work - not something they had said prior to the changes.

Good first impressions count and send important messages about a business to customers

## edexcel ::: key terms

**Brand awareness** – finding ways to make sure that customers are aware of a brand and that they choose that brand over rivals when making purchasing decisions.

**Customer loyalty** – a situation where customers prefer to buy from one business as opposed to any other in the same market and make that choice regularly.

**Motivation** – the process whereby individuals are committed and want to carry out activities on a regular basis to help achieve a business's goals.

**Customer service** – the experience that customers have in using a business. High levels of customer service improve the experience they have and encourage them to return to use the business again.

**Staff turnover** – the number of staff as a proportion of all staff in an organisation that leave in a particular time period. For example, if BCG employed 50 staff and 10 left each year then the staff turnover rate would be 20% (10/50 x 100).

The work the management team had done to highlight the importance of staff having the right knowledge about the business had also helped. This included simple things like having some awareness of the content of the films being shown, whether they were suitable for certain age groups, where the theatres were, what films were coming in the future, right down to where the toilets were.

**Improving product information** The management stressed that even though BCG was a cinema and was primarily selling a service, **product knowledge** was still vital in good communication with customers. If staff could be relied upon to provide accurate and reliable information then customers would have a better experience and would be more likely to visit again. All this was supported by investment into

## edexcel ⠿ key terms

**Product knowledge** – the ability of an employee in a business to know about the product and be able to explain its key features, benefits and limitations to a customer or other stakeholder.

**Social enterprises** – business organisations that aim to make a profit but have as their main aim social and/or environmental goals. Profits that are made may be distributed to the cause they are interested in rather than to investors.

improving the web site so that customers could find out what they wanted to know easily. This, in addition to the training of the staff, was seen as vital to improving the product information.

**Achieving other objectives** In BCG's case the different methods of communication they had adopted - between themselves and customers, suppliers, the local community and employees - had seen a number of benefits to the way the business ran, not to mention the sales it made.

However, not every business is interested in communication simply to increase sales and make profits. Charities, environmental groups and **social enterprises** are all forms of business organisation, but their main aim may be to offer a service and improve people's living standards or well being. In their case, successful communication can lead to benefits such as increased donations, increased awareness of their cause and increased understanding by the public of the social and environmental issues they are interested in. Care needs to be taken to make sure that the problems people want to be aware of are raised, but that the communication is not seen as being too 'over the top'. Images of pathetic starving children, for example, can have the effect of encouraging people to donate and/or help but if such images are used too many times it is possible that they cease to have the right impact.

## Test yourself

1.  Good communications bring benefits to a business in all of the following **except**:

    A   *greater motivation from employees*
    B   *increased costs of production*
    C   *an improvement in customer loyalty*
    D   *a fall in staff turnover*

    Select **one** answer.

2.  A successful advertising campaign is one example of good communication. A business can tell if it has been successful because:

    A   *there will be an increase in cost*
    B   *consumers will be more likely to choose a rival's product*
    C   *it will lead to an increase in competition*
    D   *the level of sales will increase*

    Select **one** answer.

3.  The level of staff skills in communicating with customers is important to a business because:

    A   *the staff have to be able to talk to each other without fear*
    B   *reducing levels of customer service will lead to increased sales*
    C   *customers can get the advice and information they require*
    D   *the customer is always right*

    Select **one** answer.

# Over to you

It had been a long wait for most passengers following the security scare at the airport, but everyone was now on the plane and ready to set off on the 10 hour journey back from Los Angeles to London. The problems started, however, when one passenger, Mary, wanted to recline her seat after the meals had been served - it was a night flight after all. The passenger behind (Gareth) - who also had his seat reclined - objected. The husband of the lady concerned (Russell) confronted Gareth who had been very rude to Mary. She was clearly upset. It all threatened to get very ugly but a member of cabin crew noticed what was going on.

The head of the cabin crew, James, took Russell and Mary to one side, gave Mary a glass of champagne and talked to them about the problems that reclining seats caused on flights. He was very sympathetic to their plight and understood they felt upset at how rude Gareth had been. James' humour and calm approach helped Russell and Mary feel much more relaxed. Meanwhile another member of cabin crew spoke to Gareth and asked him if he would like to move to another seat where there was no-one in front of him - he readily accepted. By the time Russell and Mary had finished their talk with James they felt much better and the fact that Gareth had been moved meant

that the situation had been sorted to everyone's satisfaction. All in a night's work for cabin crew.

1. Identify one example of good communication by cabin crew highlighted in the passage. (1)
2. Explain how this example might benefit the airline business running the flight. (3)

## ResultsPlus
### Build Better Answers

Jamie Oliver's restaurant, *Fifteen*, is a social enterprise. Social enterprises are businesses but they are run not just to make a profit but to tackle a social or an environmental need. Jamie Oliver set up Fifteen in 2002 with two key aims: 'to open a top class restaurant and to give disadvantaged youngsters the chance to gain professional training that would set them up for an independent, inspired and productive life'.

Source: adapted from http://www.fifteen.net/Pages/default.aspx

Building brand awareness and improving motivation amongst staff might be two benefits of good communication for *Fifteen*. Which of the two do you think is the more important benefit to *Fifteen*? Justify your answer. (8)

Technique guide: This is a question that is assessing your ability to make judgements and to break down a complex topic into easier to manage chunks (evaluation and analysis).

Think: Why are both of the items important to a business like Fifteen? Remember that this is a social enterprise as well as an ordinary business - this might influence your answer. How might the benefits of good communication link with the aims of the business?

Then: Arrive at a decision about which benefit you are going to choose - there is no right answer; the examiner is looking for your ability to make a judgement and support it.

Remember: It is not how much you write here but the quality of your answer. Make sure that you provide some balance and refer to both benefits in your answer to get into the top marks.

Plan: Try and think through how you are going to approach the answer and how you are going to structure it.

Write: Write out your answer.

🟥 **Basic** Provides a judgement about one of the benefits and gives a limited reason for the judgement. (1-2)

🔴 **Good** Provides a judgement and offers an explanation of one of the two benefits only. Appropriate terms and concepts are used as part of the explanation for the judgement. (3-5)

🔺 **Excellent** Provides a brief explanation of the role of both benefits and links them to the aims of the business. Arrives at a judgement of one and provides some explanation of the reason for the choice. Appropriate terms and concepts are used throughout the answer. (6-8)

# 6 The effects of bad business communication

## Case Study

YMA Chemicals plc has a large manufacturing plant on Teesside in north east England. The nature of the work they do means that the plant has to operate 24 hours a day. Workers had been used to a shift pattern that involved two 12 hour shifts - two weeks on and two weeks off. The management had spent some time looking at ways to improve productivity and efficiency at the plant as a result of the increase in competition they faced, especially from companies in China. The shareholders of the business had been concerned that profits had been falling for some time.

Their plan was to change work patterns. They proposed a new shift arrangement of 3 shifts, 6am to 2pm, 2pm - 10pm and 10pm to 6am. Workers would work four days and have four days off. The staff were informed through a letter sent to their homes outlining the changes. The workers did not like the new arrangements and felt that the decision had been made without any consultation with them. Most liked the existing shift arrangements because it helped them to manage their families and home lives far better. The new shift pattern would disrupt all these plans. They were also upset that management had not told them of the changes personally at a meeting at the plant. The managers argued that they would have had to have a number of meetings with the different shifts to give out the information and thought a letter was more appropriate as it informed them all at the same time.

## Objectives

- To recognise that bad communication can have major effects on businesses.
- To understand the main problems for a business that can arise from poor communications.

### edexcel key terms

**Stakeholder** – an individual or group with an interest in a business.

## When can business communication be 'bad'?

Any communication can have positive and negative outcomes. In the last section the benefits of good communication were outlined. Good communication occurs when the sender gets the feedback they are looking for but this feedback is something that the receiver is happy to give. When the receiver is not happy to give the feedback that the sender is looking for, problems can arise. There is a number of problems that arise when communication is bad.

In the case study the needs of the workers were different from that of the business. This is not a situation that does not have a resolution, every day there are conflicts between the needs of different **stakeholders** in a business. However, good communication can help to reduce the risk of problems arising. In the case above, the workers did not like the decision that had been made and they also did not like the way in which it had been communicated. In many businesses decisions have to be made that do not please all stakeholders or are likely to satisfy one more than any other. What is important is making sure that all stakeholders are aware of the reasons for a decision and to try and find ways to communicate those decisions in the best way possible.

For many of the workers at YMA Chemicals, the existing shift patterns were something that they had been used to for many years. Most had got into a routine and this routine suited their family lives and domestic arrangements. Any changes to these arrangements might cause inconvenience and plenty of time may be needed to enable workers to make alternative arrangements. The management had been under pressure to find ways of cutting costs and the new shift patterns had been calculated to save the company large sums of money each year. The management believed that an explanation of the changes through a letter was the most appropriate way of letting all staff know the new arrangements. The staff clearly felt that a letter was not the best method of communication. Their needs in the communication process did not meet the sender's.

## What are the results of bad communication

When communication breaks down the sender and the receiver may not be prepared to listen to each other. As a result messages and information do not get through. When information and messages do not get through actions are not carried out and behaviour does not change. When this happens business operations are affected in a variety of ways.

**Falling sales** One effect of bad communication with customers is that sales could start to fall. The business may not be getting the message through to customers about the quality of the products, the value of them, the technical superiority and so on. As a result consumers look elsewhere for their products and sales fall.

**Disruption of supplies** Bad communications with suppliers can lead to disruption of supplies and in some cases can even halt supplies. If suppliers do not get the right messages and the right feedback they may be in a situation where the trust and honesty between the two parties breaks down. In a similar way, bad communications between the business and its shareholders can lead to shareholders taking action against the board of directors including voting them off their position. Examples of where bad communication can take place in such circumstances are when profits are not as high as shareholders expect or where directors have voted themselves large pay rises or bonuses that do not seem justified by the performance of the business.

**The environment** There is now an increasing concern over the effects of business activity on the environment. This can range from litter from fast food outlets, pollution of rivers and the air and excessive noise right through to greenhouse gas emissions and climate change. Poor communications about the effects of business activities on the environment and the local community can lead to protest, boycotts (where consumers are urged to not buy products or use the services of a business), action by pressure groups and bad publicity for the business. Firms involved in research on animals, for example, have faced many extreme examples of protest against the business and the people who work for it. Staff at some have had their cars damaged, received threatening phone calls, have had slogans daubed on their homes and in one case, the dead relative of one family was stolen from a grave.

Businesses know that they have a responsibility in many cases, to explain their actions and to try and find ways of communicating with their stakeholders, like the local community, what they do and the benefits that their operations bring. They also try to show how they take such concerns into account when making decisions. However, if the receiver does not want to listen or the message is not clear then the communication breaks down and problems continue.

**Effects on the workforce** At YMA Chemicals, the changes being made by the management were internal. The way the changes were communicated was not what staff believed was the most appropriate, as a result there were anger and resentment amongst the workforce. Such a response is typical when employees cannot understand or see the need for a change. Unless that reason is communicated properly and through the right medium, frustration can build up and there can be longer-term problems for the business.

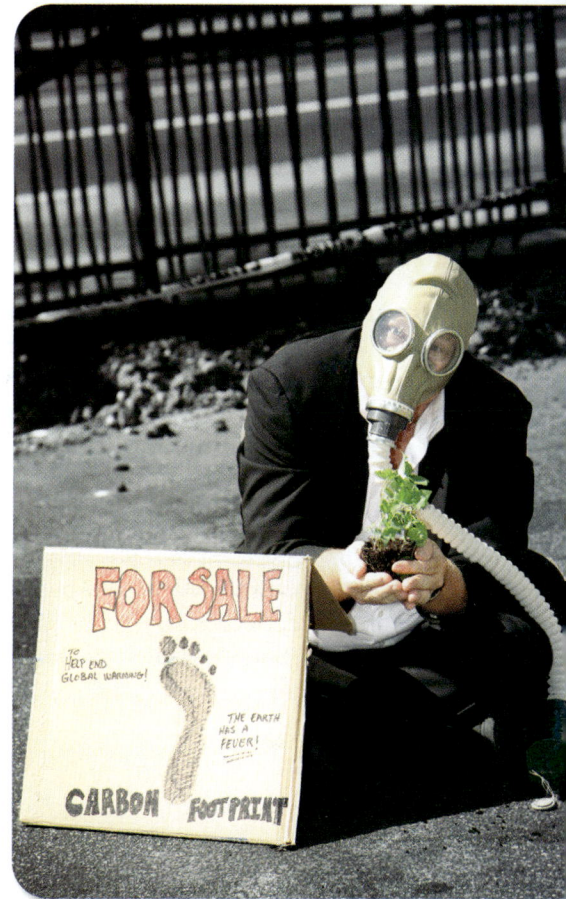

Businesses need to send a clear message about how their activities affect the environment, for example. Failure to do so can result in problems, such as protests

**ResultsPlus**
**Watch Out!**

Make sure that you remember that the process of communication is often as important, if not more so, than the method of communication. There is often more than one way to do things in a business and selecting the right one can be important.

Bad communication can lead to employees feeling de-motivated and alienated. This means that they feel apart from the business rather than belonging to it and do not put their very best into their work. They cease to feel that they belong to the business anymore. The result is often that they do not care as much about their work and their contribution. Why should they care about the business when the business does not care about them? For the business, this attitude can lead to a **fall in the quality** of goods and services produced. Complaints against staff and about products can rise and ultimately if quality declines sales will fall.

**Effects on productivity and efficiency** Having disgruntled staff also leads to a reduction in efficiency - the business does not get as much out of the worker as they could. This can also cause costs of production to rise. A fall in quality means that there may be more wastage, more returns that the company has to deal with, more repairs they have to make and so on, and all this costs money which is not being covered by additional revenue. Increasing costs whilst revenues stay the same or fall mean that profits fall and some firms can be forced to close down if the problems are not sorted out.

**Bad publicity** Poor communication can also lead to bad publicity for a business and damage to the firm's reputation. Building customer loyalty is an expensive and time consuming process but this can be undone very quickly by bad communication which affects reputation. Getting back customer loyalty can be very difficult. In 2008, the clothes retailer Primark acted very quickly to deal with reports that some of its suppliers employed child labour. Primark knew that such publicity could damage its reputation and immediately cancelled the contracts with the offending suppliers. It wanted to reassure customers that it supported the highest ethical standards in its suppliers - something that the business is keen to communicate with all its stakeholders. If it had not reacted so quickly and in the right way, the message might have been communicated that Primark did not mind using child labour. This would have been bad communication and could have had lasting effects on its business.

At YMA Chemicals, the workers were angry and frustrated by the communication. They believed the management should have consulted them in their discussions about the possible changes to shifts. If YMA's managers had done this then the workers might have felt part of the decision-making process. They would have felt that the company valued their opinions and could have made suggestions for helping the company solve its problems whilst meeting their needs as well. The letter might have explained a great deal but it told workers something that had already been decided. What may have been a perfectly good medium of communication turned into a bad one because of what had gone before it.

An alternative medium would have been to call all the staff to a meeting to present the company's plans and seek the views of the workers on those plans before they were finalised. Staff could have asked questions and heard replies from the managers themselves. They might have felt that this was a more personal and appropriate method of communication for such a change. As it was, the communication process and method chosen by the business merely caused anger and resentment.

## Test yourself

1. Poor communication is most likely to be a situation in which:

   A  the sender does not know what medium to use
   B  the receiver cannot give any feedback at all
   C  the sender does not receive the feedback expected
   D  the sender does not know the receiver

   Select one answer.

2. Falling sales might be the result of poor communication. This could be due to all of the following **except**:

   A  poor product knowledge by the staff
   B  a badly designed advertising campaign
   C  poor quality of the product
   D  an increase in competition

   Select one answer.

3. Lee sent a message via e-mail to a colleague asking them to provide a projector in the conference room for a presentation he had to make to staff. When he got to the room five minutes before his presentation was due to start the projector was not there. The conference was delayed whilst he sorted out the problem. The result of this lack of communication for Lee is most likely to be:

   A  his audience would not know what the presentation was going to be about
   B  a feeling that Lee was badly organised and inefficient
   C  the failure of his presentation to get its message across successfully
   D  bad publicity for the business as a whole

   Select one answer.

# Over to you

Colin was part way through building a small retaining wall in his garden when he ran out of bricks. It was a Sunday so he knew the local builders' merchant would be closed. However, he knew that a large DIY chain store 10 miles away would be open so he set off to buy the extra 12 bricks he needed. When he got to the store he looked in the outside area where the building materials were but could not see any bricks. He looked inside the store but could still not see any. He decided to ask one of the staff - not easy given that there did not seem to be many around. He eventually found someone at the customer service desk. 'Do you have any bricks?' asked Colin. 'What sort of bricks?' replied the assistant. Colin's heart sank. 'Building bricks', he said. 'Yes', said the assistant, 'They are outside in the garden centre area'. 'I have looked there but could not see any' said Colin. 'I will take you and show you.' said the assistant. They went outside and the assistant went to a section where there was a stack of blocks for paving. 'Here we are' said the assistant. 'Those are not bricks' said Colin, 'They are for paving'. 'Oh, we have these', replied the assistant, pointing to another product next to the blocks. 'They are paving slabs' said Colin in exasperation. 'Really, the only other things we have are those' the assistant replied, pointing to some kerb stones. 'They are not bricks' said Colin, trying to keep his temper under control. 'Oh, well those are those are the only bricks we have got' said the assistant. Colin turned and left.

1. What is meant by 'product knowledge' in relation to employees at a business like the DIY store above? (2)

2. Outline how bad product knowledge could be an example of poor communication in a business like the DIY store. (2)
3. Identify **one** effect of the lack of product knowledge by the assistant in the passage. (1)
4. For this effect, explain the likely impact on the business. (3)

## ResultsPlus
### Build Better Answers

Sarah was late for a meeting, but had to quickly send an e-mail to her personal assistant (PA), Lily, to book her a taxi for her next meeting at an important client's office for 12.30. After she got out from the meeting she found out that the taxi was not there. Lily knew nothing about ordering a taxi. The client was not happy that Sarah was late.

Which of the following might **best** explain why the communication failed? Select **one** answer.

A  Sarah typed the address incorrectly into the e-mail
B  Sarah should have spoken to her PA personally
C  The medium chosen to send the message was inappropriate
D  The receiver (the PA) did not understand what Sarah wanted

Answer A

Think: Read the passage carefully and identify where the communication failed. What might have caused the e-mail to not be sent?

Then: Go through the options.

Review: Look at each option carefully. Try to dismiss the ones that are obviously wrong in relation to the information you have been given in the passage.

Decide: Make your decision as to the correct answer.

Go through each option (distracter) and try and eliminate the ones that are clearly not right. In this case, B might be a lesson that Sarah can learn from the episode but is not the reason why the communication failed. There was nothing wrong with sending an e-mail - this is a perfectly good medium to use to send such a message - providing it is received by Lily. D is not correct because Lily did not receive the information in the first place so it was not that she could not understand it.

A is very plausible. The taxi was not there and given that Lily knew nothing about it, we might assume that she did not receive the message. Typing in the wrong address would explain why Lily did not get the message. A is therefore the **best** reason given.

**In this topic you have learned about:** what communication means, that communication involves a sender and a receiver, successful communication means the sender receiving feedback from the receiver, the purpose of communication being to transmit information, that communication involves transmitting messages to different audiences and that sometimes these messages can cause conflict, the different media that can be used to communicate information, that there is a number of barriers to successful communication, that businesses can gain many benefits from successful communication and the effects of poor communication on a business.

## You should know…

- ☐ What the communication model is.
- ☐ That communication is about sending and receiving information.
- ☐ The process of communication involves sending information, receiving it and completing the loop by sending appropriate feedback to the sender.
- ☐ The nature of communication depends on the audience to which the information is to be sent.
- ☐ Different audiences might need to be sent information in different ways.
- ☐ The different needs of audiences might mean that information sent in communication could cause conflict.
- ☐ Successful communication occurs when the sender has received expected feedback from the receiver - this could be in the form of changed behaviour or some action.
- ☐ There is a number of barriers to successful communication - things that interfere with the message being sent.

- ☐ Barriers to communication include the type of language used, cultural differences, the knowledge and expertise of the sender and receiver, the level of technical content, the trust and respect between the two parties and the status and position of the sender in relation to the receiver.
- ☐ If communication is successful there can be a number of benefits to a business.
- ☐ These benefits include increased sales, brand awareness, customer loyalty, improved image and reputation, increased motivation of staff, increased efficiency and the furthering of the aims and objectives of the business.
- ☐ However, poor communication can have many of the opposite effects.
- ☐ In addition, poor communication can lead to bad publicity, create conflict, alienate staff and reduce efficiency and productivity.

## Support activity

- Cut out the portraits of two of your favourite TV/music/film etc. stars.
- Produce a poster that shows all the different ways in which your two choices could communicate.
- Produce a mind map showing the barriers to communication and what the effects of such barriers might be on a business.
- With a group of class friends, play the game 'Chinese Whispers'. Each individual must think of a statement about a business decision - it could be any decision with which you are familiar. Set yourselves up in a line with the person whose 'go' it is first and then whisper your message to the next person in line. The person last in line must write down the message they receive. Compare the original message and the end message in each case. How different are the messages? Can you identify any patterns in the way the end messages change and why this might be?

## Stretch activity

Use the Internet or newspaper articles to find an example where communication has either:
a) failed
b) been successful
in a business.

Produce a short summary of the issue you have found. Then explain why you think the communication failed or was successful and why.

(a) Aaron had taken a phone call from a customer on Monday concerning a docking station for an MP3 player. The dock was not in stock at Aaron's store but it was available at another store nearby. Aaron assured the customer he would collect it on Wednesday when he was at the other store and would deliver it to the customer on Thursday morning as he had to pass through the village where the customer lived.

(i) What was the medium of communication used in the passage above between Aaron and the customer? (1)

(ii) Explain how the customer would know that the communication he has had with Aaron had been successful. (3)

Think: read the little passage carefully and note the information that it contains. What is the medium of communication? What is needed to make sure that communication is successful?

| Student answer | Examiner comment | Build a better answer |
|---|---|---|
| (i) The medium of communication was talking. | 🟥 This answer misses the point to an extent - clearly there was some oral communication between Aaron and the customer but how was the initial communication made - was it face to face? | 🔺 Identify the medium of communication - the means by which the information is transferred. In this case it was by telephone. Try to use appropriate terminology in your answer - 'oral' rather than 'talking'. |
| (ii) Communication would be successful if the customer spoke to Aaron. | 🟥 Again, this answer misses the point. Simply speaking to someone does not show that communication has been successful. There has to be some sort of feedback to the customer to show it has been successful. | 🔺 Use the process of communication to highlight understanding - use the term 'feedback' and identify exactly what feedback the customer would be expecting given his conversation with Aaron - the delivery of his docking station on Thursday as promised by Aaron. Only when he had received this feedback would he know that the feedback had been successful. |

## Mini Exam Paper

Mike Dean was the managing director of a retail store, Jones & Jones. He was not happy. The local newspapers had run headline stories about how the company were attempting to cheat their staff about their pension rights. This was not good publicity. It appeared that one of the staff who had worked in the offices that dealt with wages had decided to send round a confidential e-mail to other staff about the pension proposals - and they were only proposals. Some of the staff had 'blabbed' to the press and now it looked like the trade unions were getting involved wanting to know why they had not been consulted on any such changes. Mike's gut instinct was to discipline the worker who had sent round the e-mail. However, one of his colleagues on the board of directors had advised him against this saying he thought it would only make matters worse.

(a) Identify **two** possible barriers to communication highlighted in the passage above (2)

(b) For each barrier, explain **one** possible effect on Jones & Jones' business. (6)

(c) Describe **one** advantage to Mike of talking to the worker who circulated the e-mail rather than disciplining him. (3)

(d) With reference to the passage, discuss **two** possible effects of the newspaper reports on Jones & Jones. (10)

# Topic 4.2: Communication with stakeholders of a business

## Case study

The launch of a new product for any business is an exciting but anxious time. Nokia, the mobile phone manufacturer, is no different. In 2008, it launched a new phone, the N96. The phone was designed to be a competitor to the Apple iPhone and to provide **customers** with the latest mobile technology. The success of a new product is important for a number of reasons. Businesses like Nokia will want to retain their customer loyalty and so produce new products to maintain interest and keep up to date with the latest developments in the industry. **Shareholders** of the business will want to see new products be a success so that they get a return on their investment. **Suppliers** will rely on the success of new products to maintain their order books and **governments** will benefit from the taxes that firms such as Nokia pay. Mobile phones contain a number of potentially toxic chemicals and as new products come out old products get discarded. There will be environmental groups representing **local communities** that will encourage firms like Nokia to take steps to minimise the environmental effects of their business operations.

## Topic overview

This topic looks at stakeholders - the people and groups that have an interest in a business. It looks at the different ways that businesses communicate with these stakeholders. These ways include written, electronic and oral communication and also includes the use of images as a means of sending and receiving messages and information.

Nokia will have to find ways of communicating important messages about their new product to these stakeholders. In each case the message might be different depending on the audience and the interests of stakeholders. Nokia will have spent many months preparing these different types of communication. Internally their sales team will have had presentations and training on the new phone to enable them to have the knowledge and confidence to go out and sell the product to stores. Much of this communication will have been through oral means.

Nokia will also have had a large amount of written communication with its staff as the product was developed and prepared for launch. Letters will have been written, memos sent and received, the minutes would have kept a record of meetings held about the product launch so that everyone involved knew what was happening and who was responsible for what. Staff may have been kept up to date with developments through newsletters. Manuals will have had to be written to help customers understand how to use the phone.

In addition, electronic means of communication will have been extensively used. E-mail allows a firm like Nokia to keep in touch with staff and with its suppliers and customers; it is likely that the business will have done extensive market research on the product and used existing customer profiles that its databases had built up to help it reduce the risk of failure for the N96.

Perhaps most importantly of all, the design of the actual product itself and the promotional material that accompany the launch will have been carefully considered. Nokia know that good design, having the right images at the right time are an important part of building brand recognition and customer loyalty.

1. What responsibilities does a firm like Nokia have to its stakeholders?

2. Nokia uses many different types of communication in the development and launch of a new product like the N96. What do you think would be the most important methods that would allow it to communicate successfully with all of its stakeholders?

3. In the face of the growing sophistication of electronic means of communication, does written communication play such an important role in businesses these days?

4. Why might a firm like Nokia spend large amounts of time and money making sure it got the images associated with the product right?

## What will I learn?

**What are stakeholders?** Stakeholders are any individual or group with an interest in the business. A business has a responsibility to its different stakeholders and these interests often require different types of communication.

**How do businesses communicate with stakeholders?** There is a wide range of ways in which businesses communicate with their stakeholders. The method chosen will depend on the message to be sent and who is receiving it as well as the likely success of the method chosen in getting the message across.

**What types of written communication do businesses use?** Written communication is more than simply writing letters. There are formal methods of written communication such as agendas, letters and minutes and informal ones such as memos and scribbled notes.

**What types of electronic communication do businesses use?** Electronic communication plays an increasing role in business. This extends to far more than simply e-mail and fax. The developments in technology allow businesses to collect information about their stakeholders, especially customers, which allow the businesses to be able to meet their needs more directly.

**What types of oral communication do businesses use?** Speaking face-to face or to an audience is still one of the most widely used methods of communication. Different skills and considerations are needed depending on the type of communication being used.

**Images used in business communication?** The use of images is not just logos. Careful design and the use of slogans and celebrity endorsements are all part of a total package to raise awareness of a product or brand and get it known in the market place.

## How will I be assessed?

- Unit 4 is externally assessed.
- You will sit an exam of one and a half hours duration.
- There will be a mixture of multiple choice questions, short answer questions and extended writing questions.

# 7 Stakeholders

## Case Study

Times were tough for the chief executive at Bright Star Gas. The company was a large distributor of gas to homes and businesses. It had a turnover of £7 billion per year and served 8 million customers. Stewart Moore, the chief executive officer (CEO), faced a growing crisis in the business. Gas suppliers had been increasing their prices massively as North Sea gas supplies began to dry up. The shareholders in the business were complaining that the return on their investment had not been rising as they had hoped. Customers faced rising prices for their gas bills and were not happy. Employees were complaining that the squeeze on costs that Stewart had introduced was affecting the way they were able to work. In addition, he had the latest profit figures to announce. They were good, but not good enough for the shareholders. Despite this the company faced a barrage of criticism from the press about making profits, whilst customers struggled to afford their prices. To cap it all, the concerns over the environment meant he had to make some tough decisions about how the business went about its operations. His management team were divided on how the business should change the way it worked to reduce the effects of the business on the environment.

## Objectives

- To understand the meaning of the term 'stakeholder'.
- To understand the difference between internal and external stakeholders in a business.
- To understand the main ways in which businesses communicate with their stakeholders.
- To appreciate the role and importance of stakeholders to a business.

### edexcel key terms

**Stakeholder** – any individual or group with an interest in a business.

## What is a stakeholder?

The basic idea of business is very simple – find a product or a service that enough people are willing to pay a price for that is sufficient to more than cover the cost of providing that product or service. What business also involves, which makes it more complex, is people and a wide variety of people at that. Businesses have owners, managers, employees, customers and suppliers. They work in an area and their actions have an effect on the local community in which they operate. Businesses also have to consider their responsibilities to the national government. They have to pay taxes and abide by the laws of the land. In carrying out their business, they generate benefits and costs and increasingly, the costs imposed by businesses on the environment are of major concern.

All these people have an interest in the business. Employers, for example, rely on the business for their wage. Customers expect quality products and services, along with reasonable prices. Any group or individual with an interest in the business's operations is called a **stakeholder**.

- Some of these stakeholders are directly involved with the business in some way. They are referred to as **internal stakeholders**.
- There are others that are affected by the business and have an interest in it, but are not directly involved in the business. These groups are called **external stakeholders**.

The interest that stakeholders have in the business is different in each case and can sometimes create conflicts for the business, which need addressing. These conflicts represent some of the most difficult and challenging aspects to running any business. As a result, communication with all stakeholder groups is vital and has to be handled with care. For example, Stewart might need to communicate with customers of Bright Star to explain to them why the company has to put up gas prices - something few customers will like. At the same time he faces questions from the shareholders about the level of profit that the company is making. His main duty is to manage the business on behalf of the shareholders. If he puts up prices to cover the increased cost of buying in gas from suppliers then he might be able to maintain or even increase profits. If he puts up prices too high then he might face complaints from consumers. He has to try to justify his decisions to the shareholders.

The main stakeholders in a business and their interests in the business are shown in Figure 1.

## Internal stakeholders

A business has a number of internal stakeholders.

**Shareholders** Shareholders are the owners of a business. They have invested money into taking a part ownership of the business. In the case of a private limited company, the number of shareholders may be small and consist of family members or friends. In the case of a public limited company (plc), there may be millions of shareholders. Some will be individuals with a small number of shares and others will be large companies who invest in shares as part of their business, such as pension funds and insurance companies. Increasingly, the shareholders in a plc can come from many different countries around the world.

Shareholders buy shares for two main reasons. They may buy the shares at one price in the hope of selling them at a different price to make a profit. They may also buy shares because they are entitled to a share of the profits that a business makes. This share of the profits is called a **dividend**. Since the profit a business makes is one indication of its success, the more profit the business makes the happier the shareholders are, generally speaking.

**Employees** Employees are employed by the business for the contribution they make to production. They provide their labour - both physical and mental - to help the business carry out its operations. In return, employees expect to receive remuneration - a payment. This can be in the form of a wage or a salary. In addition, employees might expect bonus payments, company cars and other fringe benefits, such as pensions, paid holiday leave or subsidised canteens, depending on the company. They will also expect the company to abide by laws, ensure they work in an environment that meets health and safety rules and that they are free from harassment, bullying and intimidation. Employers will expect employees to support the business's aims and objectives and to maintain confidentiality. Employers can also expect employees to demonstrate some loyalty and commitment to the business.

**Managers** The managers have the responsibility to run the day-to-day affairs of a business on behalf of the owners. They plan, organise, take decisions and control many aspects of running a business. There is a potential problem here in that

**Figure 1** – Internal and external stakeholders in Bright Star Gas

**ResultsPlus**
**Watch Out!**

Many students confuse 'stakeholder' with 'shareholder'. Make sure you know the difference and take care when writing answers not to confuse the two.

## edexcel ::: key terms

**Internal stakeholders** – have a direct association and interest in the business - employees, managers and shareholders.

**External stakeholders** – individuals and groups not directly involved with a business or its decisions but who are affected by or have an interest in the business, the local community, pressure groups, customers, suppliers and the government.

**Dividend** – a share of the profits of a company received by people who own shares.

38

some managers are also owners. Whilst their primary responsibility is to the owners of the business, managers may have their own objectives, which might relate to the status and benefits they are able to get from being involved with the business. They may be interested in pursuing projects and new initiatives for personal gain as well as for the benefit of the business. This might be to enhance their personal CV or to improve their chances of promotion.

## External stakeholders

A business also has a number of external stakeholders.

**Suppliers** Many businesses rely on suppliers to provide them with raw materials, equipment, components and services such as banking, legal and insurance, to carry out their operations. Suppliers expect businesses to pay them within a reasonable time period and at an appropriate price for the products they supply. In return, the business expects the supplier to deliver on time and to provide goods and services that meet quality standards. There has been much written about the way in which businesses treat their suppliers, but in recent years many businesses have recognised that the relationship with their supplier is an important aspect of their business. As a result, some businesses actively seek to build closer relationships with their suppliers.

**Local community** Businesses can never be divorced from the local community in which they are located. Any business's activities will have an effect on the local community. In some cases this effect can be significant, for example, the effect that a nuclear power station has on its local community. Even small firms, however, will have an effect on the local community. Farmers, for example, have to recognise that the work they do might leave thick mud on the road or emit smells that affect nearby houses. The local community benefits from having businesses amongst them because these businesses provide employment and many businesses now seek to get actively involved in supporting the local community. This might range from providing assistance or sponsorship to local schools and sports clubs right down to sponsoring a local roundabout.

**Customers** This stakeholder is extremely important for a number of reasons. Customers are the market for the business. They provide the business with the source of sales and thus revenue - the amount of money earned by the

business through selling its goods or services. Without customers a business would not exist. In return, customers will expect businesses to provide them with goods that meet consumer law (that they are fit for purpose, not faulty, are safe and are as described) and that the goods and services meet appropriate quality standards. Customers will also expect that the price will represent value for money. Customers can sometimes be in a weak position to influence how a businesses behaves. This is because a business may be very large. As a result, various groups have developed which seek to help represent consumers. These include *Which*, the TV programme Watchdog and regulators such as Ofcom and Ofgem. Regulators are set up by the government to act as independent bodies to monitor the behaviour of firms.

**Pressure groups** Pressure groups exist to put forward the views of a group of people and to try to persuade businesses and government of the importance of their view. They hope to persuade businesses and government to change their behaviour to take into account their views. Pressure groups can be small and set up to put across a particular point of view about a very local issue, such as those protesting against the development of an eco-town on the outskirts of Leicester or can be very large organisations such as Greenpeace, Friends of the Earth, the AA and Surfers against Sewage. Some pressure groups are international organisations.

**Government** The government has an interest in businesses because businesses provide employment and pay taxes. Businesses are important in generating wealth and creating new ideas. However, governments also know that businesses can have disadvantages that can affect the public and so they pass laws and set up bodies to monitor how businesses operate. Bodies such as the Competition Commission, the Trading Standards Authority and the Food Standards Agency are examples.

Pressure groups try to persuade businesses and government to change their behaviour

edexcel ::: key terms

**Pressure groups** – groups set up to persuade businesses and government to behave in a certain way or take action in line with the beliefs of the pressure group.

# How do businesses communicate with their stakeholders?

Businesses have to remember that almost everything they do is a form of communication that sends out a message to one or more of its stakeholders. Each stakeholder might interpret the communication differently. There is, however, a number of formal and informal ways in which a business communicates with its stakeholders, as shown in Table 1.

Stewart Moore knew that the decisions Bright Star Gas had to make in the coming months were going to shape the future of the business. The demands made on the business by all the stakeholders simply could not be met. It was not possible to satisfy the full demands of every one of them. Stewart knew that he and his fellow directors would have to find a balance between the competing demands of stakeholders.

Part of the task was to make sure that the communication between the company and its stakeholders was accurate and clear. If prices had to be raised to customers it was important that they understood the reasons why. Employees had to be clear about why the squeeze on costs was so important to their future as well as the businesses - their futures were very closely linked. Shareholders had to be made to understand the importance of balancing profit with the need to maintain customer loyalty and the need to consider the impact of the business's activities on the environment.

Making sure that the right communication method was chosen to put across these messages was going to be vitally important. If letters were sent to customers, words would have to be chosen carefully to make sure that the message they were sending was clear and accurate. The written reports on the financial performance to shareholders had to contain information relating to the different challenges the company faced and the long-term benefits to them of taking painful decisions now. The web site had to provide sufficient information to all stakeholders who might want to find out about the company. The customer service team had to be well informed and understand how to deal with sometimes angry customers at the other end of the phone. Stewart knew that communication was the key to getting his messages across successfully.

**Table 1** – Methods of communicating with stakeholders

- Advertising and promotion - this could be through TV or radio but also via billboards, carrier bags, leaflets and so on. When businesses have product displays they are communicating a message to their customers - 'buy me'.
- Annual reports - these are formal documents produced by public limited companies for the benefit of shareholders and prospective investors.
- Letters - these may be in response to complaints or to provide information, for example about price changes or changes to terms and conditions.
- Magazines - a number of companies produce magazines either for their workers or for distribution to customers.
- Through the Internet - this is not only through having a web site but also providing means for customers to contact the business 24 hours a day and providing information and updates quickly to customers.
- E- mail - a quick and speedy way to contact stakeholders also used as a means of informing customers of delivery and tracking the progress of orders.
- Design - extremely important for many businesses. Design not only communicates the ethos and image of a business, it also says something about the functionality of a product. For example, the iPod's 'click wheel' was seen as being revolutionary and in the music world the Gibson Les Paul and the Fender Stratocaster guitars are almost instantly recognisable.
- Logos - as with design, having the right logo can be crucial in communicating the image and values of a business. Simple logos can help create brand identity and brand loyalty
- Mission statements - communicate what the business stands for and are a guide to all employees to help them in presenting the business to other stakeholders.
- Strap lines - these are catch phrases that a business uses to help stakeholders to remember their business. For example, 'have a break, have a ….' 'A …. A day helps you work rest and play'. Do you know the missing products?
- Technical design and specification - some products communicate sophistication and high value to stakeholders possibly with the aim of persuading customers, for example, (sometimes with good reason) to pay higher prices. BMW, Mercedes, Lexus, Bang and Olufsen and Bose are examples of brands that pride themselves on technical design and specification and want to be associated with them.

## Test yourself

1. A stakeholder is a person or group that:

   A  *is directly employed by a business*
   B  *has an interest in the business and how it operates*
   C  *owns the business and buys shares in the business*
   D  *makes decisions on behalf of the business*

   Select **one** answer.

2. Which **one** of the following is a responsibility a business has to its customers?

   A  *To make the highest profits possible*
   B  *To increase sales to a maximum*
   C  *Pay them a regular dividend*
   D  *Provide quality goods and value for money*

   Select **one** answer.

3. A pressure group is:

   A  *a group of people who try to persuade a business to behave in a certain way*
   B  *a group of people who have an interest in a business*
   C  *an organisation that puts pressure on a business to make a profit*
   D  *the legal representatives of the owners of the business*

   Select **one** answer.

## ResultsPlus
### Build Better Answers

After discussion between the directors of a business concerning their plans for the future, it was decided to hold meetings to inform all employees of these future plans.

Do you agree that this was a good idea? (4)

Technique guide: You are being asked to make a judgement in this question but to get full marks you must offer convincing support for that judgement.

Think: What are the benefits of holding meetings with employees? Will such a meeting meet their needs? Should employees have been consulted before the decisions were made?

Then: Think through how you are going to write your answer - you only have four marks to earn but this is not a question that requires just knowledge.

Remember: You need to provide some balance to the answer.

Write: Write out your answer.

**Basic** Provides a judgement but gives a limited reason for the judgement. This could simply be a statement that it was a good idea as lots of people will be there. (1)

**Good** Provides a judgement and offers an explanation of the reason for the judgement. This could state that it is a good idea because all workers will be there. This will benefit workers, who can all air their views, and the business which can get feedback. (2-3)

**Excellent** Provides a judgement and a well argued reason for the judgement. Makes a reference to the possible disadvantage of the method used to provide some balance. This could evaluate that it is a good idea from both the point of view of workers and the business. It might examine benefits such as all employees are likely to be present, all getting the same information at same time, questions can be asked to get reassurance, feedback can be given, employees can make choices and employees' feelings can be gauged. (4)

# Over to you

The latest financial figures for Bright Star were good - profits had risen by 10%. At the annual general meeting (AGM), shareholders were happy with the company's performance. They had voted on the proposed bonus package for the 12 directors, including Stewart, which rewarded them for their performance. The bonus was set at 40% of their annual salary. Newspapers reported this and claimed that Bright Star was taking advantage of customers by charging too high prices. The majority of the 70,000 employees were also very angry given that they had just negotiated a pay deal of 2.5%. When he got back to his office after the AGM, Stewart faced a large number of questions on these very issues. He had to deal with them.

1. Identify **three** stakeholders in the passage and suggest whether they are internal or external. (6)

2. Stewart faces a number of problems in meeting the needs of different stakeholders. From the passage, select **two** stakeholders and explain how their different needs in this example are in conflict. (8)

3. A letter to consumers and an e-mail to all employees would be ways in which Stewart could address the concerns that these two stakeholder groups have. To what extent do you think that these methods are the most appropriate for this purpose? Justify your answer. (10)

# 8 Methods of communication with stakeholders

## Case Study

Jordan Weidmann had called together the sales team at JK Sports. The company distributed sports equipment relating to North American sports to retailers in the United Kingdom. American football, basketball, ice hockey and baseball replica shirts, hoodies, sweatshirts, tees and equipment were its speciality. Despite a reasonably successful year, Jordan wanted to increase sales targets for the coming financial year. She gave a presentation to the team showing sales figures for the previous five years, the state of the market and the main areas that the business was going to focus on. She then had to break the bad news - the new targets. Some of the sales team shifted uncomfortably in their seats while others did not seem to be too worried by them. The targets were to be monitored on a monthly basis and there would be regular updates for the team through teleconferencing, email and a quarterly review via web cast. After dealing with questions Jordan gave a short pep talk to encourage the sales team to rise to the challenge they faced. On leaving the meeting all the sales team took a copy of the presentation handouts.

## Objectives

● To understand the different ways that businesses use to communicate with stakeholders.

● To appreciate the effectiveness of different methods of communication at different times.

## Methods of communication

Jordan's meeting with the sales team involved a wide range of communication methods. Jordan used **spoken communication**, a **visual presentation** and used **positive body language** throughout to help get the message across. She noticed that some of the sales team's body language was not so positive when she announced the new targets and noted who they were. She intended to get back to them to help support them in their task. She knew that some of the targets were deliberately challenging.

As the sales team went about their work in the next few months there were all sorts of other methods used to keep in touch. **E-mails** were used regularly to give updates and were especially useful given that all the sales team had **mobile phones** that could receive e-mail. There were times when short message service (SMS) **text messages** were appropriate and the **web cast** and **teleconferences** were also going to be important in keeping in contact with the team given that they were spread across the country.

The example above is not untypical of the ways that many businesses use to communicate with their stakeholders. The important thing in deciding which method to use depends on the **type of message/information** that needs to be communicated, **who the audience is** and the **purpose of the communication**.

The way in which a message/information is communicated is referred to as the **medium**. The media is the plural of this. Each method has its advantages and its disadvantages -depending on the nature of the communication. The main media include the following.

## Oral media

This is the spoken word - face to face communication. It is perhaps the most common way that businesses use to communicate, especially within the business. The spoken word has the benefit of being able to make a point directly, the audience can see the face and body language of the sender and feedback is often immediate. It is especially useful in situations where decisions need to be made quickly. Oral communication can be used during presentations although, depending on the size of the audience, may not allow for individual feedback in the same way.

# Electronic media

Electronic means of communication have become ever more important in business. They include a wide range of different methods including e-mail, fax, the telephone, video, podcasts, teleconferencing and webcasts and webinars. The advantage of many electronic methods is that they are quick and can enable the sender to get feedback almost immediately. Electronic communication also means that individuals are not tied to being in a particular area or place. Providing they can access the media, communication can be made 24 hours a day, 365 days a year. Electronic communication is also valuable for businesses that operate globally. Such methods can put people who live thousands of miles apart in touch with each other and help to overcome some of the problems caused by different time zones.

The development of the Internet has enabled new types of communication to be created. **Webcasts** allow files to be transferred over the Internet. The result is that businesses can use this technology to broadcast messages and information to their stakeholders either live or recorded. The advantage is that a business can contact large numbers of stakeholders distributed anywhere around the world easily. Users can access the webcasts at any time using their computers. It is possible for a business to use a webcast to report its financial performance to shareholders and employees in different countries can be given information about major events, such as proposed mergers or takeovers or important decisions affecting the business.

Web conferencing is another way in which businesses can make use of the Internet to set up meetings and presentations. Those taking part in the meetings can access the conference at their computer and are connected to all others in the conference. Depending on the software used, the leader of the conference or presentation can take control of the user's computer to demonstrate new programmes or go through new processes being introduced into the business. A **webinar** is a particular type of web conference where the organiser tends to take the lead in the session and there is limited input from other attendees at the conference. However, some types of web software enable participants to be able to take part through voting via on-screen polls, or chat facilities that allow the participant to ask questions. The advantage of such sessions is that all the information can be collated and used to help improve future services and provide a record of what was said and the feelings/thoughts of those involved.

These types of technology can be used to provide online training for employees and help cut down on the cost of bringing together people from different parts of the country or indeed the world. They are not free, however. The cost of buying the software and hardware, as well as the time taken by staff to manage and monitor these systems, has to be taken into consideration.

# Telephone

The telephone is still an important part of communications in any business. The nature of telephone communications has changed, however. The use of landlines is still important, but the development of mobile phone technology means that businesses have a far greater opportunity to be able to contact customers and suppliers quickly and at a time convenient for them. In addition, employees can now be contacted almost 24 hours a day wherever they are. This can be a disadvantage in that there can be an expectation that workers are always 'on-call'. This can lead to stress and the feeling that the balance between work and life is too far weighted to work. However, it gives some types of worker far more flexibility and can improve **productivity** and **efficiency**, as well as customer service, which benefit the business and the customer.

Many businesses will have dedicated call-centres to handle customer enquiries and provide help and support. It could be argued that if a business provides an excellent service and quality then it should not need a call centre. However, the complexity of many businesses is such that a call-centre is seen as being an

Methods of communication - face-to-face and paper-based

Methods of communication - electronic and telephone

**ResultsPlus**
**Watch Out!**

Many students think that e-mail is 'free' - it is not. Businesses providing e-mail facilities have to pay for web access, there is an electricity cost involved and many larger businesses will buy dedicated e-mail software to manage their e-mail. In addition, larger businesses will have to pay for technicians to monitor and manage e-mail. Messages have to be stored somewhere and the hardware needed can be expensive.

**edexcel** **key terms**

**Webcasts** – a means of broadcasting over the Internet.

important part of improving the overall customer experience and providing the support that customers want.

Some businesses have outsourced their call centres to countries like India. **Outsourcing** means transferring services offered by the business to another country. The main reason for outsourcing call-centres has been to reduce costs. Workers in countries like India can be employed at a fraction of the cost of workers doing the same job in the UK. However, some businesses have experienced problems having outsourced their call-centres. Customer satisfaction levels with the service have sometimes fallen. Part of the reason is that workers in India, for example, may not have the understanding of the locality or geography of the UK in the same way as those based in the UK might have. As a result queries have been left unanswered or not answered satisfactorily. This is not good for a business and some have decided that the cost savings are not as high as they expected. Some firms have decided to move their call centres back into the UK.

The increased sophistication and use of mobile phones also enables firms to contact stakeholders via e-mail and through short messaging service (SMS) text messages. There have been cases where employers have notified staff that they have been made redundant by text. However, the use of text messaging in business has to be done with care. It may be appropriate for staff to text important messages to each other that require urgent action, especially if the employee is out and about. However, the use of text messages between business and customer or shareholder might not be appropriate. The type of communication that is suitable for texts will tend to be those where the sender and the receiver know each other reasonably well and for informal communication.

## Paper-based communication

The dream of paperless business has not really happened. Developments in IT were suggested as leading to a significant reduction in the use of paper. In reality, paper-based methods of communication are still seen as being very important. **Formal letters** to customers, shareholders, suppliers and employees are still widely used. They allow the sender to think carefully about the communication, to get the message across clearly and without interruption and provide physical evidence of the communication. Such letters may be used to communicate updates about the business, changes that may be occurring, respond to complaints, aid in the recruitment process and so on.

Other paper-based forms of communication include **memos** and **scribbled notes**. These may be informal, especially the scribbled note, and only used in certain circumstances. For example, someone on a telephone call to a customer or

supplier may want a piece of information urgently and scribbles the query to a colleague for immediate response. Such a method would not be appropriate for communication between a business and its shareholders, customers or the local community, for example. Memos have tended to decline in popularity with the use of e-mail.

Other paper-based forms of communication include **posters** that may provide information on health and safety or updates for employees as well as advertising or promoting the business. **Reports** are formal documents that may be used to summarise an investigation into a particular aspect of the business, for example on why a process failed or the prospects for a new product in the market. **Annual Reports** have to be published by public limited companies by law. They provide shareholders and potential investors with information about the financial performance of the business and its future prospects.

Many businesses will record what happens in meetings through written **minutes**. These documents record the main points of a meeting and the actions to be taken as a result and by whom. Where presentations are given - possibly to customers, employees or shareholders or where a business might be communicating its plans with the local community - **handouts** are provided to help those attending to have a record of the main points of the presentation and for reference after the session has finished.

## Image and silent communication

These are less obvious forms of communication, but often reveal important aspects about a business and a situation where communication is taking place. Many firms spend large amounts of time and money thinking about the image that they want to project to their stakeholders. This image may have something to do with colour, logo, design and so on. Black and white are used to convey an image of cleanliness or mood, reds are vibrant, blues softer. The logo has to have some meaning and be something that stakeholders can identify with and associate and recognise. This type of communication is important in building **brand awareness**. The more widely recognised a brand or product the more likely are consumers to choose that product or service over those offered by rivals.

Silent forms of communication include things like body language, touch, smell and colour. The design of products may take into account smell, touch, texture and colour to make them more desirable to consumers and meet their needs more effectively. Some firms have experimented with smells to boost sales or improve the sense of well-being of customers. For example, some retail stores have used the smell of pine, freshly mowed grass or baked bread in their air conditioning systems. It has been shown that customers like these smells and are more likely to be relaxed and purchase in such an environment.

**Body language** is a subtle, but important part of communication. It refers to the signals that we give off when we are engaged in conversation or interacting with other

**Outsourcing** – transferring some operation of the business, like a call centre, to another business or even another country.

people. Imagine the signal given to a customer who arrives at the reception of a business to find a bored looking receptionist who gives the impression they really do not want to be where they are. In presentations or interviews, the body language given off can give vital clues as to whether people are engaged in the process or not. We make a number of important decisions about people as a result of their body language.

## Test yourself

1. **One** likely benefit of teleconferencing is that:

A  **it is free to all those who are taking part**

B  **it allows employees in the same office to meet easily**

C  **it can help to cut the costs of arranging meetings**

D  **the leader of the conference can see everyone on screen**

Select **one** answer.

2. A text message would be an appropriate form of communication when:

A  **a business wants to make a major announcement to its shareholders**

B  **the sender knows the receiver and requires a quick response**

C  **a business has temporarily run out of paper on which to write letters**

D  **the sender has a complicated message to send as they can use text language to shorten it.**

Select **one** answer.

3. The main purpose of a logo is:

A  **to make customers think about what it means**

B  **to provide work for designers in the business**

C  **to ensure that the name of the business is presented in a graphical way**

D  **to help stakeholders create an association with the business.**

Select **one** answer.

## Over to you

The findings of the investigation of the Environment Agency were not good. Curtis read through the report and realised that his business had a lot to explain. A local river had been polluted as a result of a leakage from a waste pipe from his factory. Local residents were angry at the smell created, anglers were equally angry that their fishing had been disrupted and the publicity the business received had hit sales. Curtis knew they had made a mistake and that he needed to do something quick to try to repair the damage to the business's reputation. He decided to arrange a meeting at which local residents, customers, employees and other interested parties could attend. At the meeting Curtis planned to try to explain what had happened, to apologise and to make it clear exactly what the business was doing to put the situation right and make sure that it did not happen again.

1. Identify **one** benefit to the stakeholders of the business of a face-to-face meeting. (1)

2. Explain how this benefit might help Curtis to get his message across more successfully. (3)

3. (i) Identify to Curtis, **one** advantage of using a slide show to get his message across to his audience. (1)
(ii) For the advantage, explain the likely effect on the audience. (3)

### ResultsPlus
### Build Better Answers

Jordan plans to provide a sales update at the end of the first six months of the financial year to her sales team. She has narrowed the medium down to two options, a podcast and a report which she will mail to all the sales team. In your opinion which of these two methods would be the most appropriate way of communicating the sales update with the sales team? Justify your answer. (8)

Technique guide: This is a question that is assessing your ability to make a judgement and to provide some reasons why you think that the method chosen is the better one. Note that there is no right answer to such a question. The examiner would be looking for the quality of the argument you put forward.

Think: What benefits would a podcast provide to both Jordan and the Sales team? What might be the problems with using this method? What benefits would there be in sending out a written report? What difficulties might there be with this method?

Then: Arrive at a decision about which one you are going to choose - remember, there is no right answer; the examiner is looking for your ability to make a judgement and support it.

Remember: It is not how much you write but the quality of your answer.

Plan: Try and think through how you are going to approach the answer and how you are going to structure it.

Write: Write out your answer.

■ **Basic** Provides a judgement about one of the methods and gives a limited reason for the judgement. (1-2)

● **Good** Provides a judgement and offers at least one advantage and one disadvantage to analyse the methods appropriateness. Appropriate terms and concepts are used and there is some understanding of the context - the role of the update to a sales team. (3-5)

▲ **Excellent** Provides a judgement of one method and provides at least one advantage and one disadvantage. The understanding of the context is very clear and the supporting argument to justify the judgement will touch on why it is a better method than the one not chosen. Appropriate terms and concepts are used throughout the answer. (6-8)

# 9 Types of written communication

## Case Study

Mahendra Lawoti was a human resources manager for MakeItEZ, a firm specialising in arranging conference facilities for businesses. He had another batch of job applications on his desk to sort through. The job that he was trying to find an employee for involved liaising with the businesses who were arranging the conference to make sure that all their requirements were met - a project manager. He was always amazed at the letters of application and CVs that arrived. The number that were badly presented, full of spelling, punctuation and grammatical errors, dog-eared or incorrectly filled in was staggering. Most ended up on the rejection pile.

## Objectives

● To recognise the variety of ways in which a business may use written communication.
● To appreciate the importance of layout, tone and language in written communication.

## Types of written communication

Written communication still forms a very important part of communication in a business. The written word can make a message or information very clear to the receiver. It is very flexible and can be used in lots of different ways, both formal and informal. Examples of formal and informal communication are shown in Table 1.

## Choice of communication method

With all of these methods of communication, the important thing is to consider **which one is appropriate** for the type of communication intended and **who the audience is**. In making these decisions, businesses will need to consider the advantages and disadvantages associated with the various methods considered. This enables the business to arrive at a decision about a method that is most likely to lead to the communication being successful.

**Table 1** – Formal and informal communication

- Letters - to employees, shareholders, suppliers, the government and customers.
- Business documentation - such as invoices that have to be clear and accurate records of what has been purchased and for how much and application forms for employment.
- Instruction manuals that accompany products.
- Newsletters used to provide updates and messages to employees or customers.
- Agendas to notify those attending a meeting what the items to be discussed and considered will be.
- Minutes - to document and record what happened at meetings and what action is to be taken and by whom.
- Curriculum vitae - a summary of a prospective employee's skills, qualifications and interests that businesses often use to help recruit new staff.

### edexcel ⁞⁞⁞ key terms

**Agenda** – a list of the main items that will be covered and discussed at a meeting.

Mahendra looked at the pile of application forms sitting on his desk. The purpose of the application forms and the **curriculum vitae (CV)** which applicants had been asked to include was to communicate the suitability of the applicant for the job advertised. Mahendra had drafted a job description and a person specification for the job, which made it clear what the job involved and what kind of skills and qualities the right person for the job needed. Looking at some of the application forms and CVs, he was beginning to wonder if those documents had been clear enough. A number of the applicants did not refer to the skills and qualities the business was looking for at all in their applications or their CVs.

Mahendra looked again at the **job description** and the **person specification**, which his team had produced. He was sure that it was clear what the job entailed and what skills the person should have. Both documents were produced on company headed paper, both had a short paragraph at the top outlining the purpose of the document and both gave a list of bullet points covering the key tasks and skills related to the job. They had also **considered the font** they used to make sure that applicants with reading difficulties could access it appropriately.

There were some applications that were relevant and very good. Mahendra was relieved that some had clearly read the information carefully and had thought about their applications. These people had **filled in the form correctly**, had clearly taken time to read the form and include the correct information. Most importantly of all, Mahendra could **easily read the forms**. Some people had very poor writing and it was very difficult to read what they had written. Such forms did not give a good impression of the applicant.

Most applicants had sent a CV as requested, but the quality was variable. Many had **written far too much** - some were over 6 pages long and included information that was also on the application form. Some had **typing errors** in them, which did not present the applicant in a good light. Others were cramped and difficult to read and used a **very small font**. Some had simply been copied from another job application, which did not say much about the desire of the applicant for the job Mahendra had advertised. Others were **creased**, possibly where the printer had jammed, and some had been photocopied and did not look very professional. These did not do a job of communicating the qualities of the applicant or their suitability for the job to Mahendra.

Looking at the CVs of the applicants who had filled out the forms correctly, Mahendra could also see that they had thought carefully about these too. Most had the usual information on them - name, address, experience and qualifications - but some outstanding ones had given a **profile of themselves** and briefly outlined their **skills and qualities** in direct relation to the person specification. This made it easy for Mahendra to see whether they had the right qualities to do the job. In addition, the good CVs provided Mahendra with information that would **help the interview** panel to ask questions. The CVs provided a brief piece of information, which the interview panel could use to find out more about the candidate in the interview.

The good CVs had successfully communicated to Mahendra and his team the qualities and skills of the applicant and made it easy for him to be able to shortlist them for interview. They had made it clear that they could be capable of doing the job and as a result Mahendra was in a position to be able to write a letter to them inviting them for interview.

The letter had to be carefully planned out. It had to contain a variety of information for the candidates which included the date and time of their interview, the schedule of the day, who they would be meeting, what tasks they would have to do in addition to the formal interview and information on how to get to the company premises. There was a lot of information to give out and Mahendra had to make sure that candidates understood it all properly. Recruiting new staff was expensive and mistakes had to be kept to a minimum.

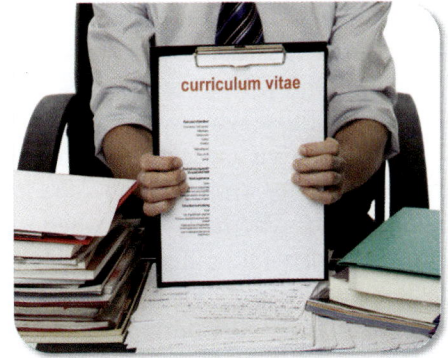
A CV says a lot about the applicant, but it also has to be relevant to the job applied for

**ResultsPlus Watch Out!**

Writing letters is time consuming and needs to be done carefully. The letter will send a message to the receiver about more than just the content and so has to give the right image of the sender and the business. Sending lots of letters can be expensive - it uses up time and money!

**edexcel key terms**

**Curriculum Vitae (CV)** – a document often required by a business to help in the recruitment process. A CV is an outline of the key skills and qualities possessed by an individual and a summary of their personal details, qualifications and experience.

In addition to the letter to the candidates, Mahendra had to coordinate the various people in the company who would be involved in the interviews. Mahendra sent round an e-mail to all those who would be involved, inviting them to a briefing meeting a week before the interviews were scheduled. At the meeting Mahendra gave out the details of the candidates who had been invited to interview. The details had all been written out and bound in a folder to make it easy for everyone to use. In it was a copy of the candidate's application forms and CV, an outline of the schedules and the questions that would form the basis of the interview. He recorded the outcome of the meeting and circulated the **minutes** to those who attended the meeting via e-mail.

Mahendra would know that his communication with the candidates was successful when they contacted him to confirm they would attend as requested in the invite and when they all turned up on time at the right place on the day of the interview and knew what they were supposed to be doing.

## ResultsPlus Watch Out!

Written forms of communication can lead to much slower but sometimes more effective communication. A business needs to balance the speed with which it needs to make the communication and its effectiveness. Written forms are useful if the business needs a record of what has been said.

## edexcel key terms

**Minutes** – a written record of the main points covered in a meeting with action points and details of those who have to carry out the actions.

## Test yourself

1.  Which **one** of the following is a written form of communication?

    **A**  A telephone conversation
    **B**  A videoconferencing session
    **C**  A text message to a work colleague
    **D**  A letter to shareholders about the dividend to be paid

    Select **one** answer.

2.  Taking written minutes of a meeting is important because:

    **A**  the person who called the meeting knows what items will be discussed at the meeting
    **B**  they can be used to discipline staff who do not carry out the actions agreed
    **C**  they provide a record of the meeting and the actions to be taken
    **D**  they accurately record the amount of time the meeting took

    Select **one** answer.

3.  The main purpose of a CV is to:

    **A**  provide a summary of the key details, skills and qualities of the applicant
    **B**  enable the human resources team to check on the applicant's IT skills
    **C**  provide a detailed account of an applicant's life and work
    **D**  provide a means of checking the Candidate Value (CV) to the business

    Select **one** answer.

# Over to you

Mahendra encountered a variety of written forms of communication as part of the recruitment process he was managing. In each case he had to think about the audience the communication was aiming at and how he would know the communication was successful.

1. Identify **two** things that Mahendra would have had to consider in writing the letter of interview to the shortlisted candidates. (2)
2. What is the purpose of a CV? (2)
3. Identify **two** ways in which Mahendra could know that his written communication with his work colleagues regarding the interviews had been a success. In each case explain how the written communication had contributed to the successful communication. (8)

## ResultsPlus
### Build Better Answers

Written forms of communication are still important to businesses because:

A **they are easy to read**
B **they make a message or information very clear to the receiver**
C **they never get destroyed like electronic ones can**
D **electronic communications are not sophisticated enough**

Select **one** answer.

Answer B

Think: Why do businesses still use written communication? What advantages do written communications provide that other forms of communication do not?

Then: Look at each option carefully. Try to dismiss the ones that are obviously wrong.

Decide: Make your decision as to the correct answer.

Go through each option (distracter) and try and eliminate the ones that are clearly not right. In this case, A is clearly wrong. For one, other forms of communication involve language such as text message or e-mail that also has to be read. Secondly, some written communication can be very difficult to read especially if it is a document covering technical issues.

This leaves you with B, C and D. D is also incorrect - electronic methods of communication are very sophisticated so this is also clearly wrong. Looking at C also reveals this distracter as being nonsense. Written documents can be destroyed.

This leaves B as the correct response.

# 10 Types of electronic communication

## Case Study

Having done her weekly shopping at a major supermarket, Marie and her husband John unloaded the bags and put their groceries away as they always did on a Wednesday evening on their way home from work. Marie picked up the post from the mat and flicked through the envelopes. One was from the supermarket and contained a leaflet about special offers. Marie noted just how many of the offers were for things they normally bought. She turned to John and said that they should keep the vouchers for the next time they shopped. She wondered if other people got the same offers as they did.

## Objectives

- To recognise the different types of electronic communication.
- To understand the ways in which businesses use electronic means to communicate with stakeholders.

## ResultsPlus
### Watch Out!

Remember that electronic means of communication have many advantages but also disadvantages - make sure that consideration is given to both sides of the coin.

## Types of electronic communication

The use of electronic means of communication has become more and more important in the last ten years. Part of the reason is simply that technology has developed to enable communication to be easier. For business, the developments in technology have meant much more than simply being able to contact stakeholders.

## E-mail

Marie knows that her supermarket and a number of other shops that she uses contact her by e-mail. She receives regular newsletters informing her of special deals, new store openings, promotions and so on. Using e-mail for sending newsletters is a useful way for businesses to keep customers informed about changes and updates about the business.

## The web

Marie also knows that she can get lots of information and do her shopping online if she wants to. The number of businesses offering online shopping is now increasing. It provides customers with a convenient way of acquiring goods and allows the business to reach a much wider market.

The web also provides the means of communicating with all stakeholders. Many company websites provide opportunities to buy goods and services. They also have information for customers - store locators, contact details, information for prospective employees about careers at the business, advice and information about how to use products, technical specifications, information about the history of the business and so on. In addition, many public limited companies will have a section for investors where details of the share price and the financial accounts of the business can be found. They will also have details about how the business is addressing its social and environmental responsibilities. A web site enables a business to be able to keep in contact with a wide range of its stakeholders.

## Fax

E-mail has enabled businesses to be able to communicate with a wide range of stakeholders far more easily, although many still use fax. The word 'fax' is short for 'facsimile', which literally means 'make similar'. Fax machines allow businesses to send documents using telephone lines. The advantage of using fax is that documents can be sent and received almost instantaneously so is far quicker than using the traditional post - now referred to as 'snail mail'.

Fax is useful for sending documents such as invoices, purchase orders and so on but is also useful for firms such as solicitors and surveyors who may need to send important documents to clients quickly. The fax machine makes a copy of the document and then sends the data through the telephone line. The receiver then gets a copy of the document. Fax has an advantage over e-mail because faxed contracts, for example, containing signatures are recognised in law whilst electronic signatures are not. This is primarily for security reasons. In addition, fax can be a more secure method of data transfer compared to the Internet where data can be hacked and intercepted.

One of the disadvantages of fax is that it tends to be cumbersome - loading the documents takes time and can be fiddly. The quality of the copy is not always good and in some businesses documents can be left sitting on a machine waiting for someone to distribute them to the appropriate person. Such disadvantages have led some large firms to invest in specialist computer systems that receive and store faxes and then distribute them to the receiver via paper or though secure e-mail. These pieces of equipment are called fax servers.

## Loyalty cards and data tracking

One of the biggest effects of electronic means of communication has been the development of systems that track information. Loyalty cards are one example of this, but there are many others. Companies like DHL, the Royal Mail, UPS and other couriers are able to track packages and parcels far more accurately and improve customer service as a result. Freight haulage - the transport of goods via lorries - is also capable of being tracked. Many businesses now ship goods across the world as part of the production process. Intel, for example, ships its silicon chips across the globe several times in their production life and electronic tracking allows the business to monitor where its shipments are at any time.

Companies that generate revenue from consumers using services such as gas, electricity, telephone calls and so on, can monitor usage more accurately with electronic systems. Meter readers can call on homes and input meter readings directly into a device that transmits the information directly to computers that can process the data and amend consumers' accounts. All these devices and systems improve the accuracy of data and mean that a business can check and monitor account information more accurately. If there are queries by the customer on their account, the business has far more accurate records and information to help deal with the query. Having more accurate information enables a business to be able to improve the flow of information between itself and its stakeholders.

The use of loyalty cards has been a very important way in which businesses have used electronic systems to improve communications between themselves and their customers and other stakeholders. This improved communication means that businesses can provide more accurate and relevant information to customers and suppliers. Such systems help to improve efficiency and reduce waste.

How do these systems work? Essentially, the use of some form of loyalty card means the business has details of the customer - their name, address and contact details including e-mail address. Every time the customer uses the card the business has a record of what the customer bought, when they bought it, how

**ResultsPlus**
**Watch Out!**

Remember that electronic means of communication includes more than just e-mail. It includes the opportunities to gather information about customers and improve communication flows between businesses and suppliers and shareholders.

**edexcel ⁞⁞ key terms**

**Fax** – a machine that copies and sends documents through a telephone line.

**Loyalty card** – a means by which the buying habits of a customer can be tracked. The customer gets certain benefits in return such as money-off goods.

what they bought matches with previous shopping trips, whether they bought particular items at particular times of the year, how regularly they buy particular products, whether the customer has responded to the in-store promotions the business might be running, and more.

Loyalty cards and data tracking provide certain benefits for businesses.

**Identifying customer habits** The business is able to build a picture about the buying habits of the customer - called a **customer profile**. The information gathered can be used to improve the communication between the business and the customer. As Marie found out, she received a leaflet with money-off vouchers that matched quite closely the sort of things that she regularly bought - as well as offering some additional products that she might be interested in given her buying habits. The data gathered allows a business to target its market more effectively. Twenty years ago leaflets with special offers were sent out but many shoppers might have not used most of the vouchers simply because they were not relevant to them. Now, those vouchers can be made more relevant and there is a greater likelihood that the shopper will return and use the vouchers. Suppliers can also be given information about the success or otherwise of products and especially new product launches as a result of gathering this type of data.

**Stock control** There are also other benefits to the business of gathering this type of data. As the day goes by, stock at many shops will be used up. The data gathered by the tills on customer purchases can be used to enable the warehouse managers to decide what stock to order and, crucially, how much to order. Few firms will want to have expensive stock sitting around in a store area not being sold. The business will have had to pay for this stock but will not get any of their money back until it is sold. This means that cash is flowing out of the business but might not be coming back in at the same rate. This can affect **cash flow**.

The use of electronic data gathering systems enables businesses to be able to keep stock levels to a minimum and keep costs under control but at the same time ensure that they meet the needs of customers. In manufacturing, the use of **Just-in-Time** (JIT) stock control systems relies on the flow of information between manufacturer and suppliers. The communication has to be accurate and reliable to enable all parties to operate efficiently and successfully.

## Summary
Electronic means of communication cover more than simply providing a different means of talking to people. E-mail has revolutionised communication but does have some drawbacks. Technology allows businesses to gather data in many different ways and to use this data to improve the communication flow between itself and its stakeholders.

## edexcel key terms

**Customer profile** – a description of the characteristics of buyers of a product or service, including features such as buying habits of a customer and income.

**Just-in-time** - a system of stock control used by manufacturing businesses to keep stock levels to a minimum and help keep control over costs. JIT systems rely on close relationships between manufacturers and suppliers and accurate flows of information between them.

## Test yourself

1. Which **one** of the following is a likely benefit of using a fax machine as opposed to e-mail?

   A   *A fax always delivers the document directly to the receiver*
   B   *Fax machines are less likely to break down*
   C   *Sending by fax can be more secure than using the Internet*
   D   *Sending by fax does not cost anything*

   Select **one** answer.

2. Data tracking systems in businesses are important because:

   A   *they allow the business to monitor production processes more accurately*
   B   *they enable the business to charge higher prices to the customer*
   C   *suppliers do not know where their products are in the production process*
   D   *a business needs to know where its workers are at all times*

   Select **one** answer.

3. Just-in-Time stock systems rely on:

   A   *the manufacturer taking all the decisions about stock control*
   B   *excellent communication between the supplier and the business*
   C   *stock being delivered at a specific time during the day*
   D   *an electronic communication at 6.00am every morning to suppliers*

   Select **one** answer.

# Over to you

Jessica Barrett worked for a firm of solicitors as a legal assistant. Her manager, a lawyer specialising in employment law, handed her a document which needed to be sent urgently to a client. Jessica was told that the document was needed because the client was in court that afternoon and had to have this information prior to the case being heard. He had to leave immediately to get to the court and so Jessica was left with the personal details of the client and a decision to make. What method should she use, fax or e-mail?

1. Identify **one** benefit of using fax and one of using e-mail to Jessica in this case. (2)
2. Which method would you choose to send this document? Justify your answer. (6)

## ResultsPlus
### Build Better Answers

1. A loyalty card is of benefit to a consumer because:

A  it guarantees them lower prices for goods
B  all their personal details are in the control of the business who issued the card
C  they can get free credit when shopping
D  communication they receive from the business is more relevant to them

Select **one** answer

Answer D

Think: What is a loyalty card? What are the benefits to a customer?

Then: Go through the options. Look at each option carefully. Try to dismiss the ones that are obviously wrong. Loyalty cards might be used to get money off goods depending on the number of points a customer has but it does not **guarantee** them lower prices. A can be dismissed. Is submitting all their personal details to a business in the customer's interest? The business might need some details but certainly not all. The customer has to be certain the information is secure and this is not always the case. B can also be dismissed. A loyalty card is not the same as a credit card and is not used to get credit (loans) from a business. C is also wrong and can be dismissed. ■

Decide: Make your decision as to the correct answer. In this case it is D. Check to make sure you are right. The business gets customer information from the use of the loyalty card, this means that the business can target the customer with more relevant information. This is a benefit as the customer does not have to put up with information which is not of any relevance to them. ▲

# 11 Types of oral communication

## Case Study

Carla spent a great deal of her first year at work in the marketing department of XciteTravel, which organised adventure holidays, in meetings with all sorts of different people including her line manager and senior managers from a range of other firms. After the first month she had got used to the meetings and felt more confident in participating. However, two things were now looming that were starting to worry her. One was her first annual performance review and the second was a presentation she had to give to a group of people from a variety of adventure holiday businesses. Her presentation was going to be on how XciteTravel would be marketing holidays to its customers in the next year. She knew this was important because the presentation could make or break a number of contracts between XciteTravel and these businesses.

## Objectives

- To recognise the different types of oral communication used in business.
- To understand when different types or oral communication are appropriate.
- To appreciate that some types of oral communication come with certain formalities.

**ResultsPlus Watch Out!**

Remember to think about the difference between formal and informal methods of communication. Different skills are required for formal methods of communication.

## Types of oral communication

Whenever an immediate response is required one of the first ways that is used is still through talking - oral communication. It might be something simple like asking where a file is on a customer or where the stapler is or could be something more complex and formal like conducting an interview with a prospective employee or making a speech in front of thousands of shareholders.

Oral communication is one of the ways in which the sender can get an almost immediate response from the receiver to check if the message has been understood. For example, if Carla asks her colleague for a file on a client and the colleague proceeds to give her the file then she knows the communication has been received and has been successful. If she asked for the file and the colleague did not hear or only heard part of the message she would also get immediate feedback. In this case it might be a frown and a shrug of the shoulders, indicating through body language that the message had not been received fully or she simply would not get the file straight away. In which case it would be a simple step to ask again.

## Face-to-face

Face-to-face communication is probably the most common way in which the vast majority of communication is carried out within a business and to an extent outside of it. Staff in a business have to talk to each other about all sorts of things relating to their work and the business. Such communication might involve asking questions, asking for information, answering questions, making requests, passing on information, right through to disciplining staff. There will also be oral communication with stakeholders outside the immediate business environment. Call centres are set up to handle customer complaints, queries, orders and so on; suppliers will be talking with businesses about their needs, problems, delays, clarification of orders and so on.

## Meetings

Many businesses have meetings every day. The purpose of meetings is to bring together people to do one of more of the following:

- discuss plans;
- be updated on issues;
- be made aware of changes or new processes;
- solve problems;
- generate new ideas;
- make decisions;
- formulate strategies for dealing with events.

Meetings involve plenty of oral communication. One of the problems is that the enthusiasm of some people to talk at meetings can reduce their effectiveness. Many members of staff in organisations complain about meetings and feel they are a waste of time. In some cases that may be the reality but this does not mean that meetings are always worthless. Much of the success of meetings depends on how they are arranged, who attends and how they are managed.

The organiser would normally provide an **agenda** to all participants after inviting them to the meeting. Such invitations can be personal or done through calendaring systems linked to PCs and e-mail. The agenda will provide an outline of the content and purpose of the meeting. The meeting would normally be chaired by one person whose role is to control the meeting - go through the agenda, make sure everyone has the opportunity to contribute where necessary and clarifying action points.

Because meetings usually involve essentially oral communication, a record of the meeting is kept through **minutes**. The minutes of a meeting outline the main points covered and what action points have been decided, who is to carry them out and by when. The role of the chair is crucial in managing the meeting. The chair must decide who to allow to speak, how long for, to cut people off if they are going on too long or invite other participants to comment where relevant. It is a highly skilled task to manage such competing oral communications within a meeting to make sure that everyone is involved and feel they will gain some benefit from the meeting.

## Formal types of oral communication

In addition to the informal role that oral communication plays in business there are more formal types of oral communication. Public limited companies have to have an **annual general meeting** (AGM) every year at which the board of directors presents an overview of the company's financial performance to shareholders. All shareholders are invited but only a small number generally attend with the majority using their right to vote via post or through secure internet connections. At these meetings (which can often be difficult, especially if the company has not performed as well as the shareholders would have liked) the speeches made by the board have to be carefully thought out. Planning is essential to enable the directors to confidently handle questions that shareholders may wish to put to them.

Carla is also facing the prospect of two types of oral communication which are more formal. The presentation will require Carla to put across information to a knowledgeable audience who will have an interest in the way the business is going to market holidays. Carla knows she will have to be confident, knowledgeable and well prepared for the speech. Her audience will not only be looking for evidence that XciteTravel have got a good plan but that someone like Carla is good enough to persuade them to put their business with the company. The presentation is more than simply giving a speech, it involves so much more; that is why Carla was anxious. She knew that it was important to the company that she presented them in a professional light.

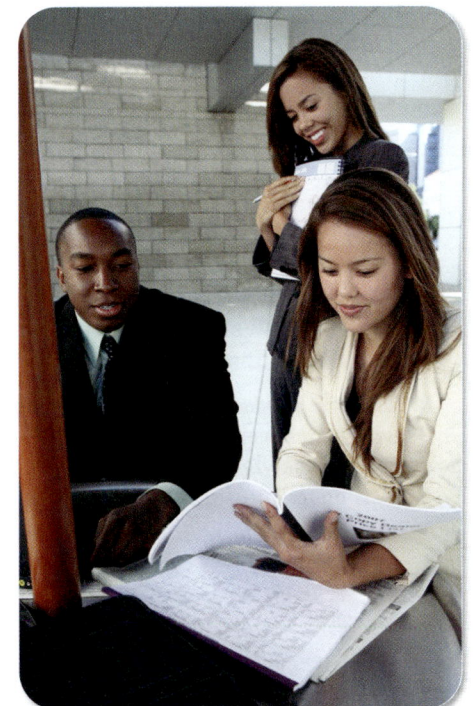

Examples of oral communication – annual performance reviews with a manager and meetings

56

The second thing Carla was worried about was her annual performance review, sometimes called an **appraisal**. Many businesses have processes in place where staff agree targets and goals for the year ahead with their line managers. At the end of the year both parties meet to discuss the year gone by. They look at what has gone well, whether goals have been met, what training needs may be required and where things might have gone badly. Carla knew that the process was supposed to be a two-way one and that she was expected to be able to review and discuss her own performance as well as making observations on how she was treated by her line manager and other colleagues. She still could not help feeling nervous about it though.

Carla knew that she had to prepare for her appraisal meeting by looking at the goals and targets she had been given and being honest about the extent to which she had met them. She also tried to note down what areas she did not do so well in and what the reasons for this were. Carla identified where she thought she might need more training and where the support she was given by her line manager, Sue, and other colleagues could have been better. This was going to be the really tricky bit - telling her boss that she could do things better.

As it turned out Carla need not have worried. The whole point of the appraisal was to help build up the relationship between Carla (the **appraisee**) and Sue (the **appraiser**) and give them both a chance to be honest about their work together and how they could improve for the benefit of the business as a whole. The meeting was not as formal as Carla expected and was almost relaxed. They agreed new goals for the year ahead, identified areas where Carla needed to improve her performance, looked at setting up training courses on specific issues and agreed ways that she could be supported better in her job.

After the meeting, Carla reflected on the role played by Sue. She concluded that Sue must have been highly skilled at managing such oral communication to make her feel so relaxed and comfortable with the process. In particular, Carla was impressed with the way that Sue listened to her comments and observations. She did not try and interrupt or impose her ideas, but instead allowed Carla to feel that she was in control of the meeting. This gave Carla the confidence to contribute to the session and also made her appreciate the comments that Sue made about her performance and the way forward.

## Summary

Oral methods of communication are vital parts of every business. Much oral communication is informal and involves normal conversations. However, the way in which people engage in oral communication is important; it helps build relationships, can build friendships and generates respect amongst colleagues that help the business to operate smoothly.

In addition to these informal methods of oral communication, there are also more formal methods including meetings, presentations and appraisals. The skills required to handle these communications well can often be overlooked but to speak to a particular audience and get the message across successfully is something that has to be worked on and developed.

## edexcel ⣿ key terms

**Appraisal** – a meeting between an employee and (typically) his/her line manager to review the goals, progress and future targets for the employee.

**Appraisee** – the employee at an appraisal meeting about whom the meeting is about.

**Appraiser** – the person who manages the appraisal meeting - often the employee's line manager.

## Test yourself

1. Which **one** of the following is the most likely way a sender can know if an oral communication has been received and understood? The receiver:

   A **asks the sender to repeat the message**
   B **acts on the message sent**
   C **asks the sender to write it down for them**
   D **acts on the message but incorrectly**

   Select **one** answer.

2. Which **one** of the following is not a benefit of oral communication?

   A **It provides the receiver with an immediate response.**
   B **Body language helps the receiver to see if the message has been understood.**

   C **The audience can identify with the sender of the message.**
   D **The sender can repeat the message and continue talking for a long time to make sure the message gets through.**

   Select **one** answer.

3. A successful appraisal is most likely to depend upon:

   A **the amount of goals that the employee can prove s/he has met during the year**
   B **how senior the appraiser is in the organisation**
   C **the oral communication skills of the appraiser**
   D **how forcefully the appraisee puts forward their case**

   Select **one** answer.

# Over to you

Darren Mailer was scheduled to present a speech at the annual sales conference of Mediate Electronics, a firm producing electronic components for games consoles. He was known in the office as a confident, almost arrogant, character who was able to talk his way out of anything. He had been given his briefing by his line manager with strict instructions to make sure that the sales team were fully aware of the changes the company were making to their components and how this needed to be communicated to the final customer - the manufacturers of games consoles. The changes in the components had to be made to meet new specifications and it was vital to the future of the business that this product was a success.

Darren prepared his slide show and leaned back on his chair. 'Are you not going to write any notes for the presentation?' asked a colleague. 'No' said Darren. 'I know my stuff'. The night before the presentation Darren was in the bar with his work colleagues at the conference hotel. He was his usual confident self but when it got to 3 o'clock when he finally went to bed he felt very ill. He was first to present the following morning. It was a disaster. The presentation slides were not in the right order, he got flustered and his usual bravado deserted him. He stumbled through the presentation and left to get a strong black coffee. His line manager was not impressed.

1. Identify **three** mistakes that Darren made prior to the presentation. (3)

2. Describe how Darren's line manager could judge whether the message he wanted Darren to get across was successfully communicated in the period after the presentation. (3)

3. Identify **two** things that you think Darren should have done that would have made his communication more successful. For each, explain how this would have increased the likelihood of success for Darren's communication. (8)

## ResultsPlus
### Build Better Answers

Which **two** of the following might be appropriate reasons to call a meeting in a business?

A  **To communicate information about a new washing up rota in the kitchen**
B  **To discuss a proposed change in shift patterns**
C  **To discipline a member of staff who has been persistently late**
D  **To address a series of complaints from a customer about the service provided by the business**
E  **Advising staff that a new member of staff is joining the marketing department**

Answer B and D

Think: What is the key term in the question? (It is 'appropriate'.) Meetings can be called for lots of reasons but which two are the most appropriate?

Then: Go through the options.

Review: Look at each option carefully. Try to dismiss the ones that are obviously wrong.

In A, the information to be communicated is relatively unimportant and is something that could better be done through an e-mail or staff newsletter. It would be a waste of time to call a meeting for such a simple announcement. A can be dismissed. ■

E is another announcement that is important but not so important that it could not be better done through other media such as e-mail. ■

A and E can be dismissed which leave B, C and D.

Decide: Make your decision as to the correct answers. Disciplining a member of staff is something that should be done confidentially and is unlikely to be done at a meeting. This would not really be appropriate. That leaves B and D. Both of these are important changes/issues that require input from a range of people. As a result it is more sensible to do this at a meeting. ▲

# 12 Images used in business communication

## Case Study

The launch of the official logo for the 2012 Olympic Games in London took place in June 2007. The logo was part of the branding for the Games - a way of making people recognise and associate the Games with London in 2012. Former athlete, Lord Coe, who led London's successful bid for the Games and heads the organising committee said, 'This is the vision at the very heart of our brand'. The Prime Minister at the time, Tony Blair, said 'When people see the new brand, we want them to be inspired to make a positive change in their life'. The launch certainly created a stir. An editor of a BBC web site focussing on the Games said 'We've had a huge reaction to the launch of the new logo - most of it negative' with one contributor saying that he had 'vomited better logos'.

## Objectives

- To understand the role of images in business communication.
- To recognise the different types of images used in business communication.
- To appreciate the importance of images in business communication.

## edexcel ⠿ key terms

**Brand** – the creation of an image or identity for a product or service that creates recognition and/or association by consumers.

**Logo** – a design which is aimed at creating an association with a product or brand.

## Business images

Many businesses can be instantly recognised by an image. Images are a powerful way in which an association can be built up between stakeholders and the business. Look at the images in this section. The chances are that you will be able to associate the images with different businesses. An image can help to give a business a reputation, an identity and a familiarity which stakeholders, particularly consumers, can recognise. As such it is closely tied in with the development of its **brand**. A brand is a means by which a business creates an image or identity that is recognised by consumers. The aim of building a brand is to help customers associate with it and thus make it more likely that they will repeat purchase the product or service over rivals. Images play an important part in building this brand awareness.

Images can be used in addition to or instead of words and sound. They can include logos, photographs, cartoons, artwork, designs, sketches and so on. Images play on the human senses. They are often easier to remember than a series of words and can generate emotions in the receiver. The **logo** for the 2012 Olympics clearly created lots of emotions in people when they first saw it. There was a large number of people who complained that the logo was uninspiring and did not reflect what people had expected about the Games.

However, as time goes on it may be that people have come to have a different view of the logo. Whatever its design faults, it has created a reaction and there are probably few people who would now not recognise it. In a sense, it has already done its job of creating that identity with the Games that its designers would have hoped for.

## The use of colour

For businesses, therefore, the use of images is an important part of their overall communication with stakeholders. Getting the right logo, photograph etc. is vital is creating an association and an identity. This might be closely linked with the use of the right colour. The drink Guinness, for example, plays on the association with black and white, Virgin make extensive use of red in their logos and advertising, British Airways is associated with red white and blue - the colours of the British flag. In recent years the oil company BP has changed its logo and colour scheme making its traditional green colour more prominent. Does this create an association with the environment? BP might have considered this in their debate on the new logo and colour scheme.

The choice of colour is also important in terms of what they are associated with. There has been a great deal of research into how the brain associates colours. The eye receives the light signal which the brain processes. Many colours have an emotional response which a business might consider when creating logos and images associated with their brand. In Europe and North America:

- reds are typically associated with danger, excitement or passion;
- blues are associated with loyalty and trust;
- yellow is associated with the sun and warmth and calm;
- gold is associated with prestige;
- green is linked to nature and health.

In the financial world, screens go red when prices fall and blue when prices are rising. When a business is in debt we say that it is 'in the red'. The use of red in businesses involved in finance might be rejected as a result.

In choosing colours for logos or advertising, businesses will have to think about where the image will be used and seen. The more colours used the more confusing it might be and the use of colours that clash is not a good idea. In addition, using colour has a cost implication - the more that are used the more expensive it generally is to produce headed paper, business cards, signs, posters etc. which include the image. The use of one colour set against white or black backgrounds is common because the contrast is high and the image easy to see and interpret.

## Principles in the use of images

Often the power of an image is greatest when it is **simple**. A simple image or logo, which is not cluttered and has clean lines and high levels of contrast between colours, is more instantly recognisable and easier to remember. The use of colour, tones, textures and shapes are all important factors to consider. In any image, simplicity is important in creating the right association. That association can be highly emotional, for example, an image of a spider and a butterfly provoke different emotional responses in many people. The use of dark imagery is associated with thrash metal bands - few would get very far if they had a logo that incorporated a cuddly toy and lots of light colours. Simple associations can be exploited to improve the effect of the image and the association in the mind of the consumer.

In some cases, however, it might be appropriate to make the image or advert a little more complex or even confusing to **create interest** and generate discussion. Again, Guinness has been very good at doing this - the imagery used seems to have no relevance to a drink at all until the very end when it all becomes clear. When tobacco companies faced restrictions on advertising before the total ban on advertising, some attempted to get round the restrictions by relying on colours or images to trigger associations with the product - even though the actual product was not in the advert at all!

If an image is simple to recognise then it can be recognised even if only part of it is seen. Some businesses use something called '**brand trashing**' to see how far consumers can recognise the brand from scraps of information. BMW has a well-known logo which appears on all its cars and promotional documentation. If the company took that logo and 'separated' it into pieces would consumers still be able to associate BMW with the pieces they are given? If the majority can, then the company might assume that it has a powerful logo and brand association.

BP is associated with the colour green. B&Q is associated with orange

A BMW logo might still be recognised even it was in pieces

59

## Other uses of imagery

The use of images does not just relate to pictures or logos, it can go much deeper than these. Many businesses will use a celebrity to help promote their business and its aims and objectives. Choosing the right celebrity is important. The celebrity will be the 'face' of the business with the intention of creating an association in the mind of the consumer with the business. The image of the celebrity will be used extensively in its promotional materials as well as 'in real life' on TV commercials, and live promotional events.

For example, in 2002 the Swiss watch maker Tag Heuer signed a contract with golfer Tiger Woods to act as a global ambassador for the business. Woods' role included product development, advertising, public relations and merchandising. What might be the reason for choosing this individual? Woods is a winner. He is seen as being a role model and an exemplary professional. His golfing skills and dedication to perfection are also well known. He has immaculate timing and precision in his game that enables him to constantly lead the pack.

Do these skills and qualities ring any bells? They clearly did for Tag Heuer because they were prepared to pay for the endorsement by Tiger Woods. They saw in Woods the perfect opportunity to match up the qualities of their product with the qualities he has. The image of Mr Woods wearing their watches, appearing at their promotional events and on advertising literature is an excellent example of how the image of a celebrity can help to boost the objectives and support the mission statement of a business.

Choosing celebrities has to be done carefully, however. Celebrities are human beings and their fame means that an association may backfire. The soft drink, Pepsi, for example, has used celebrities such as Michael Jackson, Madonna and the boxer Mike Tyson for endorsements. The tie-ups were meant to encourage young people to drink Pepsi rather than other colas, and to build customer loyalty that would last a lifetime. In some respects this has been successful, as Pepsi is a successful brand. However, all of these celebrities were dropped by Pepsi because their actions sometimes brought bad publicity which Pepsi did not want to be associated with.

**edexcel** ⠿ key terms

**Celebrity endorsement** – The use of celebrities to help promote a brand or a product and which may be designed to reflect the desired image/reputation of the product.

**Strap line** - a short catch phrase which helps the consumer to recognise and associate the brand.

The Olympic Games in 2012 has used former athletes such as Dame Kelly Holmes, Sir Steve Redgrave and Jonathan Edwards as ambassadors to help promote the Games. These were all exceptional athletes and are also seen as being role models for the young athletes and for sport that the organising committee of the Games want to attract and encourage.

This is exactly what businesses are looking for in **celebrity endorsements** - people who reflect the reputation, image, characteristics and values of the business. The use of these types of people is as much a part of the images used by a business as a logo or a photograph.

## Slogans and strap lines

In many cases firms will incorporate with logos and other images a slogan or a **strap line**. A strap line is a short catch phrase which helps the consumer to recognise and associate the brand. The aim is to help people to make purchasing decisions in favour of one brand over its rivals in the market. Similarly, slogans are used to provide a short statement to try to summarise the main benefits or characteristics (or both) of the brand or product. Slogans might be humorous and intended to try and create a need in the consumer.

Both slogans and strap lines are things that can be used regularly in advertising and promotions and because they appear regularly, on the product itself, for example, and become something the customer does not forget easily. They can also be put to music and jingles to make the slogan or strap line even more useful in advertising and promotion. Examples of some famous slogans and strap lines are shown in Table 1.

Businesses use strap lines in their marketing

**Table 1** – Popular slogans and strap lines

- Every little helps - Tesco
- A Mars a day helps you work, rest and play. - Mars bar
- Intel Inside - Intel processors in PCs and Laptops
- Let your fingers do the walking - Yellow Pages
- The future's bright, the future's orange - the Orange mobile phone network
- They're grrrreat! - Kellog's Frosties
- Just do it! - Nike
- The World's local bank - HSBC
- I'm lovin' it - McDonald's
- Beanz Meanz Heinz - Heinz baked beans

## Summary

The use of images to help promote a business and its brands has become increasingly important. The amount of information that stakeholders have to take in and the competitive nature of many markets means that new ways have to be found to make products appear different. Images can be used to help consumers remember a product or brand and to increase the recognition and association of a product or brand in the mind of all stakeholders, but especially consumers. The developments in technology mean that businesses can get their images in far more places than ever before. Logos can be put on mugs, pens, key rings, projected onto tall buildings, on digital display notices, on badges and a host of other places.

The more a business gets its image and logo placed the more likely it is that consumers will come to recognize the brand and make decisions to purchase that product or brand rather than those of rivals. The use of images as a communication medium is not without cost. Get the logo wrong and it can damage the brand. The use of celebrities is one aspect of this. The actual cost of developing the right image is, in many cases, very high and it has to work as a communication tool to get across the message about the business. The feedback to the business that the communication is working comes in the shape of increasing market share and sales.

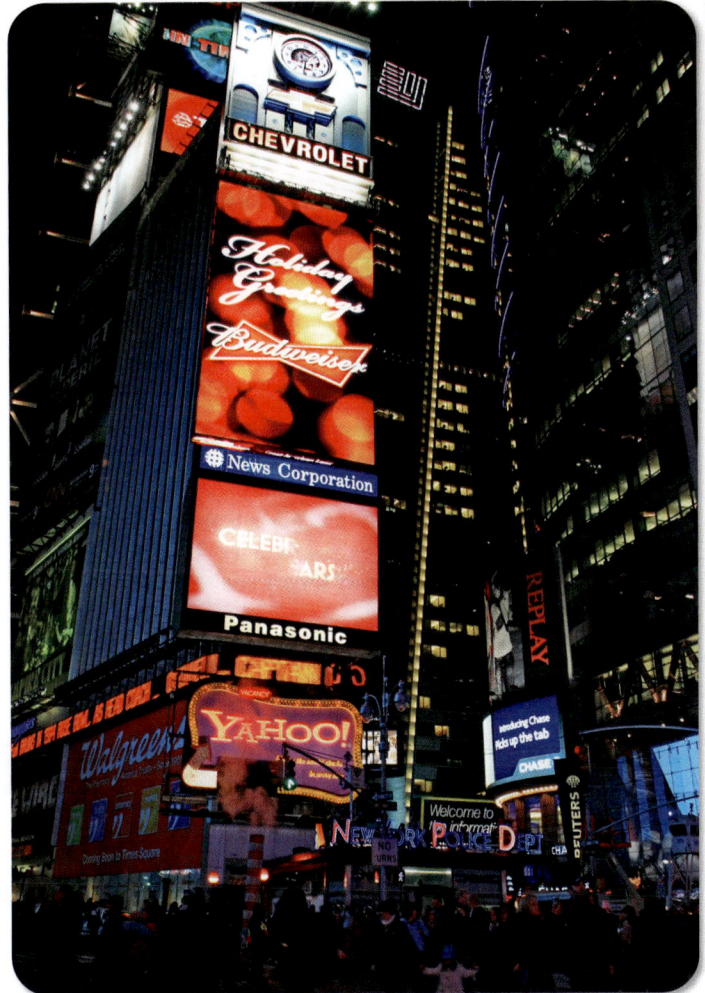

The more a business gets its image and logo placed the more likely it is that consumers will come to recognise the brand

**ResultsPlus**
**Watch Out!**

Remember that the use of images in business extends to more than just logos - they can include the use of photographs, celebrity endorsements, slogans and strap lines. Often the image comes as a whole package. The important thing to remember is the message that is being communicated and to whom.

## Test yourself

1. The main aim of building a brand is to:

A   **make it obvious to consumers that the business only has one product**
B   **create an identity for the product in the minds of consumers**
C   **satisfy the needs of shareholders**
D   **ensure that the business is able to make an immediate profit**

   Select **one** answer.

2. Careful choice of colours in logos is important because:

A   **they create an emotional response in the receiver.**
B   **the sender can make sure they clash to create a greater impact.**
C   **the use of simple white and black has little impact on the receiver.**
D   **the brain is not able to detect simple contrasts in two colours**

   Select **one** answer.

3. The most likely reason for a business to use a celebrity to endorse a product is because:

A   **the managing director really admires the celebrity**
B   **it is a cheap way of getting products known by consumers**
C   **they can help reflect what the business wants to be known for**
D   **everyone knows celebrities and this helps the business increase its price**

   Select **one** answer.

## ResultsPlus
### Build Better Answers

Kate Moss is a well known super model. She has been used by a number of companies, such as Burberry, H&M and Chanel to endorse their products. However, news of her alleged involvement with drugs in 2005 led to all three of these businesses cancelling her contract with them.

**Two** disadvantages of celebrity endorsement could be:
- The cost of hiring the celebrity is very high
- The celebrity might behave in a way that damages the business' reputation.

In your opinion, which of these two disadvantages will be the most serious for a business such as those in the passage? Justify your answer. (8)

The aim is to encourage evaluation so you will be expected to refer to both disadvantages to get to the top end of the mark range. You will be expected to be able to make a judgement of which of the two disadvantages would be the more damaging to the types of businesses mentioned. You will be expected to give some explanation of why the disadvantage would be serious to such a business thus demonstrating some analytical skills. To demonstrate evaluation skills you will place some importance or value on the disadvantage chosen on the extent of the seriousness. Will the disadvantage be very serious, quite serious or not that serious at all - and why? Remember, there is no 'right' answer here; the quality of the evaluation is the key to your answer and to accessing the higher marks.

🟥 **Basic** A judgement will be made with a simple supporting statement only. For example, 'The cost of hiring a celebrity is the most serious because it will reduce their profits.' (1-2)

🔴 **Good** A judgement will be made but at the lower level the support for the judgement will be weak and lacking in detail. There will be only one disadvantage mentioned in this level although a well developed support for the one disadvantage could get to the top of the level. Such an answer is likely to use appropriate terminology and show a clear understanding of the effect of the disadvantage on the business. For example, 'If a celebrity behaves badly then this can affect the reputation of the business. This is more serious than the cost of hiring the celebrity. This is because a company like Chanel might lose custom because people associate Kate Moss with drugs and think the business also encourages it. This could lead to customers choosing other brands and so could seriously dent the profits of the business'. (3-5)

🔺 **Excellent** At the top of the level both ways will be referred to and there will be clear development of both in relation to each other. The judgement made will be well supported. There will be clear evidence of some evaluative comment on both ways given. For example, 'Both the cost and the behaviour of a celebrity can have serious effects. The behaviour is likely to have the most serious effect. This is because a company like Burberry will have used Kate Moss to promote their products because she is a top model. Their clothes would look good on her. They would have known the cost of hiring her but have estimated that she would make them more money than the cost of using her. Her involvement with drugs will damage the reputation and as all the posters etc. will have been produced this will cost the business a lot of money. Sales might drop quite a bit as a result. However, for a big company like Burberry or Chanel, they might be able to act quickly and limit the extent of the damage caused.' (6-8)

## Over to you

The designers that had been working on the new logos for Sally's beauty salon, Face It, had delivered the different ideas that they had come up with. Sally wanted to get a logo that really captured the nature of the business and communicated the main ethos of the business - that they used only natural ingredients in their beauty treatments. She had chosen the name carefully to try and reflect the fact that many people did not know what was in the products that were used in some beauty salons and the fact that her speciality was in facial treatments. She opened the package feeling a little excited and took out the designs. Sally and her three staff then sat and discussed which of the designs they thought was the best for them to use. They wanted to make sure that the design not only reflected the business's ethos but they could apply it easily to the range of promotional materials they intended to develop. This included the new shop front that they decided they needed.

1.  Identify **three** possible factors that Sally and her staff might look for in choosing the right logo. (3)
2.  Identify **one** benefit to Sally's business of a successful logo. (1)
3.  Explain how the benefit that you have identified in question 2 above would improve Sally's business. (3)

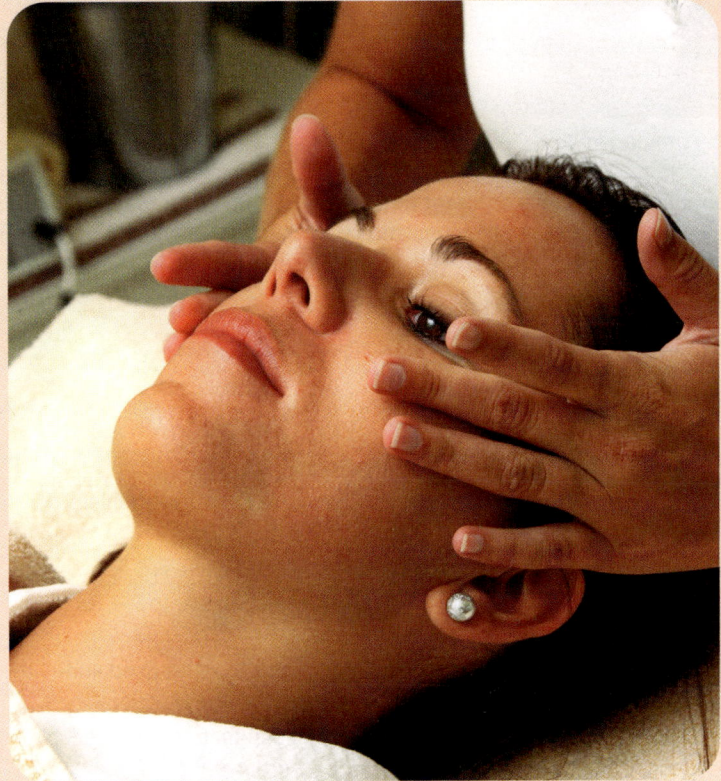

**In this topic you have learned about:** what a stakeholder in a business is, the different ways that businesses communicate with their stakeholders, the different types of written communication that businesses use in communication with their stakeholders, the range of electronic communications that businesses use in communicating with stakeholders, that written communication still plays an important part in the every day communication that businesses carry out and the importance of images in communication between business and their stakeholders.

## You should know…

- [ ] The meaning of the term 'stakeholder'.
- [ ] The difference between the internal and external stakeholders of a business.
- [ ] The interest each stakeholder group has in a business.
- [ ] The range of different ways that a business can use to communicate with these stakeholders.
- [ ] When different methods of communication should be used and how effective they are in different circumstances.
- [ ] The different types of written communication that can be used in a business in communicating with its different stakeholders.
- [ ] The importance of layout and the use of language in written communication.
- [ ] The range of different types of electronic communication.
- [ ] How electronic communication is used to communicate with stakeholders.
- [ ] The range of different types of oral communication.
- [ ] The continuing importance of oral communication in business.
- [ ] How images are used in business to help build brand awareness and promote products and services.
- [ ] The role of images in promoting the aims and objectives of a business.
- [ ] The role of celebrities in promoting and supporting a business's aims and objectives.
- [ ] The role of slogans and strap lines in promoting businesses aims and objectives.

## Support activity

Get a large sheet of paper - big enough to create a large poster.

At the centre of the paper, place the title 'Stakeholders'.

Choose a large business - for example, BP, Astra Zenica, McDonald's, BMW, etc.

Do some research to identify the main stakeholders for the business you have chosen. Include these on your poster, forming a series of spokes like a wheel.

Underneath each stakeholder create a list of **three** bullet points of the responsibility the business you have chosen has to the stakeholder you have identified.

## Stretch activity

Choose a large business such as one in the oil industry, a chemical company, a steel manufacturer etc. Go to the firm's web site and try to find out how it takes account of the impact of its operations on the environment. In some cases, this will be through a corporate social responsibility (CSR) report or under a heading for 'environment and society'.

Prepare a presentation that looks at **two** stakeholders of the business. In your presentation explain what the conflicting interests of the stakeholders might be and, from what you have observed on the web site, what steps the company you have chosen is taking to meet the conflicting needs of these two stakeholders. Your presentation should comment on the effectiveness of the communication that the business is using to get across its message to the two stakeholders you have identified.

**(a)** Ethan has been given a pile of application forms and curriculum vitae (CV) from people who have applied for the job of receptionist at his business. He is going through each of the forms and CVs to try and identify 5 people who will be shortlisted and invited for interview. The job description and person specification that was sent out with the job advert was very clear, so he is hoping that the forms and CVs will address the skills and qualities he is looking for to enable him to shortlist the right people.

**(i)** What is a CV? (1)

**(ii)** Explain how a well presented CV can help Ethan to be able to shortlist appropriate candidates for the job more easily. (3)

Think: What is a CV? What is the purpose of a CV? What is the relevance of the words 'well presented'? How can a good CV help in the shortlisting process?

| **Student answer** | **Examiner comment** | **Build a better answer** |
|---|---|---|
| **(i)** A CV is a document that has to be sent in when applying for a job. | 🟥 This answer does not get to the point of what a CV is. It is also not accurate in that not every job application has to include a CV. | 🔺 The answer has to give the main point of a CV. To do this it should point out that it is a document which summarises a prospective employee's skills and qualities. |
| **(ii)** If it is well presented Ethan can read it more easily. | 🟥 A weak answer which does not really tell the examiner whether the student knows the purpose of a CV and the value of it being well presented. | 🔺 The focus of the answer must be on the words 'well presented'. Use the passage to help you as well - there are clues in it. For example, Ethan is hoping to be able to match the candidate's skills and qualities to the job description and person specification. If the CV was well presented it would make it easier for him to do this. |

# Practice Exam Questions

Yourav is a managing director of a company which is planning to build an eco-town on the outskirts of a major city. The locals are very angry and have campaigned against such a development. The government is keen to see such projects go ahead as they meet the increasing demand for housing and take a lead in developing new technology that is environmentally friendly. The shareholders are caught between the two. Some see the development of 3,000 houses and associated amenities like shops, schools and entertainment facilities as being a great opportunity to generate profit. Others have been shocked at the extent of the opposition from local people to the plans. Yourav knows that his audience will have quite different views on the company's plans, but somehow he feels he has to address these different views and get agreement from the majority that the plans are worth backing.

**(a)** Identify **three** stakeholders in the passage. (3)

**(b)** For each stakeholder, identify **one** appropriate method of communication that Yourav can use to put forward the arguments in favour of the eco-town going ahead and explain why this method would be the most appropriate. (9)

**(c)** Describe **one** benefit of a poster campaign to a business trying to communicate a message like that of Yourav. (3)

**(d)** With reference to the passage, discuss **two** reasons why consideration of stakeholder needs is an important issue in communication. (10)

# Topic 4.3: Business communication tools

## Case study

When Jim Jeffries left his position as the business development director for a marketing firm, Nuldeaz, Corinne Sparks, the chief executive officer, took the opportunity to re-organise the business. There had been changes in the type of customer that Nuldeaz had been dealing with and the move into the digital world was long overdue. Corinne decided that as part of the reorganisation a number of new methods of working would be introduced, including the development of some new templates to standardise the communication with some of the business's key customers. Corinne also used software on the business's computer systems to design the new organisational structure. She wanted to try and improve the speed with which decisions were made within the business and so wanted to show employees how a flatter structure would help them achieve this.

## Topic overview

This topic looks at different communication tools - ways in which businesses communicate and technologies that they use to do so. It includes an overview of the use of word processing and presentation software, desktop publishing, video and teleconferencing and e-mail systems. It looks at the use of organisational charts and how ICT can be used to help construct different types of organisational chart. This topic provides lots of opportunities to try out different communication methods and carry out some practical exercises to improve your understanding of different communication tools.

Corinne knew that employees would need to know and understand what the new changes meant to the business, how it affected the way they worked, their responsibilities and their roles. In addition, she had also decided that there would be some investment in video conferencing facilities to help improve communications with Nuldeaz' overseas customers and also to reduce the costs and time involved in travelling to meetings. She knew that customers needed to be kept up to date with the changes that were happening in the business and how they had been designed to meet their needs more effectively. She had worked hard with the rest of the senior management team to put together a series of presentations to staff and key customers to explain the changes.

A series of leaflets and information booklets had been designed using desktop publishing software to help promote the new changes. These leaflets and booklets were to be given to Nuldeaz customers and so had to look professional and of high quality. Corinne had to invest in some software specifically for this. She knew that there was software that came with standard office packages but she wanted a far better quality and range of styles than was available on these and so had to pay £10,000 pounds to buy the licence and the software and also to train staff who would use this software. The results were impressive, however, and Corinne felt this was well worth the investment.

As the senior team worked on Corinne's proposals it became increasingly obvious that speedy decisions had to be made as deadlines approached. The e-mail system that Nuldeaz used was invaluable in making sure that all the people involved were in contact with each other regularly and even when key members of the team were out of the office, the mobile devices they had enabled them to respond to queries and requests quickly - whatever the time of day. For some, this was expecting a little too much but Corinne emphasised just how important the project was and most appreciated that an e-mail at 1.00am in the morning to alert them of a task that needed to be completed the next day was just about acceptable given the project.

When everything was in place, Corinne and her team set up a series of presentations to the different staff departments in the business. They identified each department and set up e-mail groups to keep them informed about when the presentations would take place and what they were expected to contribute. On one occasion, Corinne had received a call from a customer with a problem that needed dealing with straight away. Unfortunately it clashed with one of the presentations she was due to give to one of the departments. She was very grateful for e-mail to be able to contact them all quickly to alert them that the presentation had been postponed and that a new date would be set. It saved her and them a lot of wasted time.

1.  **Identify five different communications tools outlined in the passage.**

2.  **Explain two benefits to Corinne of using different tools to communicate the changes she is making in the business.**

3.  **Explain how business people like Corinne can justify spending large amounts of money investing in new communication tools.**

4.  **Evaluate two possible disadvantages to Nuldeaz of using an increasing amount of new communication tools in the business.**

## What will I learn?

**What are the principles of using word processing skills?** Word processing is a well known and popular means of communication in most businesses these days. You will learn how word processing help to improve both productivity and the quality of presentation in a business and the importance of making sure that presentation is of a high standard.

**The value of presentations in business** The number of businesses who are now involved in knowledge transfer as a major part of their business is growing. The skills needed to be able to make good presentations are not just reliant on the software and the slide show but on the skills of the presenter to complement and enhance the slide show. You will learn about the key principles involved in giving presentations.

**The use of desktop publishing in business** Producing high quality documents and publicity material used to be something that only professional designers and printers could produce. However, the development of technology has allowed businesses both large and small to be able to produce their own high quality publications using this new technology.

**The use of video and teleconferencing in business** The global nature of many businesses, the cost of travelling and concerns over the environmental effects of air travel and use of cars etc. along with new technology has led to an increase in the use of video and teleconferencing as a means of communication and of arranging meetings and interviews. They can be a cost effective alternative to face-to-face communication but are not without their drawbacks.

**Organisational charts and their purpose** Many businesses have complex structures and an organisational chart helps everyone in the organisation and stakeholders outside it to understand how it is organised, who is responsible to whom and who the most appropriate person to contact about an issue is likely to be.

**The value of e-mail systems.** E-mail is almost universally accepted as an important and very effective means of communication. Developments in technology mean that businesses of every size can make use of e-mail to keep in touch with stakeholders 24 hours a day, 365 days a year. This brings with it numerous benefits but with any form of technology there are disadvantages that a business has to balance out.

## How will I be assessed?

- Unit 4 is externally assessed.
- You will sit an exam of one and a half hours duration.
- There will be a mixture of multiple choice questions, short answer questions and extended writing questions.

# 13 The principles of using word processing skills

## Case Study

A.J. Hall Ltd is a family firm of builders run by Katie and James Hall. During a busy period the business decided to hire a 'temp' to help them in the office. Diane came highly recommended by the agency. Once she had settled to her work she felt more confident to talk to Katie and James about the standard and quality of the letters they sent out to customers and suppliers. They were impressed by the work that Diane had been doing and listened with interest to her comments. At the moment, there was little consistency in the letters. Diane showed them how the letters were badly written, with spelling and punctuation mistakes, and explained that they were all in different styles. Katie and James told her that they were often very busy and that this was probably the reason why. Diane stressed that making better use of their word processing facilities would help them to improve the quality of their letters and would save them time in future.

## Objectives

- To understand how word processing can aid communication.
- To understand the benefits of word processing for a business.
- To recognise the advantages of using templates for business communication.
- To understand the main requirements of formal business letters.
- To appreciate why layout, spelling, punctuation, grammar and presentation are important in communicating successfully.

## How can word processing aid communication?

Katie and James were communicating with a number of stakeholders. It is vital to the success of their business that their communication methods reflect the business. It is important to maintain a professional image to ensure that their reputation is not affected. Diane recognised that they were making mistakes and that it could affect the standard of their communication. By using the facilities available with word processing they could ensure that all computer produced documentation could be produced in a professional way, that would represent the business and the service they provide. They could ensure that the message they were trying to communicate got across to their stakeholders.

The first word processors were simply computerised type writers where text could just be entered and edited. Now word processors are sophisticated computer applications that can combine graphics with a variety of ways to present text, images, tables and numerical information.

Word processing allows us to:

- enter text into a document;
- store or save the text;
- edit text in a document;
- format the text to make it more attractive;
- add graphics into a document;
- enter numerical information.

When a document is written it rarely comes out perfect first time and changes often need to be made. Words can be inserted, deleted or amended or extra words can be added. Word processing provides the facilities to cut, copy and paste words from one document to another or within an existing one. Successful communication occurs when the receiver, the intended audience, is able to understand the message and acts accordingly. Presenting information in a professional way and in a format that represents the business accurately will go some way to improving the success of the communication, as well as saying something about the business itself and how much they care.

## Formatting text

Formatting means the way text and other objects like images and tables are laid out on a page. One of the main benefits of word processors is that documents can be formatted in many different ways, for example:

- margins can be changed;
- page size and page layout (portrait and landscape) can be altered;
- tables, charts and graphs can be inserted to improve presentation of information;
- images can be inserted;
- different styles and sizes of font can be used;
- a document can be produced in different colours;
- text can be given certain types of features such as underlined, emboldened and italicised;
- symbols can be easily inserted;
- comments and changes can be made, so that the original author can see what has been changed or note the comments that have been made;
- Text can be aligned, as in Figure 1.

Information to stakeholders needs to be presented in a format so that the receiver will understand the message and will be able to respond accordingly. Katie and James need to consider the information they need to send to stakeholders and the format they use to do this. Making the best use of the facilities that word processing has will enable them to establish the most suitable format for their needs. If they listen to the advice of Diane, who has experience with using word processing, they will be able to present the business in a more professional way.

It is important to the business that they have contact details on all communication that they send out so stakeholders can contact them. For example:

- address;
- telephone and fax number;
- email address;
- person who has sent the document and their position in the business;
- business logo.

This information can be integrated as a letterhead, the details on it will ensure that stakeholders can contact the business and know who to contact, which in addition will promote the business.

## Benefits of word processing to business

A.J. Hall Ltd has a number of stakeholders that it has contact with. As with other businesses, it must maintain thorough records of communication both sent and received. Word processing gives businesses the flexibility to create:

- letters;
- memos;
- questionnaires;
- reports;
- leaflets containing graphics;
- newsletters;
- personalised letters using mail merge;
- labels.

For Katie and James it will enable them to promote their business and communicate with stakeholders effectively. Word processing allows them to have consistency across all methods of communication with a format suitable for the type of business. Word processing is much quicker and more flexible than methods such as typewriters or even hand written letters. Katie and James were not using the facilities that word processing provides to the full. If they did they would find that they could produce more letters or documents (and better quality) in a shorter space of time. This means they would be more productive. They may have to invest some time to getting used to using a word processor properly, but if they did they would find that it brings a number of advantages, as shown in Table 1.

Diane is clear about what facilities are available within a word processing application and the benefits it can bring to the business. She decides to spend some time with Katie and James covering important principles of formatting using a word processor. These include:

**Figure 1** – Text

| Left aligned | | |
|---|---|---|
| | Centered | |
| | | Right aligned |

or fully justified where the text lines up with both margins to produce a neat block of text

**Table 1** – Advantages of word processing

- Documents can be stored electronically and printed
- Text can be stored and edited at a later date
- Mistakes are highlighted and can be edited
- No retyping of documents is necessary
- Documents can be professionally laid out
- Mistakes can be corrected before printing
- Documents can be attached to emails
- Easy and accessible program to use
- Graphics can be added into any part of the document

**edexcel key terms**

**Formatting** – a means of changing the physical appearance and layout of a document. This could be the style of or layout of a document. This might incorporate changing font size, font colour or the layout of a document or part of it.

- indenting text;
- adding tables;
- importing information from other applications, such as charts and graphs from a spreadsheet;
- changing the margins to match the style of presentation;
- including bullet points;
- producing automatically numbered lists;
- aligning text to improve the layout and appearance of a document;
- using the spell checking and grammar functions effectively;
- using the thesaurus;
- using automatic text correction.

It is possible to embed information into a document, which can be imported from a spreadsheet or database. Many office software programs are designed to work easily and closely together. For businesses to have access to such facilities is highly beneficial, particularly if they need to present numerical data to highlight sales, profit or predicted sales figures and so on.

## Advantages of using templates for business communications

Diane was brought in to assist Katie and James during a busy period for the business. Diane was familiar with using word processing and recognised how the facilities would benefit the business and the necessity for the business to improve its communication with stakeholders. She had the capabilities to produce a template that the business could use for all letters to be sent out. A **template** would establish a consistent approach and enable the business to produce documentation that would be professional and represent the service provided. Diane created a letter template with a letterhead that held all relevant details for stakeholders that Katie and James could access. This meant that if they needed to write a letter the business had a **consistent** style and layout. This was a much more professional approach to their communication. Diane informed Katie and James that they could create templates for producing memos, newsletters and leaflets if they wished. She

**edexcel ⠿ key terms**

**Template** – provides a way of enforcing a particular layout, style, it ensures that documents are presented in a consistent style including the size and colour of the font, layouts, borders and so on.

**Consistent** – ensuring that the same style is repeated throughout documents, establishing a corporate theme for a business.

highlighted the advantages that setting up templates would bring to the business, that it would save them time and that all they needed to do was to add text to it before printing. Katie and James were very impressed with the knowledge that Diane had and had no idea that they had access to these facilities. They could see how this could improve their productivity.

Having a consistent approach is important for business communication, it maintains a professional approach and demonstrates to stakeholders that the business is organised and takes communication seriously. A business's reputation can be affected by poor communication, which in turn could lead to a reduction in custom. Time is precious to businesses; therefore using time wisely will improve efficiency throughout a business as less time will be spent on repetitive tasks such as typing duplicate documents. Utilising the facility to create a template will contribute to the use of time and efficiency within the business together with providing a thorough and professional approach to communication.

## Understanding the requirements of formal business letters

Letters are used by organisations to communicate with stakeholders and other organisations outside the firm. The standard of letters is important in order to give the right impression about the business. The majority of firms have their logo, name and address as part of the letterhead. When a business communicates via a letter it is usually a formal letter and therefore the layout and language used is a vital element.

The layout of a letter should always have the address, including the postcode, of the person the letter is intended for, as well as their name. It should include the date and any reference numbers applicable to the topic being addressed in the letter. This will help identify who the letter is for and what it is about and allows the business to keep a record of the communication. The person receiving the letter is known as the addressee. If the person is known to the sender the letter should always start with their name, for example Dear Mrs Jones, Dear Ms Smith, Dear Catherine etc. If the person is not known then the letter starts with Dear Sir/Madam. If this is the case it should end with 'Yours faithfully'. If the letter starts with the person's name then it should end with 'Yours sincerely'. There should be five line spaces left after this, before typing the name of the person who the letter is from in full. The space is for the sender's signature.

Letters should be broken down into paragraphs to deal with each point being made. This breaks down the information into manageable chunks, making it easier for the reader to understand.

Diane is fully aware of how to write a professional letter. She is aware that the language used within the letters has to be appropriate; in a formal style given it is not a personal letter but one that is representing the business. The content of the language used will influence the person receiving the letter and should enhance the professional image that businesses strive to maintain.

## Appreciating the importance of layout, spelling, punctuation, grammar and presentation for successful communication

Diane identified that Katie and James made a lot of spelling, punctuation, and grammatical errors when writing their letters as well as the inconsistent styles. She had a discussion with Katie and James about these issues and highlighted the impact they could have on their reputation. Diane's key point to them was that their communication had to represent the business and demonstrate the elements of professionalism that ran throughout the rest of the business. Katie and James were shocked when they realised the impact their mistakes could have on the business and its reputation. They were unaware of the potential damage poor communication could cause for them. Having set up the template, Diane indicated to them that they would simply have to enter the text. James queried how they could overcome the problem of so many errors. Diane informed them that word processing software has an integrated dictionary and has the facility to set the spell check to a UK English setting. This would highlight any spelling errors, give suggested alternatives and allow them to make the necessary changes. However, not all dictionaries contain every word in the English language, particularly technical ones, and therefore it may not recognise these. Diane pointed out that letters and documents should still be checked before sending out. The software will advise them on

punctuation and grammar/order of the words and will provide them with the opportunity to read and make any necessary changes.

Presentation of a letter will say a lot about a business. Businesses which have a style and maintain consistency in their approach to communication will demonstrate they are professional and value their reputation. A letter with numerous errors will dilute the message and the receiver may question the competence of the business.

### Over to you

James had written a letter to a customer of A.J. Hall who had responded. Katie opened the letter and then replied to the query raised by the customer.

1. Identify **two** possible reasons why a customer might be confused. (2)
2. Consider why it is important for a business to ensure that it maintains a consistent approach to its written communication. (6)

### ResultsPlus
**Build Better Answers**

Stephanie was a busy entrepreneur with a growing business. One of her friends told her, however, that her written communication was very poor and let her business down. She advised Stephanie to do something about it but Stephanie said that she was not good with computers and anyway did not have time to worry about things that were not that important. Making a profit was more important.

Do you agree with Stephanie's view? Justify your answer. (6)

Technique guide; You are being asked to make a judgement in this question but to get full marks you must offer convincing support for that judgement.

Think: What are the two sides to the argument? Does Stephanie have a point? What advantages might she gain by spending more time making sure her communication is of a better quality? What disadvantages might arise if she spends more time on her communication?

Then: Think through how you are going to write your answer - you have six marks to earn. To earn these marks you must provide a balanced answer and a clear judgement in conclusion based on your analysis.

Remember: You need to provide some balance to the answer.

Write: Write out your answer.

■ **Basic**: Provides a judgement and gives a limited reason for the judgement. (1-2)

● **Good** Offers an explanation of one of the views and provides a judgement with limited support. (3-4)

▲ **Excellent** Presents an explanation of both the view points with a well argued reason for the judgement. (5-6)

### Test yourself

1. Which of the following **best** describes the benefits of setting up a letter template? Select **one** answer.

   A The business can have a standard letter ready to send out to stakeholders
   B A business has the opportunity to review how it communicates with stakeholders
   C It provides a means by which the business can save time, and set a style and layout
   D It provides the business with a variety of options for communication

2. Which of the following is **not** a facility available with word processing? Select **one** answer.

   A To be able to import other software
   B Indenting text in a document
   C Including text and graphics
   D The use of numbered lists

3. Which of the following is an important consideration when creating a letterhead for a business? Select **one** answer.

   A Ensuring the letterhead is no bigger than 10 point font size
   B Ensuring that the sender of the letter promotes the business and what it represents
   C Making sure that the information contains a strict word count
   D Making sure that the letterhead is created with different formats

# 14 The value of presentations in a business

## Case Study

Evalu8 provides training in techniques for businesses that run in-house continuing professional development (CPD). CPD is important as a means of providing staff with new skills and keeping them up to date with changes in the businesses they are involved in. Members of staff from Evalu8 go into businesses and observe a training session being given and then provide a report to the trainers about their performance and ways in which it can be improved. They then run sessions themselves to demonstrate these skills and to help trainers improve their presentational skills and the effectiveness of the training.

## Objectives

- To understand the different types of presentation techniques used by businesses.
- To understand the main principles in giving a successful presentation.
- To understand the purpose of a presentation in business.
- To understand different presentation techniques that can be used in business communication.
- To be aware of the issues to be considered in giving a successful presentation.

## ResultsPlus
### Watch Out!

Remember that a presentation is not always a slide show - it can include other techniques.

## edexcel key terms

**Presentation** – the process of communicating information to an audience.

## Different presentation techniques

**Presentation** involves communicating information to an audience. The presenter is offering information to the audience which is new and which has a purpose. The purpose may be to bring the audience up to date with changes, to encourage a change in behaviour and to communicate information they may not have known before. There are three elements to a presentation; the **audience**, the **presenter** and the **tool** used to help communicate the information. One assumption is that the only form of presentation is through a slide show using proprietary software for the purpose. However, a slide show is just one form of presentation.

**Slide shows** A slide show is a series of pieces of information which serve the purpose of helping the audience to understand the key points of the presentation. The slides act as a visual reference point to help the audience focus on the words being used by the presenter. The use of a slide show can also be helpful in incorporating other forms of visual communication such as images, maps, charts and diagrams, which can help to illuminate or exemplify the points being made. Slides can look professional and are capable of being customised in many different ways.

**Flipcharts** A flip chart is a relatively small board which has a block of paper attached to it. The paper can be written on using different colour marking pens. A flipchart is useful in recording information generated in the session and to present new ideas and thinking that might arise from the presentation. One problem with flip charts is that they tend to be suitable only for small gatherings and can look untidy and be difficult to read.

**Handouts** Some presentations, especially to larger audiences, might benefit from the issue of handouts. The handout may summarise the main points of the presentation and give the audience the opportunity of seeing what is coming, to get the big picture and to make notes and comments as the presentation progresses. Handouts may also be given out in conjunction with a slide show.

**Video projectors** The use of video as a means of communicating ideas and information is now widespread in presentations.

**Overhead transparencies (OHT)** This method of presentation is becoming less popular given the developments in slide show technology and the availability of video projectors. An OHT is a thin film of plastic which can be written on or have information printed onto it. The transparency is placed onto a machine which projects the image onto a screen. OHT projectors have the advantage of being relatively easy to move around, are easy to use and can be versatile. The problem with them is that the image is not always clear, the image is subject to a 'keystone' effect and does not look as professional as a slide show.

**Presentational software** Whilst many people are familiar with Microsoft's PowerPoint software, this is not the only software available for producing presentations. Macromedia Flash has a slide show facility and there are numerous graphics and design programmes that enable the presenter to develop quite sophisticated images, charts, graphs and other forms of visual communication for use in presentations, for example SmartDraw, PresentiaFX, Ability Graphics, FrameMaker and Corel Designer. The value of such software is to help the presenter to make the message they wish to communicate clearer and more engaging to the audience.

## The main principles in using presentation techniques

When staff from Evalu8 go into businesses and observe presentations, they identify a number of common problems that occur in many businesses and organisations. The key problem they find is that the presenter forgets the purpose of the presentation. The purpose of the presentation is to communicate information to the audience. As with any communication, the success depends on the way in which the information is presented by the sender and the feedback that the receiver/s give. A good presentation, therefore, should have lasting effects in terms of changed behaviour, new ways of working, new insights and so on, to the audience.

## What is the most important element in a presentation?

In the first paragraph, three elements to a presentation were outlined, the presenter, the audience and the tool used to give the presentation. The most important of these is the audience. The presenter must take into consideration the needs of the audience in planning, producing and giving the presentation. If this is not taken into account then the message that is being communicated will be lost and the presentation will not be as successful as it could be. Table 1 explains how to make presentations effective.

Evalu8 find that too many presenters focus too much on the actual tool itself. Using a slide show is one of the most common forms of giving a presentation and it is important to make sure that the show is lively, engaging, informative and professional. However, it is equally important to remember that the slide show is only the tool - it is one way in which the presenter can get the message across. However, it is only an aid to communication and not the main reason for the presentation.

Many students in year 10 and 11 will have had experience of using software to produce slide shows - not just in Business Studies but in many other subjects. ICT lessons will have given an introduction to producing a slide show and many students are now confident in producing attractive and interesting slide shows for a presentation. However, whilst the skills to produce a slide show may be in place there are other considerations that have to be taken into account to help

**Table 1** - Making a presentation effective

- Keep the number of slides appropriate to the length of the presentation - too many slides can lead to a loss of attention from the audience.
- Use images and charts in a presentation where appropriate - they often have more impact than words.
- Limit the number of points on a slide to a maximum of 7 - most humans can remember no more than 7 things at a time so too many points makes a slide look 'busy'.
- Be wary about using bright colours - contrast is the key. Remember, someone in the audience is likely to be colour blind so using clearly contrasting colours is going to be more effective than showing an artistic ability to use the largest array of colours possible!
- A dark background to the slide can be useful in making it easy for the audience to see text - especially if the presenter is not able to control the lighting in the room.
- Be careful what font is used - Times New Roman, for example, is not considered helpful to those who suffer from problems such as dyslexia and fonts such as Comic Sans may look rather childish and unprofessional. Remember that the reason for the text being there is so that the audience can read it.
- Think carefully before using animations. Should the whole slide be revealed at once or in stages? There are different views about the effectiveness of each. Some argue that showing the whole slide at once is a better way as the audience can see how it fits in with the whole presentation. Gradually revealing information can be frustrating but may be useful if the presenter is trying to involve the audience in a practical activity or to encourage feedback. The use of sounds, flashing introductions, rotating entry for bullet points and other 'snazzy' animations can be irritating and distracting to the audience.
- Make the font as consistent as possible throughout the slide show - use one size for headings and a smaller one for the main body of the slide.
- Make sure that the audience can see the information on the slides - wherever they are sitting in the room. This means avoiding using charts that are too small, text that is too small and so on.
- Keep the slides as simple as possible - do not include too much text and avoid using lots of different colours. Lots of artwork such as clip art can also be distracting.
- If the points that have to be made have a sequence then use a numbered list. If not then use a bullet list.

make the presentation effective in communicating the message.

## The presenter

The presenter is an important part of the presentation. Presenting successfully is a skill and an art that takes practice and requires techniques to be learned. The audience will be arriving for the presentation relying on the presenter to provide them with the information they need and expecting them to help them do their job better, improve performance, understand changes being made and so on.

The presenter is not the key element, however, the audience is and the presenter needs to remember this. The presenter needs to be well presented themselves - this means dressing appropriately, for example, looking well groomed and confident. A presenter who dresses scruffily and who has sweat patches on the armpits of his/her shirt does not inspire confidence amongst the audience.

Whether the presenter is using a slide show or any other form of presentation technique, there are some basic principles that should be borne in mind.

- The presenter has to know the material s/he is going to give to the audience. This does not mean going through a slide show, for example, and simply reading the points on the slides! The audience can read - they do not need the presenter to read this information for them. Remember the slides are there as an aid.
- Make sure that prior to the presentation all the equipment, handouts etc. are in place and that everything is working.
- Making eye contact with the audience is important; it makes them feel part of the presentation and keeps their attention.
- The presenter should not be frightened to ensure that there is some time for audience involvement - this may be through questions (see below) but may involve the presentation being punctuated by sessions that involve some practical activity or discussion. This is especially important if the session is a long one with a great deal of

information to get through. Most humans can only concentrate fully for around 20 minutes at a time - after that concentration levels fall quickly especially if there is not a break in the routine.

- It is important to be prepared to take questions. This may be at the end of a session but to encourage the audience to be part of the presentation it is often useful to deal with questions as they arise. This is not so easy if the audience is very large, however.
- The presenter should take some time to rehearse the presentation so that they can present a confident image and be in control of the presentation. This will help the audience to feel at ease and also communicate confidence to them.

It is useful for a presenter to have in mind three key messages they want to communicate to the audience and to keep these in mind throughout the presentation. This also helps the presenter to reflect on the success of the presentation at the end.

## When to use different techniques

Presentations are not all the same. Some may be a ten minute presentation at the start of an interview, some may be part of an all day training session for staff, some may be in-house and others away from the business itself in special training sessions. A presentation may involve a short briefing to a small team or a major speech by a senior member of a business to a large audience.

The presenter will have to make a decision about which is the most appropriate technique to use for the session. The main factor to consider in this respect is the purpose of the presentation - the message that has to be communicated. This is why the audience is so important in making a successful presentation. If a member of a team is giving an update briefing to the rest of his or her team then the use of a flip chart and handouts might be appropriate. If a team leader is giving out new instructions to a sales team about new products then a more formal slide show may be appropriate.

Whatever the decision, the presenter has to make sure that uppermost in their mind is the purpose of the presentation and the message that is to be communicated. If the presentation is successful the audience will have understood its purpose and the feedback to the presenter will be through the change in behaviour of those in the audience, a greater understanding of an issue or change in the business, an understanding of a new process or products and so on.

**ResultsPlus**
**Watch Out!**

The secret to a good slide show is not the slide show itself but the role it plays in supporting the presenter in communicating the message to the audience.

## Test yourself

1. The main purpose of a presentation is to:
   
   **A  communicate a message to an audience**
   
   **B  provide the opportunity for the presenter to demonstrate their presentation skills**
   
   **C  give the audience a chance to have a break from routine work**
   
   **D  present detailed and complex information to a large group of people**
   
   Select **one** answer.

2. Which of the following would be the **most likely** sign that a presentation had been successful?
   
   **A  None of the audience fell asleep during it**
   
   **B  The feedback given to the presenter was all negative**
   
   **C  The audience commented on how flashy the slide show was**
   
   **D  The audience changed its behaviour in the way desired by the presenter**
   
   Select **one** answer.

3. Which of the following is **not** a factor that should be taken into account when presenting to an audience?
   
   **A  The size of the audience and their needs**
   
   **B  The three key points of the presentation**
   
   **C  Whether the audience will think the presenter is cool**
   
   **D  The size of the font used in the presentation**
   
   Select **one** answer.

## Over to you

One particular trainer that Evalu8 had worked with had gone on to make a number of presentations to colleagues in the sales teams to explain a new product that the company were launching. After the first month of the new campaign sales were very disappointing. At a meeting of the sales team, George the Director of Sales, heard that many of the sales representatives felt they were underprepared and had struggled to understand the purpose of the new product and the message they were meant to be giving to customers. George called in Evalu8 and told them the feedback that he had been given. Evalu8 investigated further and found a number of problems that had arisen with the presentations that had been given to the sales team. The biggest problem seemed to be that the slide show was really impressive but that the message was lost amidst the sophistication of it.

1. What is the main purpose of a presentation? (2)

2. Identify **two** possible reasons why the slide show presentations that the sales team were given were not as successful as they could have been. (2)

3. With reference to the reasons given in question 2 above, recommend one way to solve each problem. Justify your recommendation. (6)

## ResultsPlus
### Build Better Answers

Jamina was called into her line manager's office just before she left work at 5.30pm with an urgent request. Could she give a presentation first thing in the morning to give a short update on a new project she is working on to a visitor from the United States? There will only be the visitor and Jamina's line manager at the presentation and it is only scheduled to last ten minutes.

Which presentation technique would you choose to use if you were Jamina? Justify your answer. (6)

Technique guide: This is a question that is assessing your ability to make judgements and to break down a complex topic into easier to manage chunks (evaluation and analysis).

Think: What are the circumstances of the presentation? What factors does Jamina need to take into consideration? What would be an appropriate presentation technique?

Then: Arrive at a decision about which one you are going to choose - there is NO right answer; the examiner is looking for your ability to make a judgement and support it.

Remember: It is not how much you write here but the quality of your answer.

Plan: Try and think through how you are going to approach the answer and how you are going to structure it.

Write: Write out your answer.

■ **Basic**: Provides a judgement about an appropriate technique and gives a limited reason for the judgement. (1-2).

● **Good** Provides a judgement on an appropriate technique and offers an explanation in support that makes use of the context. Appropriate terms and concepts are used as part of the explanation for the judgement. (3-4)

▲ **Excellent** Provides a judgement on an appropriate technique with some well argued reasoning in support. There is clear reference to the context and it is used to provide support for the judgement. Appropriate terms and concepts are used throughout the answer. (5-6)

# 15 The use of desktop publishing (DTP) in businesses

## Case Study

Blue Skies is a company providing design and marketing services to a wide range of businesses. Part of its work is to help advise clients on the design and production of a range of information including leaflets, information booklets, menus, price lists and so on. Many of the businesses they work with are relatively small and they have different access to packages to produce such information. Part of Blue Skies' work involves helping these businesses choose the right type of software package to meet the requirements of the business. There is no point in a small business having a very sophisticated DTP package when they only want to produce simple documents. Blue Skies also help these businesses understand the basics of design principles and how to focus on the purpose of the document and the needs of the intended audience.

## Objectives

- To understand the role of DTP in producing business documents.
- To understand the main principles involved with producing a business document.
- To understand how to evaluate the finished product in relation to the target audience.
- To be able to evaluate the use of different DTP packages.

## The role of desktop publishing in creating business documents

**Desktop publishing (DTP)** is a type of application that can be used by businesses to create professional looking documents such as newsletters, memos, brochures and many more. It has more facilities than word processing software. DTP allows the user to use different typefaces, specify various margins and justifications, and insert designs and graphs directly into the text together with the added extra of already designed templates to assist in the development of documents. After the design stage, the software tools can be used to set up the document, place text and graphics, and prepare digital files. The business will have a document that will look professional and be effective in communicating the message. It can be printed using desktop or commercial printing processes. DTP is quickly replacing the pre-press work done by printing professionals such as compositors and page layout workers. Its advantages are shown in Table 1.

**Table 1** – Advantages of DTP

- Lower costs of production.
- In-house control for updating and editing products, and speed of production.
- It can control the number of pages more easily than a word processor.
- Produces a professional looking document.
- More control over the way text is arranged and formatted.
- DTP can be used to bring lots of different files together on the same document.
- It allows a business to have complete control over the final product.
- Changes can be easily made.
- Different fonts can be used.
- It provides ways to effectively communicate ideas.
- Images can be imported into a DTP document from a scanner, graphics from a drawing. package, a video camera and text from a word processor.

## edexcel ::: key terms

**Desktop publishing** – a software package that allows the user to create professional looking documents which incorporate a range of styles and layouts.

Documents produced using DTP are built up using a series of frames, for example, text frames containing text, graphics frames containing images and more. The frames can be resized and moved which means it is very easy to edit by simply moving blocks of text or images around to another page if necessary. Producing a document using a word processing application can cause problems with the layout as it is not frame based and therefore if one thing is moved it can alter the position of other content. This does not happen using DTP as the frames can be moved until the user is satisfied with the design and layout.

Blue Skies need to ensure that they make their clients aware of the facilities and advantages that using a desktop publishing program would bring to their clients' businesses. For the purpose of many small businesses it would be very costly to use a large design company to design such things as menus, therefore using DTP to complete such tasks will not only save time but will reduce costs too.

## Main principles in producing business documents

A business document represents a business by communicating an image and a message to the receiver. Documents are also typically be used as a method of communication internally as well as externally. The document is an ambassador for the business and therefore it is vital that the document is produced with this in mind. A business letter is the most common method of external communication between different companies and customers. Letters are a formal method of external communication. Typically they would be sent to customers or suppliers, it is therefore important that they are accurate and well presented. Many businesses use headed paper which would include the:

* name;
* registered address;
* logo;
* names of directors and owners of the business;
* business registration number.

## Letter layout

There are several ways in which a business letter can be laid out and each business will have a preferred format. It is most common for businesses to use a blocked method, which means that all text starts at the left hand margin. A business will want to create a house style; this refers to the colours, font and logo a business will use on a consistent basis so that all its employees understand the conventions it uses in its communication. For example, a business might expect particular brands it has to be written using a certain font; it may decide how to write certain words and terms, for example, it may state that its employees use 'web site' rather than 'website'. Blue Skies will need to make sure that they advise their clients on a house style that is suitable for the business as this will reflect the initial impression the business gives to its communications. Blue Skies will need to ensure that the logo the business uses will appear on all documentation as it is either a symbol or a style of letters that are recognisable and associated with the business. They will need to advise their clients about the font to use on their documentation.

## Business cards

A business card has elements of the letterhead on it but smaller and will maintain the house style of the business. It will have the name of the person representing the business on it.

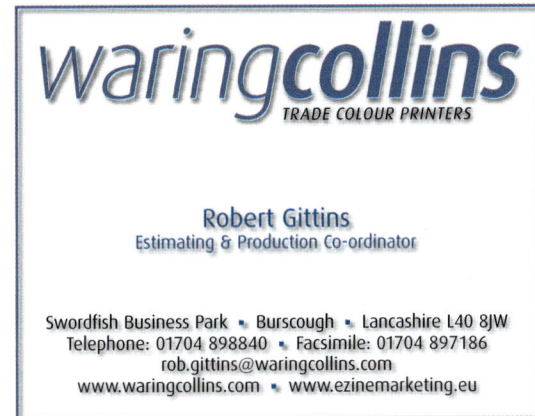

**waringcollins**
*TRADE COLOUR PRINTERS*

Robert Gittins
Estimating & Production Co-ordinator

Swordfish Business Park • Burscough • Lancashire L40 8JW
Telephone: 01704 898840 • Facsimile: 01704 897186
rob.gittins@waringcollins.com
www.waringcollins.com • www.ezinemarketing.eu

DTP can be used to produce business cards

**ResultsPlus Watch Out!**
Some spellcheckers will use an American dictionary and will not correct some English spelling errors.

Whatever the document, accuracy is important. The sole purpose of a business document is to create the right impression and communicate a message. It is important, therefore, that documents should be laid out properly, as shown in Table 2.

**Table 2** – Key points when producing business documents

- Check that the grammar and spelling are correct.
- Avoiding lengthy sentences as this might make it difficult for the reader to understand the message.
- Avoid slang or phrases that the receiver will not understand.
- Keep the layout consistent.
- Use house style.
- Ensure the communication is polite.
- Do not repeat information or phrases.

Blues Skies were approached by a business who asked for advice and guidance about creating documents that would represent the business. The business was a children's soft play area. Blue Skies advised the business that they would need to have a logo and text on their letterheads and business cards that were bright and would stand out, representing the type of service they provided. The business was advised of the information they would need to include and that creating a template for their documents would reduce time, but more importantly would ensure they maintained a consistent house style.

## Evaluating the finished product in relation to the target audience

Elements is a small successful beauty salon. Costs of salon products have risen and as a result they have had to increase the price of treatments In addition they have decided to add some new treatments and extend the range available. Elements have an existing price list available in the form of a leaflet that was designed by a friend of the owner but feel that it is a little old and needs an update. This is the ideal opportunity for them to do so.

They have decided to use Blue Skies to assist them in designing a new price list and promotional leaflets to promote the treatments available. Blues Skies has advised them to keep the design simple and to change their house style into something more up to date. They produced a draft price list and promotional leaflet. Elements thought the

change was exciting and very modern. Elements changed the sign at the front of the salon and went with the advice given to them. They used a desktop publishing package for their price lists and leaflets and were amazed at how much they could change the layout. To try out the new leaflets and price lists they decided to print a small amount themselves before making the decision to go to a printers. They were amazed by the feedback from clients. They thought the change in design was a great idea and the layout of the information and price list much easier to understand. New clients recognised the shop from their leaflets as the house style was consistent and carried through all their documents.

Elements was able to evaluate the success of the change as a result of the response from existing clients and the new clients that came to the salon as a result of the publicity. Understanding the message being given by a document is fundamental to a business's success. If the receiver understands the message then the communication via the document is likely to work much better and prove beneficial to the business.

## Evaluate the use of different DTP packages

Microsoft Publisher is not the only DTP package but is commonly used by many small businesses to create professional looking documents. Adobe PageMaker system can also be utilised to create documents and create them as Portable Document Format (PDF) files. PagePlus is another package that will allow documents to be created as Adobe PDF files if required. It is difficult to alter the layout of documents once they have been created as a PDF file and users within a business will have to have Adobe Writer to be able to open the document and adjust the layout. This will be time consuming for businesses and costly as the software is expensive.

Blue Skies have found that for smaller businesses Microsoft Publisher is the most suitable and accessible software. Their recommendations are to use such a package as users within businesses can alter the layout as details may change. It is both cost effective and user friendly for businesses. Blue Skies have found that many of their clients like the templates that are available to use which gives them a guide on layout for documents. Template layouts can be changed to suit the documents being created. Logos and images can be saved and reused as and when required.

## Over to you

Dave Moss runs a successful chimney cleaning and maintenance business in the South West of England. His business success relies on word of mouth from satisfied customers who appreciate Dave's punctuality, efficiency, cleanliness and professional approach to his job. Dave has run out of business cards and has investigated getting some new ones printed by a specialist firm but was surprised at the cost involved. His daughter suggested that he could use the family computer to produce a business card design of his own and that the cost of having them printed off on good quality card would be much less as a result. Dave was not that good with computers but together they came up with a design that Dave was very happy with. He was impressed with the flexibility of the DTP package they had on their computer and the cost was significantly less than having the cards professionally done.

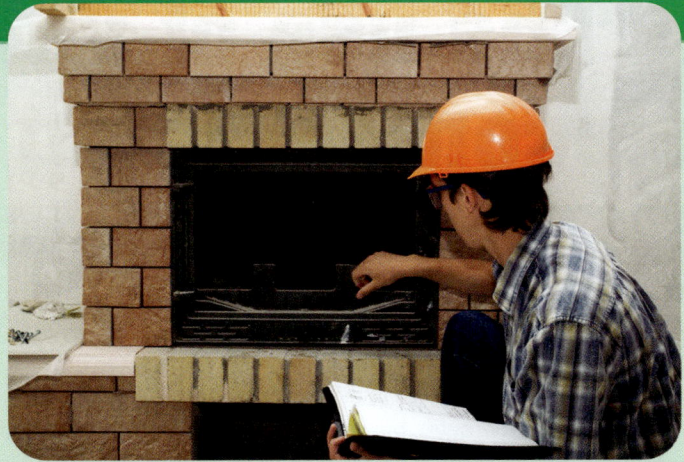

1. Identify **three** pieces of information that Dave is likely to have needed on his business card. (3)

2. Explain **one** factor that a business like Dave's might take into consideration in choosing an appropriate DTP package. (3)

3. Assess how Dave could judge the success of his new business cards. (8)

## Test yourself

1. Which of the following is **most likely** to be an advantage to a business of producing a document by a DTP package?

   A *It will guarantee additional sales*
   B *The document will look more professional*
   C *The communication can be spread over a wider range of stakeholders*
   D *The cost of the document is higher*

   Select **one** answer.

2. A DTP package has an advantage over a word processing package because:

   A *it has many more fonts available to use*
   B *images can be imported into the document*
   C *changing the layout is much easier*
   D *DTP packages come as standard with most computers*

   Select **one** answer.

3. Which of the following would be considered the most important factor in producing a leaflet advertising the opening of a new restaurant?

   A *Using as many pictures as possible in the leaflet*
   B *Checking that the number of pages is always equal*
   C *Keeping the leaflet in just black and white to make it simple*
   D *Having a consistent layout to the leaflet*

   Select **one** answer.

## ResultsPlus
### Build Better Answers

In producing documents such as information leaflets or price lists, businesses may use a 'house style'. This means they:

A    base the designs on those from a famous fashion house
B    decide to use a consistent approach to the design
C    only use one particular font throughout
D    buy the rights to use a particular design

Answer B

Think: What is house style? Why would a business want to use a house style in producing documents?

Then: Go through the options and try to discount the ones that are obviously wrong.

A uses the word 'house' but this is trying to distract you from the right answer. D is a similar answer and is not correct. C is reasonably plausible - it is something that might be part of a house style - the consistent use of a particular font but house style refers to more than simply the use of a font.

Decide: This leaves you with B as the answer. Check that the answer you have settled on matches your initial thinking about what house style meant. Once you are happy, make your selection.

# 16 The use of video and teleconferencing

## Case Study

Down Below Ltd is a business based in Scotland but which does most of its business globally. Down Below provides submersible vehicles that are used to investigate problems on oil rig platforms below the sea and conduct surveys of the ocean floor to give information for companies laying communication cables and pipelines. The business has its headquarters in Aberdeen, but has key employees located in every continent. This helps the business to respond more effectively and efficiently to enquiries from clients. The nature of their business and the fact that their workers are spread across the globe presents communication problems for it. Up to now the business has relied on the telephone, both landlines and mobiles, to keep in touch with their staff but this is becoming increasingly expensive and presents other problems such as the lack of face to face contact. Trying to convene regular meetings with all staff is also a problem. The rising price of airline tickets, because of rises in fuel prices, increases costs, as well as presenting logistical difficulties.

## Objectives

- To understand the difference between video and teleconferencing.
- To understand the main reasons why these methods have grown in popularity.
- To understand the benefits to businesses of using these communication methods.
- To understand the limitations of these methods and when they are appropriate to use.

**edexcel ::: key terms**

**Videoconferencing** – a means of connecting people from different parts of the world through audio and video equipment. It allows interaction between people without them having to be physically present at a meeting.

## Difference between video and teleconferencing

Advances in technology have meant that new ways of communicating have developed that can be very effective for businesses. Two examples are videoconferencing and teleconferencing.

**Videoconferencing** Videoconferencing allows people in different parts of the world or locations to connect and interact with one another via audio and video transmissions. It enables the participants to see and talk to each other without the expense of travelling to a meeting. There are two different types of videoconferencing used.

- A desktop system where a camera is attached to the top of a monitor and a microphone to capture the audio output. Most modern computers can be fitted with webcams that can broadcast pictures via the Internet. The quality of webcams is not as good as that of video conferencing equipment but still allows communication to take place and is relatively cheap.
- A specified system with a high quality video camera connected through a computer with microphone, television monitor and speakers to project the audio. Some of these are portable and others are set up as a permanent fixture in a dedicated room for video conferencing. The equipment can be hired to save on costs for a business but will add time to any preparation for videoconferencing. This type of set up can be expensive to install in the first place, but if the business intends to use it regularly it can be a cost-effective means of communicating, especially when high quality video pictures are important.

There may be occasions where there are more than two remote locations being used in the video conference. A business can talk to clients or another part of its business in America, the UK or China, for example, all at the same time. When this is the case a multipoint control unit is required to connect the calls from different locations.

The disadvantages of this method of communication are that:
- the equipment can be very expensive;

Videoconferencing facilities can be expensive to install, but if used regularly they can be a cost-effective and effective means of communicating

- some people do not like this method of communication - they feel self-conscious in front of a camera and therefore may not respond as well as they would normally;
- eye contact is difficult as it is an image on a screen and not someone in person therefore it can be difficult to interpret people's reactions and body language.

**Teleconferencing** This method of communication enables several people from different parts of the world to be connected by telephone at the same time which allows them to communicate with each other. **Teleconferencing** is more popular than videoconferencing as it is usually cheaper, but is less effective as the communication relies purely on a person's voice. The quality of the connection and the equipment often determines how easy it is to hear the conversation. However, teleconferencing does represent a very cost-effective means of communication between a business and its employees and other stakeholders.

Down Below Ltd uses videoconferencing and teleconferencing as methods of communication on a regular basis as a means to address issues on the other side of the globe and maintain regular contact with its employees.

## Why these methods have grown in popularity

With the cost of travelling increasing due to changing fuel prices it has become a huge expense for businesses to send people to meetings, especially those that are scheduled to be held in another country. In addition to the cost of transport there is the added cost of accommodation and the time wasted in travelling too. For Down Below Ltd it means that they can deal with any client issues that may arise more promptly and contact the relevant people. It enables them to organise a meeting at short notice without employees and managers having to spend time travelling, which for Down Below Ltd is a huge logistical nightmare due to the number of continents on which employees are located. It allows the managers to have face-to-face meetings without leaving the office providing them with the speed of oral communication and the face-to-face contact without having to travel, thus reducing the cost implications to the business. Teleconferencing is a useful tool in providing a business with the means to provide flexibility for its employees, for example, enabling them to work from home.

## The benefits of these communication methods

Companies trade globally and therefore the time differences can affect decisions that will need to be made. To have the facility to communicate through these media methods prevents delays in essential business decisions and enables

edexcel ::: key terms

**Teleconferencing** – a method of communication where more than two parties from different parts of a country or different continents are connected via telephone and are able to communicate with each other.

companies to receive and deliver information in a short space of time and to the relevant parties. This improves efficiency within an organisation and reduces costs.

Down Below Ltd have experienced many communication difficulties in the past, especially when needing to contact staff who are located in a different continent and dealing with client enquiries that only those working on the job will be able to answer. They have had to rely on mobile phones and the use of land lines. However, although these enable them to communicate, connectivity is not always at its best and conversations sometimes get cut off in mid-sentence, together with confusion over information passed on due to delays in transmission.

Utilising the facilities of videoconferencing and teleconferencing can help to prevent such issues. Problems can be rectified quickly, which leads to satisfied clients. Staff can be clearer on what needs to be done as the information relayed to them comes through from the source itself rather than being passed on by a third party. Jobs can be completed on time if not earlier, which can result in the reputation of the business increasing and the amount of new work increasing. Employees appreciate being able to have direct contact and ask questions and keep up to speed with progress as well as being able to feed vital information back to the company's base.

Down Below Ltd received a phone call from a client to inform them that some plans they had been sent for laying a communications cable were incorrect and that the correct information needed to be passed on to the supervisors involved urgently. The cables were being laid off the coast of Chile which caused an initial problem due to time differences with the UK. The boss of Down Below Ltd contacted the supervisor on the ship and informed him of the problem and that the client wished to speak directly to him and his team. Within an hour a videoconference was arranged. The client explained the changes that had been made and informed them that they were to do nothing until the updated drawings had been sent through to the team.

The methods used left the client assured that all parties involved with the job were fully informed. The facility of using videoconferencing prevented a costly error occurring and reassured the client that the supervisor was fully aware of the changes and had all the information he required.

## Limitations of these methods and when they are appropriate to use

Despite these methods of communication becoming increasingly popular with global companies the process can only happen if all parties have the right equipment to receive the conferencing. It is a large expense for businesses and must be something that they will use to justify saving on travelling expenses and regular use.

These methods limit the chance for people to establish a personal relationship and engage in eye contact, which is a strong communication itself. This can keep the meeting very

impersonal as communication is simply either a voice on the other end of a telephone or an image on a screen. No clues or additional information can be passed on by people's body language which can make it difficult to judge the reaction to a proposal or to a response. Verbal conversation in these circumstances can be difficult for people to interpret correctly as some aspects of the conversation might be formal and some informal. When the participants are not face-to-face this can be difficult to assess.

In some meetings documents need to be circulated, images shared or a presentation given to support the discussion. These methods limit the opportunities for this happening and so the participants have to make sure that any documents that are required are faxed, posted or e-mailed across to all concerned before the meeting.

One other problem that has to be taken into consideration with the use of these technologies is that, for some, meetings may occur too early in the morning or late in the evening to accommodate all parties and their locations. This can be inconvenient and involve some employees in working unsociable hours.

### Test yourself

1. Which of the following is a disadvantage to a business using videoconferencing as a medium of communication?

   Select **one** answer.

   A *The faces of the participants cannot be seen*
   B *It takes people too long to get in the right seat*
   C *The connection can be disrupted*
   D *It costs more than flying staff out to meetings*

2. Which of the following is a limitation of using video or teleconferencing?

   A *The business will have to spend a lot of time in one room*
   B *There is a lack of personal contact with other business contacts*
   C *The number of people involved in meetings will reduce*
   D *Expenses will increase significantly for the business*

   Select **one** answer.

3. Which of the following is an important technical consideration in communicating using videoconferencing?

   A *Having a method to record the amount of time spent on the videoconference*
   B *Ensuring that all staff can identify any problems with the equipment*
   C *Making sure that the software and equipment will enable communication to happen*
   D *Making sure that there is enough equipment to record the meeting*

   Select **one** answer.

# Over to you

Kamika had arranged a teleconference which included a presentation via a webex system in the boardroom of UTeach Ltd. The company developed learning materials for virtual learning environments (VLEs) that allowed students to access information wherever they were, provided they were able to connect to the Internet. The presentation was being given by a company called VitalSoft who were based in India and was due to last one hour. VitalSoft wanted to demonstrate a new piece of software they had developed that allowed multiple choice questions to be devised easily and put into VLEs. The presentation went reasonably well but the strong Indian accent of Vasu and a poor line meant that some of the 10 people who were at the conference did not hear all the things that Vasu had to say and the meeting went on much longer than expected. The poor line meant that some at the meeting were not as impressed as Kamika had been when she had visited India and had spoken to Vasu personally about the software.

1. Identify **two** possible benefits to UTeach Ltd of using teleconferencing. (2)

2. Identify **two** possible disadvantages to UTeach Ltd of using teleconferencing. (2)

3. Do the problems that are highlighted in the passage mean that teleconferencing is not as good a method of communication as face-to-face meetings? Justify your answer. (6)

## ResultsPlus
### Build Better Answers

The use of videoconferencing has grown in popularity for businesses because:

A  flat screen TVs are now much easier to move around different offices
B  the number of airlines flying to key business destinations has fallen in the last ten years
C  it helps to keep meetings limited to a particular time frame
D  it is a cost effective way of arranging meetings in a global business environment

Think: What are the main reasons why videoconferencing has grown in popularity? Availability of technology, price of air fares, cost of hotels, need by businesses to make quicker decisions etc.

Then: Go through the options to see if any of them match the reasons you have thought about.

Review: Look at each option carefully in relation to your thinking. Try to dismiss the ones that are obviously wrong and also tease out which ones might be plausible.

Flat screen TVs might well be easier to move around but that is not likely to be a very plausible reason for the growth in the use of videoconferencing, especially given the fact that there are other more plausible answers available. ■

B can be dismissed fairly quickly - if anything the choice of airlines and destinations has grown dramatically in recent years especially with the growth of low-cost airlines. ■

Many people might want meetings to be more limited but a video conference is not time limited so this is also unlikely to be the answer. ■

Businesses are increasingly concerned with keeping cost under control and this could be a plausible reason for the growth in videoconferencing. It also matches with the initial ideas that came to mind when thinking about the benefits of videoconferencing.

Decide: Make your decision as to the correct answer. D is by far the most plausible answer and it fits with the initial thinking that was carried out. ▲

# 17 Organisational charts and their purpose

## Case Study

The management at Leisure Lounge Ltd, a business providing fitness equipment to gyms and health clubs have been looking carefully at their business after two years of disappointing results. One of the problems seems to be the way in which the business is structured - on a regional basis. Customers have complained that it is not easy to know exactly who to contact about products and orders - the regional offices or the head office, situated in Wigan. The business has had a structure that requires all staff to rely on decisions being made by the senior management in Wigan. This has caused decisions to be slow in being made and as a result some customers have gone to competitors.

## Objectives

- To understand the purpose of an organisational chart.
- To understand how ICT can be used to create different organisational charts.
- To appreciate how different types of organisation structure affect communications in a business.

edexcel ⠿ key terms

**Hierarchy** – the layers of responsibility and seniority in an organisation.

## Purpose of an organisational chart

Organisational charts are usually used in larger businesses to show different roles or departments and where they fit into the business. Planning in a business can happen anywhere within the business, but direction of where it is heading often comes from those in senior positions within an organisation. People who are in senior positions have the responsibility for ensuring that instructions or decisions are passed to the relevant people or departments to be carried out. An organisational chart shows the different levels of responsibility or departments within an organisation, what roles people play, who has responsibility and who reports to who within the organisation. Knowing who to contact or answer to is important for an organisation. An organisational chart helps everyone in the organisation to understand this and helps promote good communication.

The size of the company will dictate the number of layers of management and responsibilities it has. **Hierarchy** is a term used for the level of importance within a business. Sole traders may only employ a small number of people and therefore will have few levels of hierarchy. A small business such as a local newsagent may only have the owner with an assistant, so communication is direct and is likely to be informal. Larger businesses with many employees will need a more formal method of communication and a structure to organise it to ensure they operate efficiently.

Large businesses may organise themselves in different ways.

**Function** This is found a lot with limited companies where different departments do part of the work of the business as a whole, for example, a finance, marketing, human resources and production department. The advantage of functional organisation is that those who are specialists can concentrate on a particular area. For this to be productive communication needs to be strong between different departments and a disadvantage can be that different departments may not work well together and each may pursue its own goals rather than that of the organisation as a whole.

**Product** Using a product based structure will split an organisation into different sections to accommodate different products that they sell. Large manufacturing businesses, for example, that produce many products may use this structure. It is probable that each section will be organised by function. There will be managers of each section who will be responsible and make decisions for each product. A disadvantage to this is that there can be duplication of resources, for example each department will have its own departments for other functions like marketing, production or finance and this can raise the cost of production.

**Regional** Multinational businesses tend to use this type of organisation where the responsibility is divided up into local branches or different regions making the day-to-day running of the business easier and more efficient. For example, some larger organisations split their operations into those dealing with North America, Europe, Middle East and Africa (EMEA) and Asia. Each branch or region may have its own functional departments like finance, marketing and production. The main disadvantage with this is that, as with product above, there can be duplication of functions and therefore waste with regard to resources.

All businesses want to be productive and operate efficiently. Making sure that physical, human and financial resources work effectively is important. Without good communication there can be confusion about who is responsible for a specific task. The larger the business the more difficult it is to communicate instructions or decisions.

## How different types of organisation structure affect communications in a business

There is a number of different organisational charts used to identify the structure of a business. It is vital that a business considers some or all of the following:
- what does the business do or make?
- how do they communicate with their suppliers and customers?
- how many branches or sites does the business have?
- what does the future hold?
- does the business want a hierarchical or a flatter structure?
- does it want to encourage team work or focus more on individual performance?

For a business to succeed it will need to look at its structure and communication because without a good structure communication can break down. If the structure is clear then everyone in the organisation knows what their responsibilities are and who they report to within the organisation.

## Which structure?

The size of a business will dictate which structure is most suitable. Many firms start with a centralised structure and as it increases in size will progress to a decentralised structure.

**Centralised structure** This occurs when major decisions are made by head office. This can be beneficial to the business as senior managers will have experience and an overview of the business. However, it may take time for decisions to be made and information to be passed to staff, which could lead to inefficiency.

**Decentralised structure** Here the authority to make decisions is given to different sections of the business. This enables decision-making to be shared out without having to refer back to head office and encourages everyone to be part of the decision-making process.

edexcel ::: **key terms**

**Centralised structure** – where decisions are made by head office.

**Decentralised structure** – where decisions are shared throughout different departments.

86

**Table 1** – Advantages and disadvantages of a hierarchical structure

**Advantages**
- Each layer has a clearly defined role.
- Employees have a clear career structure.
- Specialists can be employed at different layers.
- Creates loyalty to the department or management layer.

**Disadvantages**
- Depending on the size of the structure communication can be slow as there can be many different layers for messages to pass through.
- Communication between different departments can be limited.
- Departmental/management layer rivalry may exist which means the business does not pull together.
- Staff may not feel part of the business.

**Table 2** – Advantages and disadvantages of a flat structure

**Advantages**
- Many smaller organisations believe this type of structure is better as everyone within the business understands the objectives of the business.
- Encourages cooperation between departments.
- Team spirit may be improved.
- Decisions can be made quicker and the business can respond to changes in the market faster.

**Disadvantages**
- With fewer managers then there can be more employees requesting advice or information which could hinder communication.
- Workers may not be clear about who their line manager is.
- Job responsibilities and roles may not be clear.

**Table 3** – Advantages and disadvantages of a matrix structure

**Advantages**
- More efficient allocation of specialised skills across the entire business.
- Can take advantage of the shared services and skills - may not have to buy in skills from elsewhere but make better use of existing resources.
- Project managers use smaller matrix-style structures for project and team organisations so they can track skills, tasks, and resources across projects to ensure that they are being used properly.
- Individuals can be selected for projects and teams that they can contribute to rather than by seniority or management level.
- Teams can bring together different skills and can problem solve more effectively.
- Project managers have a clear budget and set of tasks to complete - makes the job very clear.

**Disadvantages**
- Putting successful teams together is not always easy.
- Staff may not know who their responsibility is to - is it their line manager or a project manager?
- Teams and projects not always as easy to monitor and may result in being more costly.

Leisure Lounge Ltd's decisions are all made at their head office. As a result of this the information or any decisions required by regional offices have suffered delays and led to disatisfied customers. This has led to them losing sales to competitors. They have realised that the problem needs addressing to get them back into a prominent market position. There are three main types of organisational chart that they could consider using.

**Hierarchical structure** A **hierarchical structure** has a clear **chain of command**. A hierarchical organisation is one in which there are a number of levels of responsibility and authority. Communication takes place up and down the hierarchy. This type of chart consists of a number of layers, with connections running between layers. At each level people take instruction from above and give instruction to those who are below. Requests or complaints are sent upwards for the people in senior positions to address.

**Flat structure** A **flat structure** is one where employees have a greater degree of similarities in the amount of authority and responsibility they have. With this type of structure there are usually fewer layers between managers and key decision makers and employees with employees working together to carry out tasks.

**edexcel** ::: **key terms**

**Hierarchical structure** – has many layers and is usually displayed in the form of a pyramid.

**Chain of command** – the lines of authority and responsibility in an organisation which show who is responsible for what and to whom.

**Flat structure** – a structure where employees have a greater degree of equal value and authority.

**Matrix structure** – where there are many different levels of responsibility.

**Matrix structure** A **matrix structure** is one in which there are different levels of responsibility, but it also has parallel departments or teams performing different tasks. Communication occurs between all sections or departments creating a multi-functional team approach. A matrix organisation reduces the possibility that skills and responsibilities could be duplicated by identifying functions or common features of the business that are shared by different parts of the business.

# How ICT can be used to create different organisation charts

Having a diagrammatic structure for staff to view will help them to know who their point of contact is, displaying a clear **chain of command** to identify the most senior staff to junior staff. The tools available within software packages enable organisational charts to be generated using the computer. Creating a combination of shapes and text could be frustrating as boxes may not be at the right level and text might not fit. Most office software has a diagram feature that includes a variety of options allowing users to incorporate diagrams into other programmes such as word processing, spreadsheets, databases, presentations and DTP packages.

There will be different templates available to create and edit appropriate organisational structures.

- 1. Hierarchical or flat organisation charts show the relationship between people as a series of layers which show the different levels of responsibility within the organisation. The more layers the organisation has the more hierarchical it is. This can often make decision-making much slower.
- 2. Circular diagrams can be used to show a continuous process where levels of responsibility are mixed. This type of chart might be used to show how teams operate with each other and tends to be associated with flatter structures which do not have many levels of hierarchy.
- 3. Radial diagrams show the relationship between different groups that have a core element (possibly the manager or team leader) and teams or departments that work with the core.
- 4. Pyramid diagrams show the arrangement of people or functions from the top of a foundation down to lower levels.
- 5. Venn diagrams can be used to show common and unique characteristics between elements. This might be useful if teams work on different but related projects.
- 6. Target diagrams can be used to show progress towards a goal and can also show how different teams operate in relation to each other and how it is possible for people to move into different teams.

Creating an organisational chart can be done using ICT. Many different types of software exist to do this. Using ICT to create organisational charts makes it easier to plan the organisation structure and to make changes as job roles, functions and the business changes. The business can take a layer out, remove a job role or alter someone's position within the company by upgrading them within the chart or altering their job title. The tools available within software packages give businesses a greater degree of flexibility to amend and create appropriate charts easily.

An example is shown in Figure 2. Additional boxes can be added by either creating a subordinate (box below) or an assistant (additional box within a layer). Lines and text can be altered. For example, text or line colour can be changed and text size or style altered to suit. The layout can be altered to fit the structure of the organisation. By using ICT amendments or additions are easily made without the whole structure having to be re-drawn. This saves time for a business and enables them to maintain an up to date structure and issue updated versions to staff quickly. This helps to avoid confusion and provides a clear visual structure for staff to refer to. The chart helps to highlight positions, job roles and titles, together with identifying responsibilities for a department or specific individuals.

**Figure 1** – Templates to create organisational structures

**Figure 2**

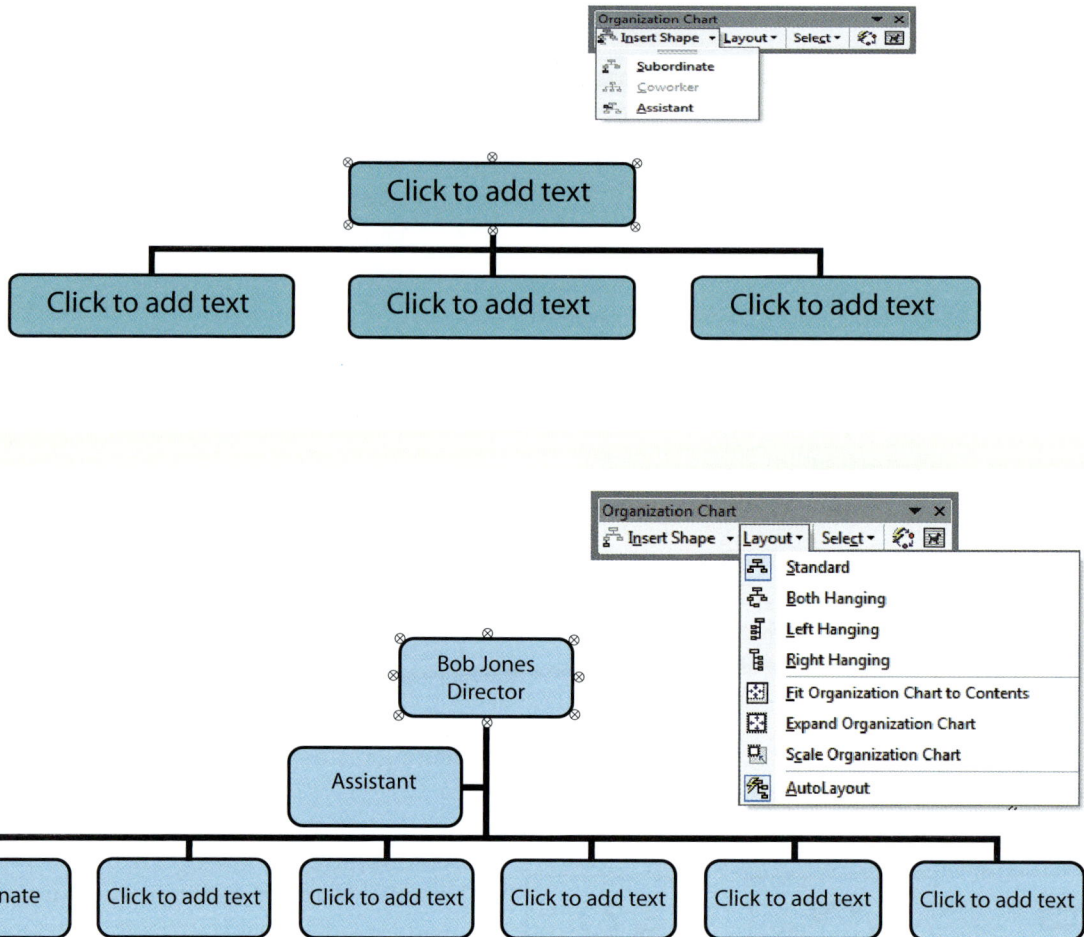

## Test yourself

1. Which **two** of the following are the **most likely** factors that a business should consider in deciding on an appropriate organisation structure?

   A   *How many different departments does the business have?*
   B   *Will all the stakeholders understand the structure?*
   C   *Does the business have the appropriate IT facilities to create the chart?*
   D   *What sort of working relationship does the business want to encourage?*
   E   *Will the new organisation structure match those given in business textbooks?*
   F   *What sort of structure does its main rival have?*

2. A centralised business structure is where:

   A   *there is only one main office*
   B   *the business is located in the middle of a country*
   C   *decisions are only made by one person*
   D   *decision-making is made by head office*

   Select **one** answer.

3. Businesses may choose to have a flat organisational structure when:

   A   *the managing director makes all the decisions in the organisation.*
   B   *it only has a small number of workers.*
   C   *it wants to reduce the levels of management*
   D   *it is aiming to cut costs as far as possible*

   Select **one** answer.

# Over to you

The new chief executive officer (CEO), John Setters, at Chelford Manufacturing had been in post for two months and had been reviewing the way the business was organised. He had decided to make some major changes to the business and needed an organisation that would be able to meet the challenges of the market place, which was changing fast and was increasingly competitive. The business had been run on a very hierarchical basis prior to her arrival with a relatively large number of levels of management and responsibility. John wanted to replace this with a flatter structure and encourage greater emphasis on team work.

1. Identify **two** possible disadvantages that might be associated with a hierarchical organisation structure. (2)

2. Identify **one** advantage and one disadvantage to Chelford Manufacturing of a flatter organisation structure. (2)

3. Explain how the advantage and disadvantage that you have identified in (2) above might affect Chelford Manufacturing (6)

## ResultsPlus
### Build Better Answers

Casey runs a medium sized company which makes high quality building materials. Changes in the industry mean that she wants to change the way the business is organised . She needs to have an organisation that is able to respond quickly to changes and which can work together. She has decided upon a matrix structure. The most likely reason for this is that a matrix structure:

A   allows her to make all the decisions herself
B   means that everyone knows what their responsibilities are
C   allows her to move people around to the most suitable use quickly
D   means that there are few layers of management

Think: What is a matrix structure? What are the main features of this structure? How does the information given in the question help me in selecting the answer?

Then: Go through the options.

Review: Look at each option carefully. Try to dismiss the ones that are obviously wrong.

A is referring to a hierarchical structure - exactly what Casey does not want. B also is one of the characteristics of this type of structure so this can also be dismissed. Fewer layers of management are characteristic of a flat structure so this can also be dismissed.

Decide: This leaves C as the option to choose. Check to make sure that your choice is right - a matrix structure does have various projects which people can move in an out of as needed. This is something that Casey may feel is important to the future of the business. C is therefore the correct answer.

# 18 The value of e-mail systems

## Case Study

Goods Travel is a global shipping company delivering packages and parcels for businesses world wide. The developments in electronic communication have helped the business improve the service to its customers considerably. It can keep in touch with its customers whatever time zone they are in; they can use email to record when a pick-up has taken place, where the product is en route and when delivery can be expected. E-mail also allows the company to provide an enquiry service to potential customers about delivery times, prices and so on. E-mail has revolutionised its business but it is not without its problems. If addresses are wrong they can lose valuable customer contacts and simple human error can mean incorrect information being sent to the wrong customer. The company also have to ensure that staff do not abuse the system and use email for its proper purpose. They even have to think about making sure that they tailor their e-mails to the requirements of customers in countries where language and culture may be different.

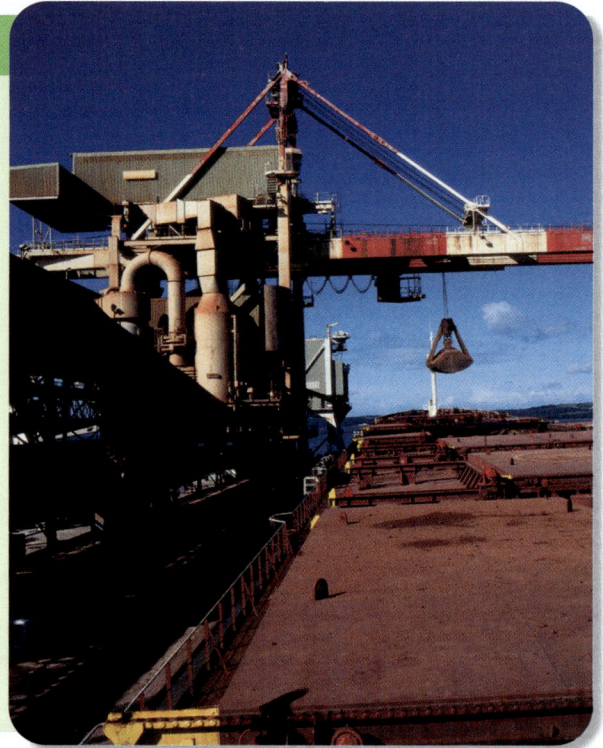

## Objectives

- To understand how e-mail works
- To appreciate the main purpose of e-mail in businesses
- To recognise some of the advantages of using e-mail in business
- To recognise some of the disadvantages of using e-mail in business
- To appreciate what constitutes appropriate use of e-mail in business
- To recognise the importance of e-mail in business

**edexcel ::: key terms**

**e-mail** – a means of creating, communicating, storing and transmitting text and other files using digital communication systems.

## How are e-mail systems used in a business?

Electronic mail, which we know more familiarly as **e-mail**, is a means of creating, communicating, storing and transmitting text and other files using digital communication systems. The development of e-mail systems has revolutionised the way that people in businesses communicate. It is not only people within a business that make use of e-mail, it is between the business and a wide range of its external stakeholders. The main purposes of e-mail can be summarised as follows.

- It allows employees in a business to communicate quickly and easily within the business.
- E-mail enables queries to be sent and dealt with quickly rather than an employee having to move to talk to a colleague - in larger businesses this might involve walking a considerable distance which wastes time and is inefficient.
- Communication with customers can be improved - it allows the customer to contact the business 24 hours a day and may be a more convenient method of communication than letter or telephone.
- E-mail provides a means of recording conversations and thus can be used to settle disputes or grievances between the business and employees and between the business and customers and suppliers.
- Changes to meetings, venues, times, dates etc. can be communicated to all parties quickly - it serves as a very efficient notice board.
- E-mail can be accessed almost anywhere given the right technology (for example, the use of BlackBerry devices or e-mail facilities on mobile phones). This means that there are more opportunities for businesses to allow more flexible working and to contact stakeholders at any time.
- Customers and suppliers have access to information about their orders/delivery etc. and can ask questions and get information sent to update them on the status of their order/purchase.

## Advantages of using e-mail

The advantages of using e-mail include the following.

**Almost instant communication** E-mail is a very fast and effective means of communicating both within the business and with external stakeholders. If the receiver is at the other end of a device that can receive e-mails then the communication can be quick and effective as an immediate response can be gained. This helps speed up decision-making and in the case of customer queries can ensure that there are improved levels of customer service. E-mail allows people to communicate whether they are in the same building (and many larger businesses have large premises) in offices elsewhere in the country or overseas.

**Cost-effective** Using an e-mail system can be relatively inexpensive - there is a number of e-mail systems available, such as Microsoft Outlook and Mozilla Thunderbird, linked to web browsers, which are effectively free. There are also other systems that have additional functionality and which may be more appropriate to a business setting such as Mulberry, i-Scribe and Pegasus. Regardless of where the receiver is, it is possible to be able to communicate far more cheaply than may be the case through telephone or face-to-face meetings.

**Easy to use** Most e-mail systems are relatively easy to use and require limited training to use them. The vast majority of people now have their own private e-mail accounts at home and so using e-mail in the workplace is something that they are familiar with.

**Versatility** Whilst e-mail is useful for communicating text based messages it is far more versatile than this. E-mails can be used to transmit a variety of other files in the form of attachments such as documents, presentations, images, movie clips, sound and so on. This versatility is extremely valuable; for example, an individual who may be planning to give a presentation to a sales conference can e-mail their presentation in advance of the session so that it can be loaded up on the venue's PC and be ready to use. This saves time and avoids the problems of loading up presentations etc. when the presenter arrives at the venue.

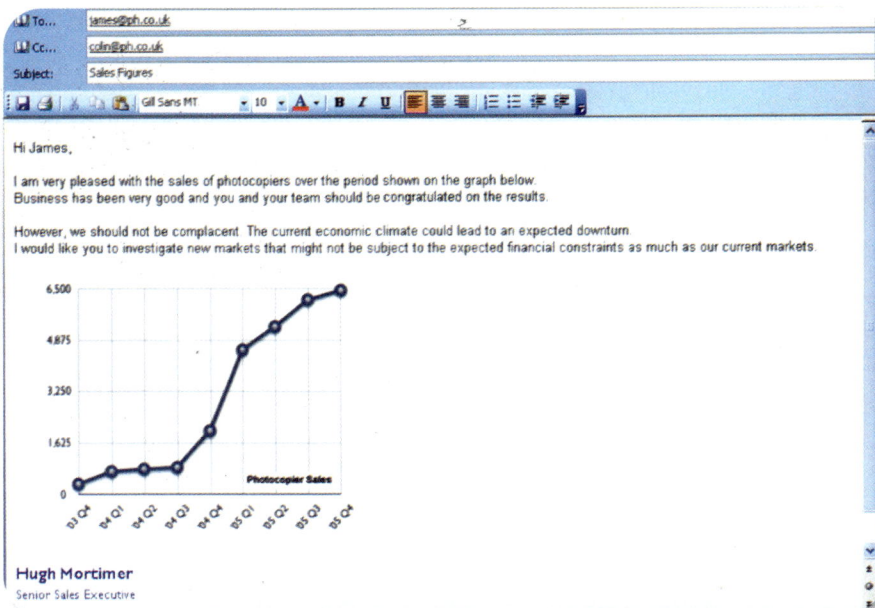

E-mail can be used to send text, images and other information

**Efficient communication** The ability to create e-mail groups can mean that communications can be very efficient. A large business with different offices in different locations and with different departments can set up e-mail groups to send messages to all those in the group. This can be far more efficient because it avoids sending messages to people who will not find the information relevant.

**Appropriate** Depending on the type of organisation, e-mail can be used as a less formal means of communication - it can be more 'chatty', be briefer and more conversational than other text based communications systems.

## Disadvantages of e-mail

It might be very easy to think of a number of advantages of using e-mail, but as with anything there are also disadvantages that need to be taken into account.

**Time** One of the main problems with e-mail systems is the time they take up. It has been estimated that many workers spend up to two hours a day sorting, reading and responding to e-mails. The ease with which it can be used may mean that people send messages that are not really necessary and this can take up valuable time and also reduce productivity.

**Cost of managing systems** Contrary to popular opinion, running an e-mail system is not 'free'. In large business organisations managing the e-mail system can be a full-time job. The number of e-mails sent and received, the need for storage space, dealing with queries when the system does not work, maintaining the security of the system against hacking and spam all take time and cost business money. A smaller business may not have the same size of problem but even small businesses need to make sure that their e-mail systems are secure by having appropriate software to protect them from spam, scams and individuals and criminal gangs seeking to gain access to computer systems to extract data and information for inappropriate use.

**Lost production and time-wasting** In addition to the above many businesses find that there is also a cost in terms of lost production or reductions in productivity through inappropriate use of e-mail. Most large organisations have a strict policy on the use of e-mail and any violation by employees of the policy can result in disciplinary action. Abuse can take the form of sending inappropriate e-mails around the workplace such as jokes or offensive material and images, or using e-mail to harass, victimise or bully another person.

**Possible breakdowns in communication** One of the benefits of personal communication is that it brings people together, improves relationships and builds understanding. E-mail can be used as an alternative to this and it can lead to a breakdown of the relationships in a business and actually hamper communication rather than help it.

**E-mail has to be checked** Successful communication requires sender and receiver to interact. E-mail can speed up that process but not necessarily. It requires the receiver to be able to access the e-mail and indeed to want to access it. The sheer volume of e-mails for some individuals in an organisation may mean that important messages can get ignored or buried amongst large amounts of other messages. The receiver does not know if they have been sent an e-mail until they check their inbox and this is not always possible. The result of all these things is that communication can break down and important messages can get 'lost' in the system.

**May be misused** E-mail is useful in many cases but is not always appropriate as a formal medium of communication. Its use has to be appropriate to the situation and the message being communicated.

**Whether it is appropriate** The length of an e-mail might also be a factor in how successful it is in being an effective means of communication. If the reader gets bored of the e-mail because it is too long, too technical or too complicated then it may not be received properly. The fact that many people see e-mail as a quick way of communicating a short message means that care has to be taken to think about whether e-mail is the appropriate medium for the message being sent.

**Security** E-mail does open up increased possibilities of security breaches. Some businesses have systems that allow the employee to access their e-mail anywhere outside the office through web based e-mail systems. This further increases the threats from those who might want to find ways of getting into a business's systems and extracting information. Making sure that systems are secure is important to protect confidential information that a business does not want its rivals to see or which is meant to be secure, for example, the personal and banking details of its staff.

**Possibility for misunderstanding** Misunderstanding is a key barrier to successful communication. Because e-mail is quick and instant it can be that the message sent is not what the sender really wants to send. For example, there have been cases of employees coming home from work after being out for the evening having either brooded on something that happened during the day or reading their e-mails late at night and sending a hasty reply that in hindsight they would not have sent. In addition, the speed with which people often type a response to an e-mail might mean that **typos** creep in and change the tone of the message. The receiver does not have body language, tone of speech and so on with which to judge whether an e-mail is serious, angry, flippant, rude etc. and so misunderstandings can arise.

## The appropriate use and format of e-mails in a business context

Because e-mail is used in wide variety of different contexts as a means of communication it is important to realise that the way it is used might need to vary according to different circumstances. An e-mail to a friend asking them if they are free to come to a party on Saturday night might be very informal. An e-mail to a colleague at work might need to be written in a different way and an e-mail to a customer might need to be different again.

Within business, employees use e-mail to contact each other about a range of things. The type of language used and the formality of the message may vary. An e-mail sent to a group inviting them to a meeting may be written in a formal manner with a salutation at the beginning ('Dear all', 'To all in marketing') and at the end ('Regards', 'Best wishes''Yours sincerely') etc. An e-mail to a customer is also likely to be formal but an e-mail sent from one colleague to another may

## edexcel ::: key terms

**Typos** – spelling mistakes or words that have been mis-typed by the sender and which might change the tone of a message

be more informal and not have 'Dear…' or 'Best wishes' etc.

Many businesses will have policies in place to provide guidelines for staff about appropriate use of e-mail. It will be expected that staff use appropriate spelling, punctuation and grammar, for example, when sending more formal e-mails. If a customer receives an e-mail which is littered with spelling mistakes or uses text language, the impression that gives is not a good one so most businesses would want to avoid such informal use of language. Most e-mail systems have a spell check facility which can be automatically switched on to alert the user to any errors before the message is sent. The use of capital letters in e-mail can be interpreted as the electronic equivalent of shouting and is, therefore, discouraged.

In any business, the way in which e-mail is used has to be done on the basis of who the message is being sent to, why it is being sent and the urgency or importance of the message. Systems will have different tools to inform the receiver whether the message is of high importance or not and therefore whether it needs dealing with immediately. There are also tools to allow users to store messages, set up reminders and alerts and have links with a calendar to enable the user to be able to manage their e-mail messages effectively and efficiently.

Many organisations will also have policies in place to impose limits on the amount of e-mails that can be stored or saved or an archive system so that users can store important e-mails without the danger of them being deleted. In many cases, larger organisation will have means of tracking e-mail use by employees and to be able to retrieve e-mails that have been deleted from the user's PC. This may be required to maintain security, make sure that e-mail policies are being

## Test yourself

1. E-mail is a versatile means of communication because:

   A  it does not require a telephone line to communicate
   B  it enables additional files to be sent quickly
   C  there are different e-mail systems available
   D  only the user is able to access the relevant files

   Select **one** answer.

2. Which of the following would be an example of an appropriate use of e-mail in a business setting?

   A  Contacting a group to alert them of a change to the venue for a meeting
   B  Sending round an image of an employee who got drunk at a staff party
   C  Sending the personal details of a group of employees to an e-mail group in a business
   D  Using the system to store personal e-mails to friends and family

   Select **one** answer.

3. Janice was in charge of the customer services team at a large tool suppliers. She noticed that the response time to deal with customer comments and queries had fallen by 25% in the past six months. Which of the following might best explain why this might have happened?

   A  The number of customer enquiries had fallen by 50%
   B  Customer services staff had increased their productivity
   C  Staff had been spending too much time answering personal e-mails
   D  A new e-mail system increased the efficiency with which queries could be dealt with

   Select **one** answer.

followed and be used to trace issues or problems should they arise.

Ultimately, there is a responsibility on the individual to use the system appropriately and to make decisions about what is acceptable in the use of e-mails. Sending round a joke may not be an appropriate use of e-mail in 99% of occasions but there may be odd times when it is appropriate. Ultimately, the user has to make a judgement and think about the consequences of the message they send and the effect it will have on the recipient/s.

## Summary

E-mail is now widely used by most business organisations. Whether the business is in the public sector or the private sector, whether it is large or small, e-mail has become an essential part of communication for the reasons described above. Its use has to be monitored and there are concerns about the amount of time taken up with dealing with e-mail.

However, it is generally regarded as having benefits that outweigh the costs.

For businesses where contact with customers is vital, e-mail has helped to improve the speed and efficiency with which customers can access and be sent information. In being able to alert customers about when packages etc. have been sent, when they should expect to receive such packages and providing the means for customers to give feedback it can be extremely useful in building up higher levels of customer service and also gathering useful marketing information. As with any system, its limitations have to be borne in mind and balanced against the benefits it provides.

---

### ResultsPlus
### Build Better Answers

The use of accurate spelling, punctuation and grammar in an e-mail to a customer is important because:

A   it sends out a message that the business has a good spell checking facility on its e-mail system
B   the customer is always right
C   accurate presentation of an e-mail sends out an image that the business is professional
D   without it the customer will not be able to read the message at all.

Think: Why is accurate spelling, punctuation and grammar important? What are the effects on a customer if the message has poor spelling etc?

Then: Go through the options.

Review: Look at each option carefully. Try to dismiss the ones that are obviously wrong and also tease out which ones might be plausible.

The system might well have a spell checking facility but these are not always 100% effective so a well written message does not always mean that the company has a spell check system or that it is used by those sending messages. ■

The customer may always be right but this does not have any relevance to the reason why accurate spelling etc. should be used to communicate with customers. ■

C is a plausible answer - good presentation of an e-mail to customers does send the right message to customers.

D is also possible but even if the spelling etc. was poor would this stop the customer reading it at all?

Decide: Make your decision as to the correct answer. In this case it is C. Check to make sure you are right. C is a better answer than D because poor spelling can make it harder to read a message but not impossible as implied by the words '…at all' at the end of the option. ▲

## Over to you

Goods Travel uses e-mail a great deal in its everyday business operations. Communication is not only needed between employees, but also between the business and its thousands of customers, most of whom are other businesses who want to send parcels and packages to other businesses. It has recently encountered a problem, however, when it had its systems hacked and the credit card details of 50 of its customers were stolen when the e-mail system was invaded by a hacker.

1. Identify **two** possible benefits to Goods Travel of using e-mail in its business. ( 2)

2. Does the increased security risk involved in using e-mail mean that it is not a good idea to use e-mail in business? Justify your answer. (6)

**In this topic you have learned about:** the way in which word processing can provide advantages to a business in improving communications, the different presentation techniques that can be used and the key principles to consider in making successful presentations, how and why businesses use desk top publishing (DTP), how to produce an appropriate DTP item and to consider its value in business communications, why more businesses are using video and teleconferencing as a means of communication, the purpose and use of organisational charts in different types of business and the use, advantages and limitations of e-mail in business communication - with a variety of stakeholders.

## You should know…

- [ ] Why businesses use word processing and the benefits of using it.
- [ ] How templates can help to improve written communication.
- [ ] How a standard business letter is laid out.
- [ ] Why accurate spelling, punctuation, grammar and presentation are important in successful written communication.
- [ ] The range of different presentation techniques that can be used.
- [ ] What the main principles are in making a successful presentation.
- [ ] How different presentation techniques are appropriate for different circumstances.
- [ ] An understanding of some of the dos and don'ts in making a presentation.
- [ ] The basics of using a DTP programme.
- [ ] How to use a DTP package to produce a piece of business communication.

- [ ] How to evaluate a business communication with regard to the purpose of the message and the effect on the audience.
- [ ] What benefits video and teleconferencing can bring to a business.
- [ ] The circumstances when video and teleconferencing may be appropriate and when not.
- [ ] The different types of organisational structures that businesses may use.
- [ ] The role of organisational charts in helping business communications.
- [ ] The ways in which businesses use e-mail to communicate with their stakeholders.
- [ ] The advantages and disadvantages of using e-mail in a business.
- [ ] Why using appropriate language and formats with e-mail in a business is important.

## Support activity

- Select a business and choose one product that the business offers for sale.
- Imagine that the business concerned is just about to release the product you have chosen.
- Use a DTP package to produce an advertising leaflet which is designed to make customers aware of this 'new' product.

Assume that you work for a business which operates a shift pattern. The business has decided to reduce the number of shifts per day from 3 to 2 - from 6am - 2pm, 2pm - 10pm and 10pm - 6am to two 12 hour shifts - 6am - 6pm and 6pm - 6am.

(a) Write a letter addressed to employees telling them of the change. Insert one paragraph that explains why the shift pattern has been changed. Ensure that you lay out the letter appropriately and that you pay attention to the spelling, punctuation and grammar.

(b) Produce a slide show of not more than 6 slides explaining the change and the reasons for it that could be used as part of a presentation to the workforce. It would be helpful if you were able to actually give your presentation to others in your class and get their feedback about whether they believe it is successful in communicating the message.

## Stretch activity

Many businesses now provide presentations of their annual financial and corporate social responsibility reports on the web. Two such examples are given by the links below:

http://www.shell.com/home/content/investor/news_and_library/presentations/2008/dir_presentations_2008.html

http://www.mcsaatchiplc.com/saa/ir/reports/

- Either use the links given or find an appropriate example yourselves through using a search engine.
- Access the presentation and look through it.
- In the light of what you have learned about presentations in this section of the course, write a critique of the presentation you have chosen.
- Comment on the key message it is putting across, the construction of the slides, the use of colour and fonts, images and charts, how engaging it is, who you think the intended audience is and whether you think it communicates the message that it intends to its audience.

### ResultsPlus
### Build better answers

(a) Anne had a particularly difficult letter to write. A customer had made a serious complaint against a member of staff and she had to respond to the comments that were made. There was no evidence that the allegation was accurate but Anne was mindful of the need to avoid bad publicity for the firm, especially given that there was no proof of what had happened between the customer and the member of staff. She was using the standard complaint template that was available on the company intranet and set about writing a letter to the customer to try to meet their concerns but also to avoid laying any blame with the member of staff. This would be a tricky one.

(i) State **one** advantage to Anne of using a template to produce a business letter. (1)

(ii) Explain why appropriate layout and presentation of a business letter like the one Anne has to write is important in good communication. (3)

Think: What is a template? What is the purpose of a template? How can a template help a business produce better letters?

| Student answer | Examiner comment | Build a better answer |
|---|---|---|
| (i) A template is a set way to write a letter. | There seems to be some hint of understanding but this has not been made clear. It is difficult for the examiner to know whether the student really does understand what a template is or not. | Be more precise in the use of terminology to leave the examiner in no doubt that the term is understood. For example, mention that a template is a document that has certain items like the address and salutation already completed and which saves time for workers like Anne in preparing a letter. |
| (ii) If it is well laid out then it makes it easier to read. | A weak answer which does not address the question fully nor give the detail necessary for this type of question. There is no reference to the context at all. | An explain question requires a bit more detail - what sort of layout and presentation is considered appropriate - accurate spelling, punctuation and grammar, for example, well laid out paragraphs, logical progression of the letter and so on. The context is also important; this is a difficult letter to an angry customer so Anne has to be very careful to make sure she sets the letter out appropriately to ensure the communication is successful. |

## Mini Exam Paper

Clearview Publications PLC is a large international publishing house producing mainly educational books for schools, colleges and higher education in a variety of subjects. It has just been taken over by a firm of venture capitalists who are planning on making some changes to the business. The changes include a restructuring of the organisation of the business into a flatter structure and some changes in the responsibilities of teams who work in the EMEA part of the business (Europe, Middle East and Africa) in who they report to and how they work. Because it is a large business, the new owners have planned a whole staff meeting at its headquarters in Manchester but have arranged for staff in its EMEA offices to be involved through a video conference. At the staff meeting the new owners will give a presentation to outline their vision for the future of the business. Some staff are concerned that the takeover might lead to job losses so the meeting is being eagerly awaited to find out what the plans are.

(a) State **two** possible advantages to Clearview of using videoconferencing. (2)

(b) What is meant by the term 'flat organisation structure'? (1)

(c) Explain **one** possible benefit to Clearview of a flatter organisation structure. (3)

(d) Given the nature of the staff meeting, what sort of presentation technique would you recommend the new owners of Clearview use? Justify your answer. (6)

(e) The new owners of Clearview have decided to produce an information leaflet using a DTP package aimed at staff to summarise the new organisation structure. Analyse **two** key issues they need to consider in the use of a DTP package to produce this leaflet. (8)

# Topic 4.4: Communicating via the web

## Case study

Amazon is one of the most recognised businesses in the world. It might come as a surprise to realise that it is quite a young company. It was started by Jeff Bezos in 1995 and took until the last quarter (three months) of 2001 before it made a profit. The cost of setting up the business was very large, but Bezos believed that the possibilities of the new technology that was starting to take off provided him with a great business opportunity.

Amazon was one of the first companies to see the potential of the World Wide Web - the global network of connected computers. There were others that started around the same time as Amazon. Many business people, as well as those in financial markets that helped raise large sums of money to get these businesses going, believed that the web was the future for business. Their optimism meant that share prices in so-called dot com businesses rocketed making some of the business owners of these companies very wealthy indeed - at least on paper.

Many of the businesses that started at this time did not survive. The web did provide many business opportunities. However, it also had some limitations which needed to be addressed, not least the fear of some customers about the safety of their personal details when making electronic transactions. Since that time, the benefits of the web have been appreciated by many customers. In the UK, online retailing has grown rapidly. Over Christmas 2007 around 27 million people shopped online and spent £15 billion. Around £4 billion is spent every month in online sales.

The ease with which people can now access the Internet means that organsiations are exploring new ways to do business and using the Internet to gather vital information and to keep in regular contact with their customers. The benefits of the Internet are not shared by every business, however. Having a web site is not something that is appropriate for every business and setting up a web site is not a guaranteed route to success. Many businesses have to think carefully about the costs associated with setting up and running a web site, as well as the messages they are sending out to their customers and other stakeholders. For example, a web site that is out of date and poorly maintained sends out completely the wrong message to stakeholders and may even send out inaccurate information.

1.  **What benefits do you think the web provides to businesses like Amazon?**

2.  **Is the Internet and the World Wide Web the same thing?**

3.  **Why do you think that some early businesses failed in the dot com crash?**

4.  **Are there any disadvantages to a business of using the Internet?**

5.  **Why might a web site not be appropriate for every business?**

## Topic overview

This topic is designed to introduce the growing role of the World Wide Web (the web) in business communications. The web has revolutionised the way we work and in how we access information. It has also provided massive opportunities for businesses to develop communications with their stakeholders. This section will look at what the Internet actually is and how it works. It will explore some of the advantages and disadvantages that such technology brings to businesses.

## What will I learn?

**What is the Internet?**   There will be a brief overview of what the Internet is and how it works including some technical terms. An outline of the main opportunities open to business of the Internet will be given.

**Benefits and limitations of business web sites**   There are many benefits to businesses of having a web site. It can not only help with sales but provides the business with all sorts of information that it can use to help understand its market. However, setting up a business web site is not something that will guarantee success and there are lots of things to consider. The cost of setting up and the cost of running the site are two of these things.

**The principles of setting up and running a web site**  Setting up a business web site has to be done with a great deal of planning to make sure that it is right and that the benefits can be maximised. There are a series of stages that it is wise to go through and the business must have some understanding of some key terms and technical issues to make it work properly.

**Some of the legal considerations that a web site has to consider**  The government passes a number of laws to help protect vulnerable people in society. Some of these laws will influence the way in which businesses design and run their web site. They must take these laws into consideration otherwise they could face the prospect of being taken to court!

**Ways of measuring the success of a business web site**  There are different ways of measuring the success of a business web site - not just in terms of the number of sales it generates. The purpose of the web site has to be taken into consideration. Not every business web site is set up to sell products or services; some will be to provide information only. This section will look at the variety of ways in which success can be measured.

### How will I be assessed?
- Unit 4 is externally assessed.
- You will sit an exam of one and a half hours duration.
- There will be a mixture of multiple choice questions, short answer questions and extended writing questions.

# 19 The Internet

Mark Norton owned a high street hardware store in a small market town. The business was a successful family run business that had been in existence for many years. Mark was aware that his larger rivals, such as B&Q and Homebase, had a web site. Customers were able to use these sites to order from the comfort of their own homes, as well as to find information about products and prices. Was it time for him to invest in getting a web site?

## Objectives

● To understand what the Internet is and how it works.

● To recognise the range of opportunities to businesses that are provided by the Internet.

● To explain some advantages and disadvantages of the Internet for business communication.

**ResultsPlus**
**Watch Out!**

The web is not the same as the Internet. The web is just one type of information exchange which makes up the Internet.

**edexcel ⠿ key terms**

**The Internet** – a global network of computers that are able to exchange information.

**The web** – one part of the Internet which contains documents that are all linked together and which can be viewed at a computer or other device.

## What is the Internet?

Computers that are linked together form a network. Such systems enable information to be shared across computers. The **Internet** is a global network of computers that are able to exchange information. It consists of billions of people, ranging from individuals in their homes through to governments and multi-national businesses, all connected together and capable of sharing information.

This information might be mail, chat lines, video, music, files, gaming and documents. The power and value of the Internet is the flexibility it provides in helping people and businesses to access and share such a wide range of information. The Internet, therefore, is essentially a global communications network, putting people in touch with each other in a variety of different ways.

The Internet developed as a result of research by academics and by government and military establishments from around the 1940s. It was not until the 1980s that the general public really became aware of the Internet. For many people it was not until the late 1990s and into the early twenty-first century that the power of the Internet began to be appreciated. Figure 1 shows the number of users in different parts of the world.

The World Wide Web, or 'the **web**' was created by Sir Tim Berners-Lee in 1989 whilst working for a nuclear research facility in Switzerland. The web is a system of documents that are all linked together, which can be viewed at a computer or other device, such as a mobile phone, through a browser. A browser is the software that enables the user to access information and data on the web. There is a number of different browsers available. Microsoft's Internet Explorer is the market leader, with Netscape, Mozilla Firefox, Safari and Opera being examples of others.

**Figure 1** – Internet users in the world by geographical region, 2008

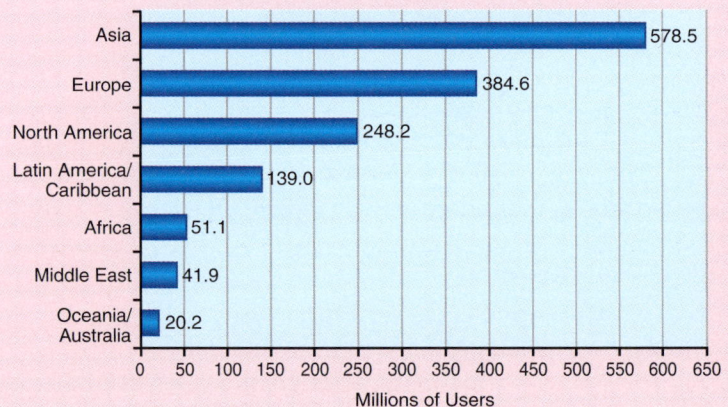

| Region | Millions of Users |
|---|---|
| Asia | 578.5 |
| Europe | 384.6 |
| North America | 248.2 |
| Latin America/Caribbean | 139.0 |
| Africa | 51.1 |
| Middle East | 41.9 |
| Oceania/Australia | 20.2 |

Soruce: adapted from http://www.internetworldstats.com/stats.htm

## Advantages and disadvantages of the Internet

The Internet has opened up many opportunities for businesses. These include:

- being able to share information;
- accessing information, for example, about customer purchasing habits;
- providing a means of selling products and services through e-commerce 24 hours a day, 7 days a week;
- improving the speed and flexibility of communication, for example, through e-mail or providing video or audio files;
- providing new means of marketing products and services;
- enabling businesses to control and cut costs;
- providing different ways of working;
- providing the opportunity to be available to customers at all times.

Mark had tried to consider some of these advantages for his own business. He could see that there were possibilities to be able to provide information to his customers about the products that he had in stock, prices, opening and closing times, special offers, guides about how to do DIY jobs and using different tools, for example. He knew that his rivals sold products online and that many customers liked the convenience of this type of service. A web site was certainly an attractive proposition.

One of the main ways in which Mark's business competed with its rivals was through the quality of the service he offered. Customers trusted his advice and judgement and he thought that providing the opportunity to contact him through e-mail would be another extension to this service. He also had an idea that he could find new suppliers, new products and get updates on new developments in his business area through using the Internet. He even wondered whether it would be sensible to have short video clips showing how to do basic DIY jobs to help his customers.

However, Mark had also done some research about the disadvantages to his business. He knew that he would have to find someone who could design the web site for him. He was aware that there were certain legal requirements that he had to adhere to. As a result he had to have someone who knew what they were doing. Then he would have to pay for the hosting and maintenance, manage the technical problems that might arise and also consider the limitations of a site for his business. It would be difficult, for example, for him to have an e-commerce facility to allow customers to buy direct from him. He simply did not have the staff or resources to be able to manage such a distribution method. If customers were able to contact him at any time through his web site, would he have the time and energy to deal with all the requests for information or communication he received?

Mark knew that one of the advantages of e-mail is the possibility of quick communication, but that might mean he spent more time sitting at his computer checking and replying to his e-mails than running the rest of his business. Answering queries was one thing, but unless they translated into sales it would be of limited value. When he checked about the cost of producing mini-videos he was surprised at how expensive it was and at the fact that he would need to consider whether his customers could access the video and which format he would need to provide.

Mark was also aware that he would have to learn a whole new language to understand the technicalities of the Internet and the web. Whilst he was aware that he did not have to have any major technical skills to run the site, he did want to make sure that he had at least the basic understanding of how everything worked. The disadvantages Mark faced were typical of those faced by many businesses which are planning to have a web site.

## How the Internet works

Remember that the Internet is like a huge network of connected computers around the planet. To make the network successful the computers have to be able to 'talk' to each other and they do this through 'protocols'. To successfully

**Figure 2** – HyperText Markup Language (HTML)

```
<!--whatsnew-->
<h2 class="imageheading"><a
href="/homeinfo/whatsnew.htm"><im
g src="/images/title_whatsnew.gif"
width="187" height="28" vspace="4"
alt="What's New" class="homepage"
/></a></h2>

<p class="mainsmall"><strong><a
href="/cgi-
bin/homepage/redirect.pl?where=/edu
cators/16-
19/tourism/operations/activity/enviro
nment.htm">Tour operators: Take-off
or grounded?</a></strong>
(14 Oct)<br /><a href="/cgi-
bin/homepage/redirect.pl?where=/edu
cators/16-
19/tourism/operations/activity/enviro
nment.htm"><img
class="whatsnewborder"
src="/images/homepage/thomas_cook
_1950_wide.jpg" width="370"
height="90" alt="A Thomas Cook
poster from the 1950s" /></a></p>
<p>In this new travel and tourism
resource, we look into the performance
of the major tour operators, analyse
the impact of XL Group's failure and
ask if there is any room for new
entrants in the travel industry.
</p><div
class="homeimagetext"><div><a
href="/cgi-
bin/homepage/redirect.pl?where=/dat
aserv/chron/quiz/"><img
src="/images/homepage/mq.jpg"
alt="Multi-choice card/A white
question mark on a blue flag"
width="90" height="67"
class="whatsnewborder" /></a>
```

### ResultsPlus
**Watch Out!**

Remember that the Internet has advantages and disadvantages to a business. Do not just assume that having a web site is a 'good' thing for every business and that it will automatically bring benefits.

communicate there has to be a system where each computer on the network is identified. Computer devices connected to the Internet are identified through an **IP address** - an Internet Protocol address.

## Accessing a web page

When a user types an address into their browser, the address is sent to a server operated by an Internet Service Provider (**ISP**). The server then communicates with other servers to identify where the web address is located and also the IP address of the user. A **web server** stores web pages and ensures that the page is routed to the correct IP address. The server then knows where the web page is and can deliver it to the user's browser where the user can view the page/s.

The whole network is very complex but it might be useful to think of it like a postal network. The post person has to know the address to deliver the right letter. The postal sorting office takes in and sends out millions of letters every day. It has to sort all these letters and make sure that the right letters are delivered to the correct addresses. The web server is like the main sorting office. It receives millions of requests for web pages from millions of users. It has to identify the right address and making sure that it sends the correct web page to the right address.

It is important, therefore, that when typing in a web address you get it right. If not then the web server will not be able to identify the web page and an error message will be sent. Every document on the web has its own specific address called its URL which stands for Universal Resource Locator.

A typical web address or **URL** looks like the following.

### http://www.bized.co.uk

where
- http:// stands for HyperText Transfer Protocol - the means by which web pages are transferred between computers.
- www denotes the **server** on which the web pages concerned sit.
- bized - the **domain name** which enables the web server to recognise where a collection of pages belong to.

- .co.uk - the **host name**. In this case .co.uk implies that the organisation is a company based in the UK. Other host names represent the type of organisation. .ac.uk is an academic institution like a school, college or university in the UK, .gov.uk is a government body, .org.uk is an organisation. Other countries have their own identification, such as .in (India) and .ca (Canada).

You are also likely to see more extensions to a web address in your browser. Typically, these show the directory structure of the web page. Many web sites have different sections with different sub-sections off these and such extensions help to identify where in the web site the page being looked at sits. **http://www.bized.co.uk/index.htm** will tell you that you are looking at the index page on Biz/ed for example.

To construct a web page, a particular language is used which a browser is able to read and translate into what we see on the page. **HTML** stands for HyperText Markup Language. The language tells the browser exactly what the page should look like - the size and description of images, the font used, the colours and so on. An example of the language is shown in Figure 2. For the user, the browser will translate the language into a web page. An example of a web page is shown in Figure 3.

## E-commerce

Many businesses have seen the advantages that the Internet can provide for e-commerce - selling goods and services over the Internet. An e-commerce facility means a business can make sales 24 hours a day, 7 days a week. However, setting up an e-commerce facility which allows customers to order and pay for goods and services is something that needs careful thought. The customer has to believe that the facility is secure. They will be asked to submit a variety of personal details including their address and credit card information and this can make some people nervous. Stories in the news about hackers breaking into databases and stealing personal information are something that businesses are very keen to

## edexcel ⠿ key terms

**IP address** – the means by which a computer connected to the Internet is identified.

**ISP** – Internet Service Provider, a business that provides a service, usually a server, which allows the user to access the Internet.

**URL** – Universal Resource Locator, the specific address of every document on the web which enables the server to identify it.

**Server** – a computer running software that receives information, usually a request of some sort, processes that information and sends out the resulting information back to another computer.

**HTML** – HyperText Markup Language, the language which tells a browser what a web page should look like.

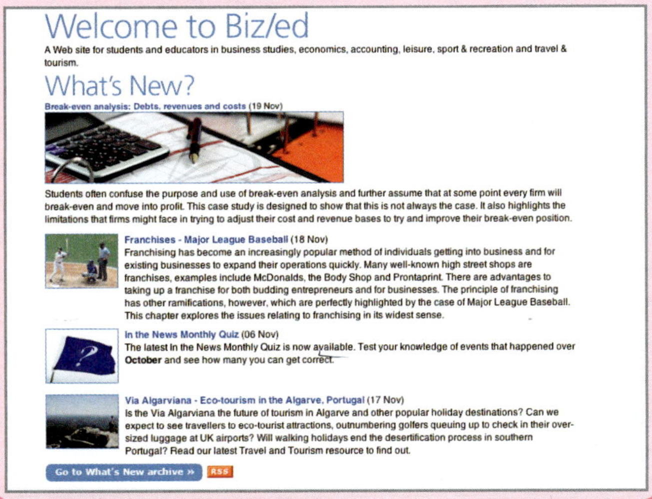

**Figure 3** – An Internet page

## Welcome to Biz/ed
A Web site for students and educators in business studies, economics, accounting, leisure, sport & recreation and travel & tourism.
### What's New?

Break-even analysis: Debts, revenues and costs (19 Nov)

Students often confuse the purpose and use of break-even analysis and further assume that at some point every firm will break-even and move into profit. This case study is designed to show that this is not always the case. It also highlights the limitations that firms might face in trying to adjust their cost and revenue bases to try and improve their break-even position.

Franchises - Major League Baseball (18 Nov)
Franchising has become an increasingly popular method of individuals getting into business and for existing businesses to expand their operations quickly. Many well-known high street shops are franchises, examples include McDonalds, the Body Shop and Prontaprint. There are advantages to taking up a franchise for both budding entrepreneurs and for businesses. The principle of franchising has other ramifications, however, which are perfectly highlighted by the case of Major League Baseball. This chapter explores the issues relating to franchising in its widest sense.

In the News Monthly Quiz (06 Nov)
The latest In the News Monthly Quiz is now available. Test your knowledge of events that happened over **October** and see how many you can get correct.

Via Algarviana - Eco-tourism in the Algarve, Portugal (17 Nov)
Is the Via Algarviana the future of tourism in Algarve and other popular holiday destinations? Can we expect to see travellers to eco-tourist attractions, outnumbering golfers queuing up to check in their over-sized luggage at UK airports? Will walking holidays end the desertification process in southern Portugal? Read our latest Travel and Tourism resource to find out.

Go to What's New archive »  RSS

avoid because it discourages customers from using e-commerce.

In addition to the cost of setting up payment facilities, the business will also have to ensure that it has distribution networks in place to make sure that the right goods are delivered speedily to the right customers. For a small business this might mean a daily trip to the post office but for medium and large businesses, the planning and organisation of its distribution can be expensive and difficult to manage.

## Test yourself

1. Which **one** of the following is the best definition of the Internet? The Internet is:

   A  **the software that allows the user to view a web page**
   B  **the World Wide Web**
   C  **a global network of connected computers**
   D  **a superfast means of accessing information**

   Select **one** answer.

2. Which **two** of the following are possible opportunities for business provided by the Internet? Select **two** answers.

   A  **It enables a business to spy on its rivals**
   B  **Communication can be much quicker**
   C  **It provides businesses with the chance to market their products differently**
   D  **Generating revenues becomes much easier**
   E  **It allows every business to improve its sales**
   F  **It enables a business to advertise for free**

3. Which **one** of the following would be a reason why a small business might not want to set up a web site? Select **one** answer.

   A  **Because they would have to attend college to learn HTML**
   B  **Setting up a network and a server would be too expensive**
   C  **The cost of running the site would not be covered by the revenue generated by it**
   D  **Finding an ISP with exactly the right web address would be too time consuming.**

## Over to you

Mark Norton had given the idea of setting up a web site serious thought. He had done a large amount of research and felt that he had enough information to make a decision. He had drawn up a list of 'good points' and 'bad points' to help him make his decision. These are summarised below. Using the information above and that given in this section, write a short report of no more than 300 words advising Mark whether a web site would be appropriate for his particular business. (10)

| Good Points | Bad Points |
|---|---|
| Other stores had web sites | The cost of setting up and running the site is high |
| He could keep in contact with his customers 24/7 | Keeping the site up-to-date is time consuming |
| He could generate additional sales | He would have to set up a mail delivery system |
| He could provide useful information to his customers | He could not afford to send large items by post |
| It would be another key part of his commitment to customer service | His customers tended to be local only |

## ResultsPlus
### Build Better Answers

(i) Identify **one** opportunity open to businesses of the Internet. (1)
(ii) Explain how this opportunity might benefit a business. (3)

Think: How might a business use the Internet? How can this help the business?

🟥 **Basic** One opportunity is given to answer part (i) of the question but the rest of the answer is left blank. (1)

🟠 **Good** One opportunity (for example, providing different ways of working) is given to answer part (i) of the question. For the second part a link is made between different ways of working and a benefit to the business. For example, it can help a business do away with expensive premises and focus on selling online instead. (2-3)

🔺 **Excellent** The opportunity is given along with a link but this link is then taken further. For example, doing away with expensive premises can reduce overheads and help cut costs thus boosting profit margins. Use of business terminology is in evidence. (4)

# 20 Business web sites

## Case Study

Beauty at a Snip is owned by Josette Nichols. Josette owns three salons in towns across the West Midlands. The salons provided a range of hair care services and beauty treatments. She had been in business for 10 years and had been pleased at the way that the business had grown in that time. Up to now she had not believed that a web site was an appropriate form of communication for her business as she believed it was too localised to warrant one. However, her customers had increasingly been telling her that they had tried to find the business on the Internet but were surprised that she did not have any online presence. Josette decided that it was time to do so and had employed a web design company to get everything set up for her. As she discussed the project with them, she was surprised at the extent to which the web might be able to help her business communicate.

## Objectives

● To understand the meaning of the term 'online presence'.

● To appreciate that an online presence allows a business to reach a wider market.

● To understand that online presence allows a business to gather useful information about its customers.

● To appreciate that a business can communicate with a range of stakeholders through the web.

● To appreciate some reasons why a web site is not appropriate for all businesses.

## edexcel ::: key terms

**Online presence** – having a web site that allows people to see/get information about the business.

**Niche market** – a very small or specialised part of an existing market where customer needs are not currently being met.

## What is an 'online presence'?

An **online presence** simply means having a web site for the business. This means that anyone, anywhere in the world, is able to access and find out about the business. This brings its own advantages and disadvantages, however. How relevant is the information the business gives out to all those millions of people who might look at the site? Who are the people that will want to look at the site? What sort of information and facilities will they want? Do they have particular problems that you have to consider to enable them to view the site properly and get the information they need?

Setting up a web site will be done for a variety of reasons. These include:

● providing information to customers and other **stakeholders**;

● making the business available to a wider audience;

● Increasing exposure to the market - especially if the business serves a **niche market**, for example nail care;

● helping to cut costs;

● providing advice and support for customers and other stakeholders;

● selling products and services through an e-commerce facility;

● gathering information to track customers of the business;

● giving stakeholders 24 hour access to the business.

Some businesses have web sites that are really dedicated to giving out information. It is not appropriate for the business to use it as a means of selling its goods or services. Other sites will be almost exclusively for selling. The range of reasons for having an online presence makes it important that a business thinks carefully about why it wants to have a website.

Josette knew that she could not sell hair and beauty treatments online - clients would have to come into her salons for this to happen. However, she did think that a web site might help her to gain more clients and/or make it easier for new and existing clients to access her business. They could make appointments online, enquire about availability, find out opening times, prices and the range of services that she offered. Josette also thought that providing this sort of information online might help reduce the amount of time staff had to spend answering these sorts of questions. Whilst they were dealing with queries which often were exactly the same sort of questions, they were not doing work that was actually generating revenue for the salon. A 'frequently asked questions' (FAQ) section on her website might well help customers and save costs.

In addition, Josette thought that it would be useful to have information about different hair types, colours, the sort of products they used in the salon, things that clients need to think about when considering beauty treatment and hair styling. Clients would be able to come to the salon with a far better idea of what they were looking for and what was possible and not possible if they could be directed to the site beforehand. In addition, she felt that she would be able to show why the salon chose to use high quality but more expensive products and how clients benefitted from this decision.

One of the things that had always made Josette put off the idea of a web site was that she felt that, being a small local business, it was not worth it. Why would web site users in Malaysia or Argentina be interested in her little salons in the West Midlands? It was no use, she thought, having an online presence because the vast majority of users would never see her site and even if they did they would not find it useful or be interested.

Having talked to a web site design team, Josette realised that it was not the fact that someone in Argentina would not find the site useful if they came across it, it was more important to consider how useful someone in Wolverhampton or Walsall would find her site. She began to understand that size was not the issue, but that an online presence allowed her to meet her customers' needs more effectively.

Josette's business is a small sole trader and the outline above provides some reasons why an online presence can be of benefit to such a business. Many of the web sites we might use on a regular basis are linked to businesses at the other end of the spectrum - they are associated with very large multi-national companies. These companies have a global presence. They have operations, stores, factories or interests in many different countries in the world. They have millions of customers who might be able to make use of the site in different ways. However, it is important to realise, again, that very large businesses do not always want to have an online presence to sell things.

## A tale of three businesses

The web sites of three businesses can be used to illustrate the different functions of web sites.

**O2** O2 is a leading communications company for consumers and businesses in the UK. In September 2008 O2 had over 19 million mobile customers and over 260,000 fixed broadband customers. Telefónica O2 UK Limited is part of Telefónica Europe plc which is a business division of Telefónica S.A. and has 44.9 million customers.

**BP** This is a multinational company. It searches for and extracts oil and gas. It then refines these products to make a whole range of other products like jet fuel, petrol, diesel, lubricants, waxes and asphalt. It also sells products to customers - there are plenty of BP garages selling petrol and a range of other products. It has over 1 million **shareholders**, employs over 97,000 people, has operations in more than 100 countries and has a **turnover** of over £170 billion a year.

**CosmoGirl** This is a magazine aimed at teenage girls. Its web site contains a range of information and articles covering fashion, beauty, advice, gossip and 'fun'. CosmoGirl is a part of the Hearst Corporation which is involved in publishing, broadcasting and communications. It takes a bit of searching through the site to find that it is part of this company but that is not the main reason why users would go to this site.

All three companies have web sites. The reasons for their sites are different, although there are similarities. The home page of each site helps to provide an indication of the purpose of the sites.

• O2 is mainly organised to help customers find information about buying O2

Business websites

edexcel **key terms**

**Shareholders** – owners of a business. Shareholders may own a small part of a business but have bought a share of the ownership of the business.

**Turnover** – a measure of the amount of sales generated by a business over a period of time. Turnover is the same as sales revenue. A turnover of £50,000 a year means the business has sold £50,000 worth of goods or services in that year.

services whether it be broadband or buying a mobile phone and finding a tariff that suits the customer.

- The customers are recognised as being both individuals and businesses.
- The whole of the home page is geared towards those who either have an account with O2 or are looking to open one.
- The opportunities to buy online are made easy and clear.
- BP's home page is primarily organised to give information.
- The information covers the history of the business, the sort of work that BP undertakes, latest news about the business and its financial results and performance.
- CosmoGirl is primarily designed to provide information and be attractive and inviting to its users.
- It provides the opportunity to access a number of free areas to give information on fashion, advice and so on.
- There are adverts to subscribe to other magazines in the group such as Seventeen.
- There is also the opportunity to register to 'My CosmoGirl' where there are additional benefits for members. Subscription is free.
- All the sites have opportunities to contact the business and BP and O2 have information for those looking for jobs or careers with the company.
- BP and O2 sites provide a means by which customers can find their nearest store or petrol station.
- BP and O2 have some information about the business itself.
- CosmoGirl and O2 have sections where to get further information you have to register or subscribe.

## The needs of different stakeholders

We can see from these three sites that the needs of different stakeholders are met in different ways. For O2, the main stakeholder is the customer. The website is a means through which the customer can buy services - to register an account and buy phones, broadband services and so on. A web site is ideal to enable the business to be able to do this.

For BP, selling petrol online is clearly not possible. They provide information for customers, for example about local petrol stations, but the main focus is on giving information to other stakeholders like shareholders and the local community. BP has a special section devoted to investors where details of the company and its financial performance can be gained. It also has a section on 'environment and society' which shows what the company is doing to reduce its impact on the environment and to show how it is trying to be environmentally friendly.

In the case of CosmoGirl, the emphasis is on the user - the **target market**. Many of the articles and features on the site will be of little interest to those who are not in its target market. Why does CosmoGirl ask its users to register? In registering the user has to input certain information such as date of birth, e-mail address and post code. In submitting this information, CosmoGirl can start to build a profile of the type of user of the site and use it to get a better understanding of its

customers' needs.

The primary focus of a business web site is an important part of the online presence. The business has to consider who its main users are likely to be and what they will want from the web site. In some cases, a business will have to make it very clear that there are two different sections to their web site - one for selling and one for information - to satisfy the different needs of possible users. This is why many students often have difficulty finding information about a business when doing research.

If, for example, a student is asked to find information about Marks & Spencer doing an Internet search usually takes the user to a home page that provides information about its products aimed at customers. The user has to search around for a link to take them to information about the company. There is often a link called 'Investor Relations' where information about the actual business itself can be found.

## A website for all?

Josette had thought for many years that her business did not need a website. It may be that at the time she was right. A website is not appropriate for every business. Many small businesses do not have web sites. The reasons why they may choose not to have one could include the following.

### Test yourself

1. Which **one** of the following might be an important consideration that a business thinking of setting up a website would have to take into account?

   A *Whether the likely users lived close enough to the business*
   B *Who the likely users were and what their needs would be*
   C *Whether users had access to a computer or not*
   D *Whether the potential users had access to a telephone line*

2. Which **two** of the following are the most likely reasons why a business might choose to have an online presence?

   A *It almost guarantees that the business will make a million quickly*
   B *The future of business is going to be dependent on the Web*
   C *All other businesses have web sites so it makes sense to join them*
   D *It can allow the business to provide information to its customers*
   E *An online presence is the only way to gain information about customers' needs*
   F *It provides the possibility of being able to sell products to new customers*

3. Which **one** of the following is **not** a reason why an online presence might not be appropriate for every business?

   A *It increases access to the business for customers and other stakeholders*
   B *The cost of setting up the site might be too high*
   C *The type of business is not appropriate for a website*
   D *The business might have a tried and tested means of getting new customers*

- The cost of setting up and maintaining a web site.
- The fact that many of its business contacts are made through personal recommendation rather than through random searches.
- Products or services could not be sold through a website.
- The availability of e-mail contact may serve the purpose of enabling the business to be in contact 24 hours a day without the need for a web site.
- The time needed to monitor and keep the site up to date

may not be something the business feels it can afford.
- The sort of information that could be provided is not relevant for its customers or stakeholders.
- The benefit in terms of additional sales or interest in the business would be less than the cost of setting up and running the website.
- be a success. However, he knew there was a risk that the market research could be wrong. If there were too few customers, his business would fail.

107

## Over to you

Sainsbury's is one of the leading grocery retailers in the UK. Like other retailers, it has developed an online presence to complement its many stores around the country.

1. Identify **three** possible stakeholders that are being targeted by the Sainsbury's website. (3)
2. Explain how each stakeholder might benefit from the web site. (9)
3. To be able to shop online the user has to register. Discuss **two** benefits that this provides to the business. (8)

Source: http://www.sainsburys.co.uk/aboutsainsburys

## ResultsPlus
### Build Better Answers

An online presence is likely to be **most** important to a business if:

A the cost of setting up the web site is cheap
B it believes all its competitors also have a web site
C it wants to open up its business to a wider audience
D it is suffering a slump in sales

Select **one** answer.

Answer C

Think: What is an online presence?

Then: Think about why an online presence may be important to a business.

Remember: Not every business has an online presence or indeed needs one.

Review: Look at each option carefully. Try to dismiss the ones that are obviously wrong.

Decide: Make your decision as to the correct answer.

The four options above have to be read carefully.

An online presence is about having a web site.

A - Is the cost of setting up a web site important - yes - but what

does 'cheap' mean? Cheap might mean not good quality. It is more important to consider the benefits of having the online presence.

B - Whether all its competitors have a web site or not is not important. The business has to decide whether it will benefit from a web site.

C - This will be an important consideration for many businesses - even if the audience can only access the business from a local area. An online presence opens out the business to customers who may not know it is there.

D - An online presence may help to boost sales in some cases but we have seen that an online presence is more than just trying to sell goods and services. Even if a business has an online presence it is no guarantee that its sales will rise. There might be other reasons for the slump in sales - maybe the product is not meeting customer needs.

The two possible answers are A and C.

C is the better response because it applies to the vast majority of businesses.

# 21 Creating a simple web site

## Case Study

Carlisle Winters was nuts about music. He thought that his prowess with music technology would stand him in good stead to transfer his skills to designing a web site for his business. Carlisle's business involved creating jingles for local radio stations and TV adverts and being a session musician. Session players are professional musicians who get booked to play their instrument or contribute their music in a wide variety of different musical environments. One week, Carlisle could be playing guitar for a recording of a theme tune for a TV show. The next he might be in the studio recording with a top band. The success of his business relied on word of mouth recommendations, but increasingly he knew that producers were looking to gather more information about session musicians via the web. Carlisle thought that the web provided the perfect vehicle to display his CV and enable a wider audience to contact him.

## Objectives

- To understand the main factors that need to be considered in setting up a simple business web site.
- To understand the importance of balancing the cost of development with the anticipated use of the site in decision-making.
- To understand the importance of technical issues in setting up a web site.
- To appreciate the role and importance of development, testing and implementation in the process of setting up a web site.
- To understand that a business web site needs regular monitoring and maintenance.

## What factors have to be considered in setting up a web site?

Setting up a business web site is different from setting up a personal web site. The consideration of the main purpose of the site is something that was covered in the previous chapter. There are many other factors that also have to be thought about before the web site becomes a reality.

Carlisle spent some time studying web design and web technology. He was right, his technical prowess did give him an advantage but there was still a great deal to learn. Carlisle invested in a software programme to help him design and build his web site. There are plenty of these types of software available from something simple like Microsoft's FrontPage to more sophisticated packages like Dreamweaver and Xara. There were even free software packages that could be downloaded from the Internet, like WebPlus.

Having mastered the actual design elements of the software, Carlisle knew that there were other even more practical things that had to be considered, which will now be explained.

## The available budget

Setting up a web site takes time and, in business, time represents a cost. It was important for Carlisle to set aside a certain amount of money to provide some discipline in the amount he was going to spend. If Carlisle was going to spend two months designing and developing his web site, that was time when he would not be earning money. The price of the software he bought was also not cheap - it was over £300. The more sophisticated his site and the more things he wanted to include, the more expensive the design was going to be.

Carlisle knew that if he wanted to spend £15,000 or even £20,000 developing his web site he could easily do so, but he thought that it was more appropriate to limit his budget to a more modest sum. He settled on setting aside £5,000. He arrived at this figure through research about the time it would take, the equipment and software he would need and the specialist help he would have to hire to do the more complex work he wanted on the site. He also asked a number of professional designers how much they would charge to do the work for him.

The range of quotes he received surprised him. Some were expensive, whilst others seemed very cheap.

Carlisle could have got someone else to do it for him for £5,000, but he wanted to do the work himself and build new skills. He believed that you never quite know when such new skills would come in useful in the future. Some large companies have slick, sophisticated and large web sites, with hundreds of pages. These organisations might be able to afford to use specialist web design companies and in some cases will employ their own web design specialists to manage and develop their web sites. Carlisle's business was a little more modest.

## The type of content

One of the key considerations in setting up a web site is to decide what will actually be in it. This may sound obvious, but it can often be forgotten in the excitement of developing the site. Some of the considerations might include the following.

- Will there need to be an e-commerce facility?
- Should the site have the facilities to present Web 2.0 tools such as forums, wikis and blogs?
- What messages does the business want to put across for the users of the site?
- Will the content of the site be primarily written content or will it include video clips, music or other presentation means such as Flash animations?

Carlisle wanted to include MP3 files of some of his work and a video clip where he introduced himself and his work. He knew that this was a little more complex than a simple web site that just included text. His research into this suggested that making video files available on the web was more challenging than he

**ResultsPlus**
**Watch Out!**

Developing a business web site has to be done with a great amount of thought, care and attention. The costs of developing the site have to be set alongside the benefits that the site can bring. Saving a bit of money on the development can lead to a far greater loss in the future if the site is badly designed and has lots of errors which turn customers away.

**Figure 1** – Carlisle's home page for the website

110

expected. Putting music clips onto the site was more straightforward. He decided that he could produce the written material easily enough himself and would also record and upload the music clips. However, he decided to get the video shot professionally and to employ a company to edit and process the video for his site.

## The potential users of the site

Carlisle had made some initial sketches of what he wanted on his web site. However, he soon realised that he was being quite ambitious and that the site was going to get too big. Considering the potential users of the site was very important. For Carlisle, the web site was meant to be a means by which he could market his skills and talents. He was selling himself. He did think about putting all sorts of material onto the site that covered technical issues about music technology, but he realised that this was not what the main users he hoped to attract would want. They would want to find out who he was, what range of skills and abilities he had, what his experience was and how to contact him. This helped to focus his mind on what was going to be important about the site. Figure 1 shows the site ideas he finally decided upon.

Carlisle also knew that he could use a social networking site such has Facebook or MySpace to do the same job - portray himself and his work. If he was not planning to sell anything directly then this could have been a very cost-effective way of setting up a web site. He could register, set up his own profile and include information about himself in the same way as he was planning.

However, after much thought he decided to go with his original plan to set his own web site up. He would own the content and his own site, which might give him greater exposure to people looking for his type of skills through search engines.

## Technical considerations

The decision to include video clips and music meant that there were various technical issues that had to be considered. Whilst Carlisle knew that many people now had access to **broadband**, he also knew that there was a wide range of speeds that people had access to. He knew that

including things like music and video took up more space and so he had to think about **download speed**. The inclusion of graphics and animations also had an impact on download speed. He wanted to make sure that users did not have to wait too long to see the site. He had seen some company web sites that included a Flash animation at the start and it took twenty to thirty seconds to download before the user could see it and even then the animation did not help the user to get to the information they needed quickly even though the animation looked very professional and impressive.

Carlisle decided to make sure that users got to the key information as quickly as possible. He also wanted to make sure that the site was structured to make it as easy for users to get information as quickly as possible, with the least amount of clicks of the mouse. This led him to having to think carefully about the **navigation** - how easy it is to get around the site and to get particular pieces of information.

He also had to consider other technical issues, such as how consistent the site would look. There would be different parts to his site, such as contact information, a site map, help pages, his recent and his past projects and a site search facility. He wanted to make sure that when the user visited these different pages they had a consistent look and feel. He spent some time researching **cascading style sheets** (CSS). CSS is used to control the look and feel of text and to position the text in a consistent way on different pages. What this meant was that the font, its size, the colour and the spacing of the text would all be consistent whatever page the user looked at.

Carlisle knew that this was important because his users might be looking at his page in different browsers. Whilst many people use Microsoft's Internet Explorer, there are other browsers such as Firefox, Opera and Safari. He also had to bear in mind that not everyone accessed the Internet via a PC. More and more people use their mobile phone or other mobile devices to access the Internet. He wanted to make sure that whatever device they had, users could see his site properly.

## Testing

The development process took Carlisle much longer than he thought it would. He came across lots of issues and problems in setting up the site. They were not insurmountable but he did have to do more research and learn more new skills than he thought he would have to. As he created the site, he made sure that he spent time testing it to make sure it all worked. He wanted to make sure that the navigation worked properly, that all the links he had included worked and that the video and music clips downloaded quickly. There were times when he got **error messages** when checking the site. In most cases the reason was simply that he had made a typing error in the code or had forgotten to include a tag in the code.

**edexcel ⠿ key terms**

**Broadband** – a means of connecting to the Internet, often at relatively high speeds. Broadband allows users to always have a connection to the Internet and also allows larger amounts of data to be transferred more quickly.

**Cascading style sheets (CSS)** – a language used to specify the way in which a document is presented on the web. It ensures that pages are presented in a consistent style including the size and colour of the font, layouts, borders and so on.

One of the things that helped Carlisle in the testing process was using a **validator**. Validation is the process of checking web documents against a standard. The standard that Carlisle used was produced by the Worldwide Web Consortium (or W3C). By validating his web pages, Carlisle could be confident that he had not made mistakes with his coding and that his pages would look as he wanted them to for his users. He knew that, in some cases, a web page can appear completely blank in one browser whilst looking perfectly fine in another. He wanted to make sure that his users did not have this sort of experience.

## Implementation and roll out

Having spent quite some time on the development and testing of the site, Carlisle finally felt that he was ready to release the site to the general public. He went through all the pages and made some amendments and additions. Having done that he then made sure that he gave it a final quality check to make sure everything worked and that all the pages validated against W3C standards. The site then went live.

## Maintenance

In the early stages of the new site, Carlisle monitored things carefully. He received a number of e-mails through the contact section of the site. Some noted where there were still mistakes that he had not picked up. By following a rigorous programme of regular maintenance, Carlisle was able to make sure that any errors were quickly corrected, to make improvements to parts of the site and to make sure that the information was as accurate and as up to date as possible. There were other little things that he also had to remember, such as changing the dates on the site in the New Year to make sure that the copyright information was accurate and adding any new music, photos and his latest recording session details.

## Summary

The development of the web site took Carlisle much longer than he expected. In the end he exceeded his budget for the site by £1,000. However, in the process he had developed a range of new skills and was pleased with his efforts. He was also pleased that he had control over the development of the site and did things his way rather than having to spend lots of time going back and forwards with a web developer.

However, he had been surprised at the amount of things he had not initially thought about. These included how **web pages are displayed** in different browsers, the consideration of different **screen resolutions** that users might be using, how **legal issues** affected the site and how certain designs that might seem 'good' actually made the site difficult to use.

Carlisle reflected on his experience. He thought that, whilst he enjoyed the challenge of doing it himself, he would have hired a professional developer if he did it again. He certainly felt that this would be a benefit to a larger company, which might have a far more complex set of requirements than he had settled on.

A web site may be one of the first ways in which a potential customer comes into contact with a business. If the site looks wrong, does not work properly or contains lots of errors and links that do not work then it sends out a bad impression of the business and might mean that users do not come back to it again. Most businesses do not want to lose potential customers and so making sure that their web site is of high quality is important. Getting a professional to do it might be more expensive, but it might end up being money well spent.

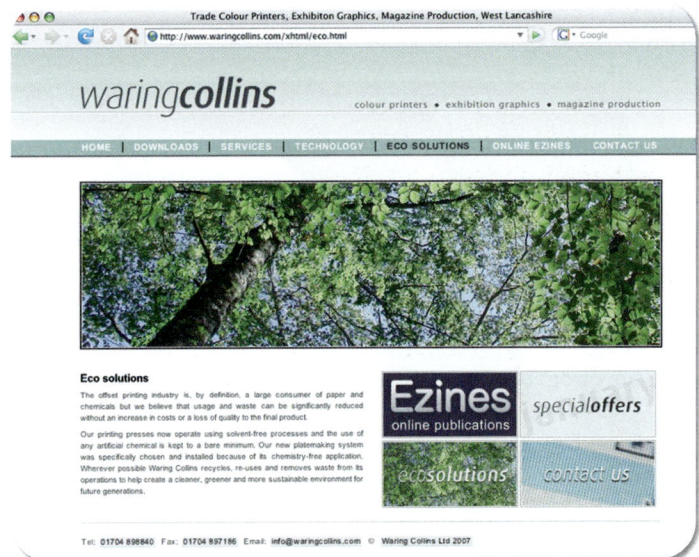

Effective websites are easy to use and are well maintained

edexcel ⋮⋮⋮ key terms

**Validator** – a means of checking a web page against a standard as laid down by the W3C.

## Test yourself

1.  The budget available for a web site is important because:

    A   *the more the business spends on a web site the better it is going to be*

    B   *businesses need to think about how much they are going to receive from the web site in revenue*

    C   *it provides a means by which the business can set a limit on what it spends*

    D   *it tells the business how much the tax it has to pay will be*

    Select **one** answer.

2.  Which of the following is not a consideration about the content of a web site that has to be taken into account? Select **one** answer.

    A   *If the business will be selling products and need a means for customers to pay*

    B   *What features the site will contain*

    C   *Whether it will include text and graphics and other forms of communication like video*

    D   *The number of users that the web site might attract*

3.  Validating a web site is important because:

    A   **without it users will not be able to see the site**

    B   **it reduces the cost of developing the site**

    C   **validation reduces the risk of errors on the site and maintains a standard**

    D   **validation means that the web site will have a value on the Internet**

    Select **one** answer.

## ResultsPlus
### Build Better Answers

Deciding on an appropriate budget and considering the potential users of the site are **two** considerations in designing a web site. Which of the **two** do you think is the more important consideration? Justify your answer. (8)

Technique guide: This is a question that is assessing your ability to make judgements and to break down a complex topic into easier to manage chunks (evaluation and analysis).

Think: Why are both of the items important? Can a web site be developed without one or the other?

Then: Arrive at a decision about which one you are going to choose - there is NO right answer; the examiner is looking for your ability to make a judgement and support it.

Remember: It is not how much you write here but the quality of your answer.

Plan: Try and think through how you are going to approach the answer and how you are going to structure it.

Write: Write out your answer.

■ **Basic** Provides a judgement about one of the ways and gives a limited reason for the judgement. (1-2)

● **Good** Provides a judgement and offers an explanation of one of the two considerations only. Appropriate terms and concepts are used as part of the explanation for the judgement. (3-5)

▲ **Excellent** Provides a brief explanation of the role of both considerations. Arrives at a judgement of one and provides some explanation of the reason for the choice. Appropriate terms and concepts are used throughout the answer. (6-8)

# Over to you

Chelsea Phelps had some experience of web design whilst at college, where she created her own web site. She had included this fact on her CV and when her employers, Bradd, Crickmore and Stubbs, a partnership firm of building surveyors, asked to see her about it she was intrigued. The company had a problem with the firm that had been hired to develop the company's new web site. It had gone into receivership and the business was left with a partially completed site.

At the meeting, Chelsea pointed out that she only had limited experience, but she was happy to help out temporarily until a more permanent solution to the company's problem could be found. Her employers were delighted and told her she would be given three days a week to work on completing the site as much as she could, but that, first, the company wanted a report on how she would approach the task.

Chelsea went to work and the first thing she did was to run the existing work that had been done on the web site through the W3C validator. She was shocked to find that the validator reported back a large number of errors on the site. She set about writing a report to her employers explaining some of the implications for the company of the problems and outlining her strategy for dealing with them, as well as finishing the site.

Before you answer the questions it is useful to have a look at what a validator does and what the report it provides looks like. Paste the URL of your school into the address bar of the W3C validator which can be found at http://validator.w3.org/ and select the 'check' button. See what comes up.

1. Identify **three** possible factors that Chelsea might have included in her report to her employers about the process for developing the site. (3)
2. Explain why validation is such an important part of the development of a web site. (8)
3. Testing and maintenance are two important parts of building and running a web site. Which do you think is the more important of the two to get right? Justify your answer (8)

# 22 Domain names and hosting

## Case Study

Alissa Ford had decided to set up her own web site for her business which involved selling framed photographs which she had taken. The business had been quite successful in the three years she had been operating. Alissa felt that having a web site would allow her to display the range of photographs and styles to a wider audience more effectively and help generate new orders and commissions. Her business was called Ford Photographs, but Alissa knew that she did not want to have a web site with an address that was that long. So she decided to simply call it Ford and www.ford.co.uk would be perfect as a web site address, she thought.

## Objectives

● To understand the meaning of the term 'domain'.

● To understand the process involved in buying and registering a domain name.

● To understand the meaning of web hosting.

● To appreciate that web hosting can be done via a network or a server.

## edexcel ⣿ key terms

**Domain name** – the means by which a business can provide a unique identity for its web site that its stakeholders can recognise and associate with the business.

## What is a domain name?

A **domain name** is the unique way that a business's online presence is presented to its stakeholders. It provides the identity for the business. It also provides customers and other stakeholders with the means of finding and accessing the business quickly and easily. For many businesses the domain name will have something to do with the name of the actual business, but not always. For example, B&Q has the domain name www.diy.com. There may be good reasons for this. One might be that using an ampersand (&) in a web address can cause some problems, but it might also be that the domain name 'B&Q' was not available to use.

In the case of B&Q the domain name chosen does have something to do with the business. It may also be that many people might use 'DIY' as a term in a search engine and that is most likely to link through to B&Q. It is usual to try and get a domain name that relates to the specific business. For example, Manchester United's web address is www.manutd.com. The club is likely to have chosen this domain name because it is short and easy to remember, as well as identifying the club. The longer it is the more likely users are to make mistakes typing the address into a web browser. Imagine if the address was www.manchesterunitedfootballclub.com

## Some basics in choosing a domain name

Having a short and easy to remember domain name means that users will be more likely to be able to remember it and thus get back to the site more easily. The domain name can also be incorporated into e-mail addresses, which again help to market the business. For example, if one of Alissa's business e-mail addresses was contactford@tiscali.com then the promotion would be for the brand Tiscali rather than for Alissa's business. Compare this to 'contact@manutd.com'. Here it is clear that the business concerned is Manchester United.

The key things to think about in choosing a domain name, therefore, are to try to:

• make it as easy to remember as possible;

• make sure that the name is as directly related to the business as possible;

• make it so that as many people as possible will get to the site easily - even if they make some basic errors in the name;

• think carefully about the type of domain name extension - do you want .co.uk, .com, .net, .org, .eu or any other? If the business is international then .co.uk might be of benefit in identifying to users that the business is based in the UK or it may be seen as being a disadvantage in that it is too small or 'local'. In addition these extensions tend to vary in the degree to which they are familiar to users - few people will recognise .tv for example;

- avoid a name that is similar to another (possibly larger) well known business.

Alissa used a search engine to find out how to get a domain name. There was plenty of information. She found a company called ukdomains.com that sold domain names and entered 'www.ford.co.uk' into the search facility, as illustrated in Figure 1. She was rather surprised when the search results came up and a list appeared in red with all the names already taken. Then she realised that, of course, there was the Ford Motor Company and that they had probably already registered the Ford name.

There is a number of companies that will register a domain name, but because there are now so many people wanting to register names, there is an organisation that oversees and manages domain name registration. **NOMINET** is a not for profit limited company that maintains a register of UK domain names and carries out other services that help the Internet run smoothly. Domain names need managing so that duplicates are not made which could cause confusion. It is possible, as Alissa found out, that the desired name a business wants to register has already been registered by someone else around the world. Some people have specifically bought popular domain names in the hope that they can then sell them back to businesses for a profit.

Alissa had to rethink her domain name. She decided on Fordphotos and found that this was available. She also found that the extensions .co.uk, .org.uk, .biz and .uk.com were all available but that .com and .net were not. She decided that she would initially use .co.uk but that she would also register .biz and .com.uk as well. She did this so that she had the flexibility in the future to expand her web presence and also to help prevent others from taking a name that was similar to hers. The price she had to pay for the registration ranged from £9.99 for two years to over £60. It seemed that if the registration was a universal one such as .net this was more expensive.

Assuming that the name is available, a business like Alissa's can lease the name for a fixed period of time, usually a year, with the right to extend the lease after that time. If the lease is not extended then the name will expire and later will become available for registration by others. She had to complete various forms to register her domain name and then received confirmation that her name had been registered.

## Hosting

The next stage in the process was to find a way of **hosting** her web pages. Hosting means having a server that stores web pages. Alissa knew that she could buy her own web server and network, but this was an extremely expensive and quite complicated process. A number of large companies do have their own servers and networks but they can afford to employ specialist staff to manage their systems. The more appropriate option for a relatively small business like Alissa's was to use an Internet Service Provider (ISP) and host her site on their server. An ISP host provides a service; they will rent space on their server for storing web pages. The ISP takes the responsibility for maintenance, security and upgrades and this seemed to be the most cost-effective method for Alissa.

Alissa found out that there was a large number of companies that provided such a service. She had to carry out some research about what to look for in finding a good host. There were three main things she was looking for.

**Price** What price did they charge for the service they were offering? For a small business this might be a very important consideration but on its own it is not sufficient. There is a number of free web hosting services but Alissa had found out that these were not always good value especially for a business. They tended to

**Figure 1** – An example of a business that will sell domain names

Source: http://www.names.co.uk

**edexcel** ::: **key terms**

**NOMINET** – the organisation that manages domain names and registration for UK domains.

**Hosting** – renting space on a server to store web pages. The host is the company that rents space.

116

have lots of pop-up advertising and were often slow so she was advised to steer clear of them. She found out that the average price for hosting a web site was between £10 and £30 per month depending on the number of features and the quality of the service. The price charged has to be balanced against other factors.

**The range of features that the host provided** Alissa knew that she would have to upload new content to her site; that she wanted to have the facility for **e-commerce** on the site which included **secure access** for customers. (This can be checked because when using an e-commerce facility the web address should have an 's' after the http - https:// - to indicate that customers can be confident their credit card details are secure.)

Alissa also wanted to make sure that she could have access to **sufficient space** to host her site. This was very important to her because of the amount of images that were on her site. If she wanted to use Flash animations or have video then these would also use up bandwidth so it was important to choose a host that provided sufficient space.

Alissa had also been told by a friend to make sure that the host offered the facility to **run scripts** that enable users to do a range of things. These scripts are parts of the computer language that trigger certain processes. This might include filling out forms, taking part in forums, ordering a product or running regular updates. Alissa had to make sure that she found a host that offered this facility.

Finally, Alissa wanted to make sure that she could have **various e-mail accounts** linked to her web site. She wanted to have separate e-mail accounts to process orders, receive queries, ask for information, monitor administration issues and so on. The host she chose would have to be able to provide these sorts of services. The more services and features she wanted, the higher the price was likely to be, but Alissa thought that this was worth it to ensure safety, security and quality of her site to her users.

**The level of customer service** Alissa was not experienced in using web sites and even less so in the technical aspects of running a site. Her naivety over the domain name had clearly highlighted this point. It was important to her that the host she went with had an excellent customer service facility. She wanted access to FAQs to help her but also to make sure that she had access to 24-hour support. She would never know when a problem would arise and she did not want to lose potential customers because of a technical problem that took too long to solve.

**edexcel :::: key terms**

**E-commerce** – the facility on a web site to allow customers to buy products or services.

## Transferring web pages

Alissa finally settled on an ISP and completed all the documentation and payments for the service she was going to receive. She then had to transfer all her web pages to her ISP's server. Here again she came up against a choice. She could have used what is called FTP (File Transfer Protocol). FTP is a common way of transferring files but it can lead to security issues. Usernames and passwords can be identified by third parties. A more secure way of uploading her pages was through SSH (Secure Shell) programs. Using this method meant that the data transfer was secure so she decided to choose this method.

## Summary

Creating the right web site is not just a case of making sure the pages look good and do what the business wants them to do. There are plenty of other considerations to take into account not least the support and services of the host and making sure that the domain name is appropriate. If it is not then no matter how good the web site, if there are not enough people visiting there will be a limit to the extent to which it will be successful.

### Test yourself

1. Which **one** of the following is the best definition of 'domain name'? It:

    A  *is a unique means of identifying a business on the web*
    B  *shows where the business originates from*
    C  *is the home page of a businesses web site*
    D  *tells the user the name of the owner of the business*

    Select **one** answer.

2. An important consideration in choosing a domain name is:

    A  *making the name long to ensure it is distinctive*
    B  *ensuring that it can easily be translated into a variety of other languages*
    C  *making it no more than 20 characters long*
    D  *trying to avoid a name that is too much like other businesses*

    Select **one** answer.

3. A domain name needs managing because:

    A  *it gives web site users the chance to locate a web address*
    B  *without it the Internet would crash*
    C  *it prevents duplication of names and possible confusion*
    D  *the database has to be located in a central place directed by the government*

    Select **one** answer.

## Over to you

Krystyna and Jerzy had come to the UK from Poland and had set up in business selling Polish food in Luton. There was a reasonably large Polish population in the area both due to recent migration and from the period after the Second World War. The business was called Kielbasa, named after a Polish sausage and the pair had found that the domain name 'kielbasa' was available to register. They had produced their own web site and were very pleased with the result. The main aim of the web site was to provide information which included recipes for traditional Polish meals and details of the different types of ingredients that are used in these meals. They hoped that the site would encourage people to come to the shop to buy the ingredients and also help spread information about the Polish culture and lifestyle.

The pair found a free web hosting site and decided to make use of it. The other option was to use an ISP to host their web site but they felt that the price that was being charged, £20 per month, was too expensive. They managed to get their web site up and running but soon ran into problems. People came into the shop and complained that the site took a very long time to load and that there was a number of very annoying pop up adverts that kept appearing. Krystyna and Jerzy began to wonder whether the free hosting represented false economy.

1. Explain the meaning of the term 'web hosting'. (3)

2. Identify **two** advantages that Krystyna and Jerzy would have gained from choosing a paid-for web hosting service. (2)
3. Explain how the advantages you have identified in Question 2 above would benefit Krystyna and Jerzy's management of their web site. (6)

## ResultsPlus
### Build Better Answers

Which **two** of the following are important features that a business should consider in its choice of host?

A  That the host is a well known Internet company
B  That it is possible to disable e-commerce facilities to increase security
C  Ensuring there is sufficient space for the site to develop and expand
D  That there is a limited number of e-mail accounts to prevent confusion
E  That the host can offer secure e-commerce facilities
F  That the host also provides free server hardware
G  That the price charged is as low as possible

**Answer C and E**

Technique guide: This is a question asking you to choose two correct options from a choice of seven. It is important that you try to eliminate the obviously wrong ones first - so go through them all carefully.

Think: Try to recall what the three important main features of choosing a web host are - price, features and customer service.

Then: Look through each option.

It does not matter how well known the host is - it is the quality of the service they offer. Few businesses want to disable e-commerce facilities and in any event, how would this improve security?

It is not how low the price is - again, the business has to balance out the costs with the quality of the service they require.

This means that A, B and G can be discounted. ■

This leaves you with C, D, E and F - two from four.

D is not right because a business wants the flexibility of having a larger number of e-mail accounts at its disposal if possible. F is nonsense but uses the term 'server hardware', which might sound persuasive. ■

This leaves C and E as the remaining options. Most businesses will want to expand and having a web site that is also capable of expanding as the business grows is definitely important. Equally, if the business is intending to sell online then having a secure e-commerce facility is going to be vital to encourage customers to have the confidence of spending online.

So, C and E are the correct answers. ▲

# 23 Legal obligations of web sites

## Case Study

Michael Dykes had always been good at art and design technology at school. He also had a skill with computers. So when he decided to leave school and set up his own business few of his friends and family were surprised. Michael set up a business selling chicken houses. The houses were quite ornate and much more attractive to look at than traditional chicken runs. Michael had used his design skills to the full in producing the chicken houses. After demonstrating them at a local county agricultural show he received a large number of phone enquiries from prospective buyers. He decided to set up a web site to promote his business further and looked forward to getting to grips with the design of his site. He also decided that he would use his IT skills to set up a database to gather the names of possible customers. He planned to include a requirement that customers register on the site and give some personal details. This would allow him to build up a picture of the sort of people visiting his site and who might be possible customers.

## Objectives

● To appreciate that web sites have a number of legal obligations that have to be adhered to.

● To understand that these legal obligations extend to accessibility, data protection, copyright, consumer legislation and privacy.

● To understand how the legislation can affect the design and functionality of a web site.

**edexcel ::: key terms**

**Legislation** – the laws passed by national and international governments that businesses (and everyone else!) must adhere to.

## What is legislation?

In the UK as in most countries, governments pass laws. These laws help to provide rules by which people can live. Most laws are passed to give help, support and protection to people who, individually, may not be able to help themselves or protect themselves. The growth of the Internet has presented governments with new issues and problems which require laws, or **legislation**, to meet and overcome these challenges. This section will look at how some existing laws have an effect on how businesses set up and use web sites and how new laws have been passed to address particular issues that have developed, partly, but not exclusively, because of the growth in the use of the Internet.

## Issues with web site designs

Michael set about the task of designing his web site with enthusiasm. His ideas were really flowing and he could hardly wait to get them down on paper. The idea of using the animation of a chicken house which the user could gradually open up with a simple click of the mouse to look inside and get the detail of the construction was particularly good, he thought. He wanted to attract attention to his latest deals. So he thought a flashing, starred banner detailing these would really draw in customers' attention. He would also have a scrolling 'ticker' across the top to give prospective customers other news. He further aimed to attract their attention by having bright colours. The idea of having a video clip that showed how the houses were built and how to keep chickens was a must. He had already worked on this and had produced a 20-minute masterpiece. He had found a number of other images of chickens from Google Images and thought they were perfect for illustrating his site.

Michael then set about work on the database. He decided on the appropriate fields and the information he wanted customers to input. He had heard that there was money to be made in sharing customer details. Michael wanted to design the database to make sure that he had plenty of information that would be useful to other businesses.

**Table 1** – Potential problems with website design

- Bright colours - all very well, but what if your users are colour blind?
- What about the degree of contrast in the colours that he intended to use?
- How would the site, as designed, look to users who were partially sighted or totally blind?
- The video - few people would view for 2 minutes never mind 20. In addition, how would those who were hard of hearing be able to follow the video?
- The animation - how would partially sighted people know what was going on in the animation?
- Mouse clicks - what if the user was unable to use a mouse or did not have access to one?
- Tickers and flashing banners - had Michael considered how this might affect people who suffered from epilepsy? In any event, flashing signs and tickers were often seen as being annoying and irritating by many users.
- The Images - had he acquired permission from the copyright holders to use the images for a commercial enterprise?
- The data gathering -had Michael thought about the security of the data he collected? Did he realise that there were strict laws on the way in which data can be gathered, stored, used and shared?

At the same time that the design for the pages began to take shape, Michael had been investigating hiring a firm of web developers to do the work of constructing the site for him. His clear ideas on what he wanted would make it much easier for them to do the work, he thought. He finally chose a company and thought that it was time to reveal his grand designs. The developer he was going to be working with was called Ian. Michael arrived at Ian's office and proudly unwrapped his sheets of designs from the cardboard tube he had brought them in.

The next three hours were very uncomfortable for Michael. Ian looked at the designs and highlighted a large number of things that he advised Michael not to do. Some of these seemed to totally kill off his great ideas. Michael was shocked. He thought he knew a great deal about design, but in the context of a web site some of those principles were clearly not applicable. Table 1 shows some of the issues.

Michael left the meeting under no illusions that his enthusiasm had run away with him. The comments that Ian had made were very logical and Michael could see the importance of the points raised. The problem was, he realised, that he was simply not aware enough of the laws and directives relating to the use of web sites. Ian had also made him realise that to meet the various accessibility guidelines and legislation in existence would mean quite significant changes to the way the site was designed and how it would have to look. Michael also realised that the cost of developing the site would rise by a relatively large amount. Ian tried to counter this by pointing out that if he was sued because of breaking the law then the additional cost of the development was going to be small in comparison. So it made sense for Michael to take the points Ian had raised into consideration now, rather than later.

## How laws affect website design

Michael decided to get some further information on the main laws he would have to adhere to. They would affect his web site in a number of ways.

Businesses must create web sites that are accessible to people with disabilities

**ResultsPlus**
**Watch Out!**

There are lots of things that a business has to consider when setting up a web site. Some of these are considerations that can depend on the type of business and the product/service in question. However, businesses HAVE to abide by the law. If they choose to ignore the law or claim they did not know the law then this is no defence against legal action.

120

**Accessibility Accessibility** means making sure that anyone, whatever their physical or mental condition, is able to access, get onto and use (in this case) a web site. The main laws that cover this issue are The Disability Discrimination Act (DDA) and the Special Educational Needs and Disability Act (SENDA). The DDA states: 'a person has a disability if he has a physical or mental impairment which has a substantial and long-term adverse effect on his ability to carry out normal day-to-day activities'. (Source: http://www.opsi.gov.uk/acts/acts1995/ukpga_19950050_en_2#pt1-l1g1). The legislation gives the responsibility to businesses that have web sites to ensure that the services that it provides are accessible to all users regardless of their physical or mental state. This means that those who have hearing or visual impairments, those who are wheelchair bound, who may have physical deformities or maybe have lost the use of limbs must be given the opportunity to access a web site and all its features in the same way that an able bodied person can.

Users who have a visual impairment might use a **text-to-speech reader** in conjunction with their computer. This is a piece of software that converts written text into spoken words. What is on a web site, therefore, must be capable of being read by a text-to-speech reader - and make sense! That means that if the user scrolls their mouse over an image, the text-to-speech reader has to be able to identify the image to the user. This is done through the provision of '**alt-text**' which are written words describing the image.

Users with a **hearing impairment** will need to have audio transcribed so that they can read what is happening in the audio clip or video clip. Imagine the problem for such users with Michael's proposed 20 minute video 'masterpiece'. In addition, care must be taken with the **colours** used on a web site to make sure that those who may be colour blind are not discriminated against. This means using well defined contrasts in colours especially with regards to the use of words and the background colour on which they are presented.

The designer of a web site cannot take for granted the assumption that everyone who uses the site will be able to use a mouse let alone to be able to 'click' or 'scroll'. If you were not able to use a mouse for some reason (maybe because you had lost limbs or had severe arthritis) then a request on a web page to 'click to confirm purchase' would not be that easy. This means that businesses have to consider how they are going to provide the means by which such disabilities are catered for so that those suffering them are not discriminated against. Businesses must make every effort to ensure that they have made sites as accessible as

possible, therefore.

A web developer can check the degree to which a site is accessible by using the guidelines and checklist issued by the W3C. This organisation has three checklists of differing degrees of rigour from the bare minimum (Priority 1) to the most rigorous (Priority 3).

**Data protection** The gathering, use and storage of data is governed by the Data Protection Act (DPA). The DPA gives individuals the right to find out what information about them an organisation has in its possession. The increased use of the Internet and the web by business has meant that companies have been able to collect large amounts of data about the users of its web site and services.

Take Amazon, for example. Every time a customer browses the site or buys a product the company is able to gather a large amount of information about the user. This includes who they are, their interests, buying habits, preferences, home address, contact details and credit card information. Such a service is incredibly useful to customers. It allows Amazon to provide individual services to its customers to make sure they are kept up to date with products they are interested in and not bombard them with products they are not interested in.

However, Amazon, like every other business, has a responsibility to use the data it has collected within the law as laid down by the DPA. The main points of this law are shown in Table 2. The DPA can be a very confusing Act, but

**Table 2** – How the Data Protection Act affects businesses

- Any data must be processed fairly and lawfully - gathering information by deceit when the user does not know, for example, may not be considered fair.
- Any information gathered can be used for specific purposes. This means that sharing information might not be allowed and cannot be used for purposes other than that for which it was gathered.
- Users can be asked relevant and appropriate information to the purpose for which it is to be used - but no more. Excessive gathering of information is not allowed.
- The information gathered must be kept up-to-date to ensure it is accurate.
- Information must be kept no longer than is necessary - this means that in some cases data on customers must be destroyed after a period of time.
- Any information gathered must not infringe an individual's rights.
- Information must be kept secure.
- Information gathered cannot be transferred to countries outside the European Economic Area unless certain measures are imposed and agreed.

edexcel ::: key terms

**Accessibility** – making sure that anyone, whatever their physical or mental condition, is able to access the services of a business.

it is an important one. The consequences of ignoring it can be severe, not only because of the possibility of legal action, but also in the loss of trust that a business might experience if it misuses data.

**Copyright** Copyright is a legal right for the creator of an idea, work of art or literature, image, musical material or filmed work to produce and control that work for a specified period of time. This means that businesses must ensure that they have the rights to use images, video clips, music and so on, used on the site. If a business wants to use a piece of copyrighted material such as a piece of music for a soundtrack, then they must get permission from the copyright holder. This can often mean having to pay a sum of money for the right to do so. If a business tried to use a picture, for example, without the permission of the copyright holder, then they could be open to legal action and be sued for damages.

Copyright, like the DPA, is a complex area. There are lawyers who specialise in this field. The greater use of the web has increased the issues that arise with peer-to-peer file sharing and sites such as You Tube facing challenges about the way that copyrighted material is used. Some sites that began as free music sharing sites like Napster have been forced to close down and re-invent themselves to keep within the law.

**Consumer legislation** Any business is obliged to abide by various pieces of consumer law such as the Sale of Goods Act, the Trade Descriptions Act, the Supply of Goods and Services Act, The Weights and Measures Act and the Consumer Credit Act. It is not necessary to know the details of these laws. They govern the way in which businesses provide goods and services to consumers so that consumers are protected. They help to ensure that if a customer buys 200 square metres of lawn turf from an online business they will, indeed, receive 200 square meters. It covers how customers can send back faulty goods, or goods that are not as described (for example, photographs on a web site showing a luxurious holiday destination when in fact the place is a building site), that any credit agreements adhere to strict guidelines and that customers have the right to replacements, refunds or compensation in the event that goods are not fit for purpose or of appropriate quality.

These laws apply to all businesses. Businesses trading online are not exempt from these laws and so consideration has to be given to making sure the laws are adhered to and that consumers are aware of their rights when using a web site and buying online.

**Electronic Communications and Privacy** The development of the Internet has opened up new ways in which businesses can reach customers. So-called guerrilla marketing and viral marketing make use of electronic communications such as e-mail to very quickly spread the word about a business and market it. There are, of course, plenty of legitimate uses of such new techniques but inevitably there are those that will abuse the opportunities and cause problems. Spam messaging, attempts to commit fraud through scams, phishing (where bogus messages are sent from banks or credit card companies asking the user to provide confirmation of their personal details, pin numbers and account information which is then used to access the account) and e-mails that the user has not agreed to receive are all examples of how electronic communication can be abused by businesses.

In the UK the Information Commissioner's Office is working with other international organisations to try and reduce the incidence of these types of problems. The Privacy and Electronic Communications Regulations details the rules which companies must adhere to in contacting individuals and the rights of those individuals. Legal action can be taken against those who breach the regulations but to date few businesses have been taken to court and successfully prosecuted. The very nature of the web makes it difficult to catch businesses that do break the rules!

## The effect of legislation on a business

The main effect of any legislation related to web sites and their use in business is likely to be that the cost of developing and managing the web site will increase. This is because additional features will have to be built into the site to ensure that it does meet the legal requirements laid down.

In addition, costs will rise because businesses have to ensure that they take steps to protect data. There have been some high profile cases of businesses which have had databases hacked. This means that criminals are able to access the data and if they do, the information can be used for a variety of criminal purposes including fraudulent use of credit cards, selling personal data and identify theft. If such a breach of security happens then businesses can lose the trust of their customers and sales and profits can fall quickly. In April 2007, for example, the retailer TK Maxx announced that it had had its computer systems hacked and that data relating to 45 million customers' payment cards had been accessed by the hackers.

## edexcel ▦ key terms

**Copyright** – the legal right for the creator of an idea, work of art or literature, image, musical material or filmed work to produce and control that work for a specified period of time.

**Viral marketing** – using the power of the Internet to spread information about a business through a reliance on individuals sending on the message to friends and colleagues.

**Guerrilla marketing** – the use of non-traditional methods to make consumers aware of a product through, for example, chat rooms, forums, discussion boards, e-mail, blogs and Yellow Pages.

## Test yourself

1. What is the main reason why governments pass laws which affect businesses? Select **one** answer.?

   **A** *The government want to raise as much in taxes as possible*

   **B** *Laws help to provide businesses with new customers*

   **C** *Laws are put in place to protect consumers*

   **D** *Laws are passed because they help reduce business costs*

2. Which **one** of the following would be **most likely** to break the law relating to Data Protection?

   **A** *Asking a customer buying a product online for their address and telephone number*

   **B** *Encrypting customer databases so that the information could not be hacked*

   **C** *Destroying the data records of a one-off customer of a hire car business after six months*

   **D** *Getting as much information as possible about the customer and their lifestyle when asked to register to receive a newsletter*

3. The design for a business web site is governed by certain laws. Which **two** of the following are factors related to these laws?

   **A** *The ethnic origin of the prospective web site user*

   **B** *Whether the user has access to broadband*

   **C** *Whether permission is needed to host a video clip of a TV advert*

   **D** *Whether users like fluorescent colours or not*

   **E** *The religious conviction of possible users*

   **F** *The ease with which users who might be deaf can hear audio files*

### ResultsPlus
### Build Better Answers

1 (a) Identify one legal consideration that a business needs to take in creating a web site. (1)

(b) Explain one possible consequence to the business if it did not take notice of the legal consideration you have identified in 1 (a) above. (3)

Technique guide: This is effectively one question split into two parts. In the first you are being asked to recall some knowledge and in part two to offer an explanation to highlight how ignoring the law might affect a business.

Think: Think carefully about both parts of the question. Try to choose a legal issue that you can easily explain in part (b).

■ **Basic** Identifies one possible legal consideration but offers no further comment or explanation. (1)

● **Good** Identifies one legal consideration and offers some explanation on how it might affect a business if it ignored the law. For example, it could lead to legal action against the business or it might put some potential users/customers off the site. (2-3)

▲ **Excellent** Identifies one legal consideration and provides an explanation that makes at least three links regarding the impact on the business. For example, legal action could be taken, the business could be sued which in turn might cost the business large sums of money and even cause it to have to close down. (4)

## Over to you

This chapter has outlined how Michael's initial enthusiasm for the design of his web site led to him making a number of mistakes in the plans for his design. Go back over the plans that Michael initially had on page 118 and using the points raised by Ian on page 119, make a list of the main ideas that Michael originally had that are likely to conflict with the laws covered in this chapter.

Using the information from the W3C organisation below, outline how Michael might keep some of his ideas alive but modify them to make his web site more accessible. You can get more information on how to do this from the W3C organisation at http://www.w3.org/WAI/quicktips/

1. Images & animations: Use the alt attribute to describe the function of each visual.

2. Image maps. Use the client-side map and text for hotspots.

3. Multimedia. Provide captioning and transcripts of audio, and descriptions of video.

4. Hypertext links. Use text that makes sense when read out of context. For example, avoid "click here."

5. Page organization. Use headings, lists, and consistent structure. Use CSS for layout and style where possible.

6. Graphs & charts. Summarize or use the 'longdesc' attribute.

7. Scripts, applets, & plug-ins. Provide alternative content in case active features are inaccessible or unsupported.

8. Frames. Use the 'noframes' element and meaningful titles.

9. Tables. Make line-by-line reading sensible. Summarize.

10. Check your work. Validate. Use tools, checklist, and guidelines at http://www.w3.org/TR/WCAG

# 24 Successful business web sites

## Case Study

Mithali and Ian both enjoyed using the coffee bar near to their workplaces. Mithali worked for a company selling office supplies. The business traditionally sold its goods through the distribution of catalogues to businesses throughout the country, but had developed a web site five years ago and the way that people ordered goods had now changed. Ian worked for a motor vehicle support service. The company provided advice on all aspects of owning a motor vehicle, from legal advice on motoring issues to insurance advice and information on the reliability and value for money of garage services. His company also had a web site. When they were talking one day, they realised just how much their businesses had changed as a result of having an online presence. The changes, however, were very different for each of them.

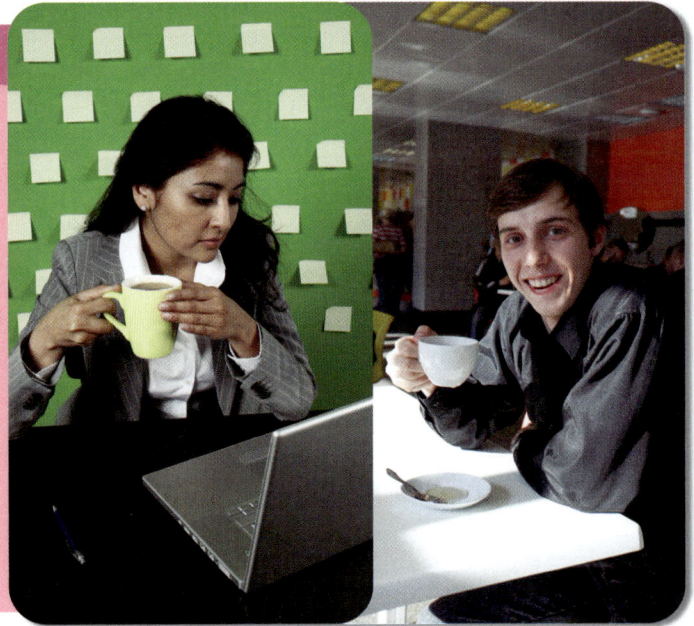

## Objectives

● To understand that 'success' can mean different things to different businesses.

● To understand the key ways of measuring the success of a business web site.

### edexcel ⣿ key terms

**Success** – the achievement of a goal set.

**Brand** – a means by which a business creates an identity for a product or service that enables customer to associate or recognise the product more effectively.

## What is success?

Most businesses will set up a web site with a specific purpose in mind. In some cases it will be to try to boost sales. For some it will be to provide information and others will have a combination. Some business web sites will aim to try and help promote the business with the information that they have on the site. Others will be keen to provide a means by which customers can be in touch with them 24 hours a day.

The **success** of a web site has to be measured against the main purpose it was set up for and what the business hoped to achieve as a result of setting up its site. For example, if a business set up a site with the intention of driving sales, to get a measure of how successful this would be would require the business to have some idea of what the increase in sales would be that would be seen as being 'successful'. If it set a target of increasing sales by 40%, but the web site had led to a rise in sales of 60%, then the business could argue that the site had been a success. If sales grew by 35% it might not believe that the web site had been as successful as it had hoped.

## Judging success

There is a number of different ways in which the success of a business web site can be measured.

**An increase in brand awareness** A **brand** is a means by which a business is able to create an identity for its product so that consumers have something that they associate the business with. The more aware a consumer is of a brand and what it stands for and represents, the more likely they are to choose that brand over rivals when making purchasing decisions. Being able to promote the brand via the web means that the number of potential customers that can be reached is huge - global in fact.

One good example of how businesses use the web to build brand awareness is when new movies are released. James Bond, Star Wars, Indiana Jones, Harry Potter, The Matrix and Alien might all be films but they are also brands. Movie makers can use the power of the Internet to show tasters, run promotions, provide information about characters and plots and a whole host of additional features. Many of these would not be possible without the web. The web site is able to build interest and awareness of the movie and the brand as a whole.

**Sales from e-commerce** One of the most obvious ways of measuring success is the extent to which a web site can be used to generate sales. Many traditional businesses (often referred to as 'bricks and mortar' businesses) now have web sites which allow customers to buy products (this is called 'clicks and mortar'). John Lewis, Tesco, Argos, Sainsbury's, Asda, Toys R Us, Marks and Spencer and many others have a web site for selling products as well as their traditional shops.

Success can be measured by how much a web site contributes to the additional sales of products. For many users the availability of a web site makes shopping far more convenient and less stressful. The growth of online sales is a testament to this fact. To really make online selling successful the e-commerce facility, the means of processing sales and making payment, must be easy and convenient as well or it could put off prospective customers.

**Market reach and market share** Many small firms have found that the opportunities to reach new markets and customers have been greatly increased by the use of a web site. The development of search engines means that many more people might come across a small business web site selling products or services that previously were only available in a local area. For example, a search for 'hockey sticks' will bring up a large number of businesses offering such an item for sale. Many of these are smaller businesses who, provided they are able to deliver the products quickly and cheaply, are able to increase their market reach, sales and market share more than they would have been able to do without the web.

In addition, the development of systems that monitor web use allow firms to gather information about their customers' spending habits, behaviour and other useful information. This helps the business to tailor its marketing to its customers' needs.

One example of how a business can use the web to target markets more effectively is the use of **Google AdWords**. This is a system where businesses can create adverts that will appear on other, related, web sites. The adverts contain key words or phrases. These key words relate to the particular business, for example, a business selling toys might use key words relating to specific toys. When users enter a search term into Google if one of the search terms includes one or more of these key words the business's advert might appear next to the search results. If users then select the link to the business then it triggers a payment to Google but the business concerned is able to target specific customers who may be interested in the business more effectively.

**Meeting customer needs** The relationship between a business and its customers and wider stakeholders goes much further than the purchase of a good or service. Stakeholders want information, service and support as well as the opportunity to buy goods online. Firms like electricity and gas suppliers, water companies, rail companies and so on can give customers lots of information and provide a means to answer questions. Many firms will have an e-mail contact service to enable stakeholders to contact them 24 hours a day. Information can be given out quickly and efficiently. For example, train companies are able to warn passengers of engineering works that may be taking place and advise on alternative routes and the length of possible delays to a journey. This helps passengers plan in advance to take account of the situation.

For many businesses, a call centre is an important part of their operations. However, call centres are expensive to run and the provision of information and FAQ sections on a web site can help to reduce the pressure on call centres and

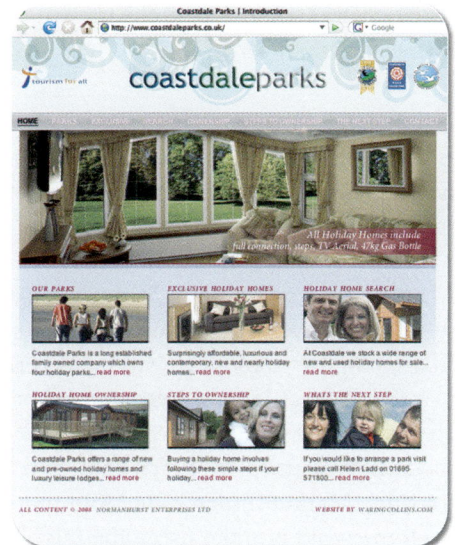

125

The opportunity to reach new markets can be increased by the use of a website

**ResultsPlus Watch Out!**
In dealing with questions asking for a judgement of success, always try to make your judgement in relation to a target. Do not just assume that any rise in sales or reduction in costs, any promotional campaign that leads to an increase in awareness, for example, represents success. Success has to be judged against the expectations that the business has of the change it makes.

**edexcel key terms**
**Market reach** – the number of potential customers a business is able to target and make contact with.
**Market share** – the proportion of total sales in a market accounted for by a particular business.

126

allow customers to access the information they are looking for far more efficiently.

## Success from different perspectives

As Mithali and Ian chatted away, they realised that they were talking about different views about the success of their respective company's web sites.

**Mithali's perspective** In Mithali's case, the company released the web site because customers were telling them that using the catalogues was inconvenient. Customers wanted to be able to browse the web site and make their choices online - the ease of using the e-commerce facilities made life much easier for customers who were often pressed for time. Market research had told the company that customers did not like using the telephone to make orders as it was often slow, especially in busy periods. The web site could be used 24 hours a day and was much quicker in processing information as well as being able to store personal account details of customers, which made payment even easier. Customers also said that ordering by post was slow and irritating; the forms that were in the catalogue were often too small to fit all the information requested in.

The release of the web site had seen sales rising by 28% a year. Further market research had showed that 72% of users had said that they preferred to use the web to make their orders and 84% said that they found it more convenient, quicker and efficient. The company bosses had been very pleased with the results of moving to a web based system although they still retained the catalogues. Mithali told Ian that around 56% of sales now came from the web site and that she could easily see the day in the not too distant future when the catalogue would be phased out.

**Ian's perspective** Ian's story was quite different. Mithali could not see how his company really benefitted from a web site nor how he could say that the web site had been a success. 'You do not sell anything through your web site' said Mithali, 'so how can you tell whether it has been a success?' Ian had to explain that the company had been very successful in building up new members. Members had to register for the site to get information but it was free. The success of his business was based on how good the information given was and how often members used that information.

Ten years ago the company had to spend large sums of money on setting up a call centre to answer member queries. At that time, to be a member individuals had to pay £50 a year. Now the service was 'free'. 'How do you make any money?' asked Mithali. Ian explained that the company had decided to abandon the membership fee because member numbers started to drop. The call centre had been very popular but it had been overwhelmed and many members complained that they had to wait too long to get their queries dealt with. Many of the queries needed to be answered quickly and using the postal service was often not good enough to help answer member queries quickly.

Now that the business had set up a web site and made membership through registration free, the change in the business was significant. The call centre had been slimmed down, partly because many of the queries members had were often the same. The web site had included a FAQ section and many members were able to find what they wanted from this section. The web site also allowed the company to post lots of other information on the site that members needed to know. The design of the web site had been thought about very carefully and the navigation was easy. Members said they were very satisfied with the ease with which they could find what they wanted to know and liked the fact that the provision of an e-mail service and the continued existence of the slimmed down call centre if they really wanted to talk to a human was a perfect combination.

The slimming down of the call centre had cut costs for the business considerably. The fact that members were getting their queries answered quickly, when they wanted them answered, was the key measure of success for the company Ian explained. In addition, the membership, measured by the number of registrations had increased by 140% and the site was receiving page accesses running at 5 million a month! The company had decided to allow the use of advertising on its site and this was generating revenue. The volume of traffic meant that other businesses in the motor industry, including insurance companies, were keen to advertise on the site because they knew they could target interested and relevant customers.

The company had also made use of a service provided by the search engine company, Google. **Google AdSense** is a system that sends through adverts to Ian's company site. The adverts it sends appear down the sides of the main pages and so are not intrusive. However, the great thing about it, Ian said, was that the adverts were all associated with his business - the motor industry. The adverts might be for companies providing motor insurance, breakdown services, maps and other travel services, motor vehicle accessories, car dealerships and many more. Whenever a user selected one of the AdSense links, Ian's company got a small amount of money. The real success of the site, he said, was that the increase in the volume of traffic to the site meant that the advertising revenue from AdSense was quite healthy and helped to maintain the business.

**Results Plus**
**Watch Out!**

Some businesses have found out that a web site might boost online sales but they have also experienced a knock-on effect in terms of falling sales in their stores - an excellent example of a trade-off.

## Summary

The conversation between Mithali and Ian highlights how different businesses have different perspectives (viewpoints) on what is meant by success in the context of a business web site. Mithali's company measures success on the basis of how many sales the web site helps to generate. Ian's company measures success on the volume of traffic that use their services - the provision of information.

There is no right answer to what a successful web site means - it means different things to different businesses. What is more certain is that the importance of the Internet and the web in helping businesses and improving their performance and success is likely to grow in the years to come and who knows how it will change and what the Internet will provide for businesses and customers in the next ten years?

## Over to you

The different perspectives offered on the success of web sites by both Ian and Mithali on page 126 highlight the fact that a successful web site means different things to different businesses. Read the two accounts carefully again.

1. Identify **one** target that Mithali's and Ian's company each appeared to have in setting up their respective web sites. (2)

2. How might each company have measured whether the setting up of their web site was a success? (3)

3. Assess **one** possible benefit and one possible cost to either Mithali's or Ian's business of having a web site. (10)

## Test yourself

1. Elicia owns an independent driving school and has set up a website to try and increase the number of enquiries she receives. She hopes the web site will increase enquiries by 50% a month. Which of the following outcomes would be considered a success? Select **one** answer.

A *The number of enquiries rises from 45 to 54 each month*
B *Enquiries increase by 47%*
C *Enquiries rise and so do appointments*
D *The number of people contacting her rises from 60 each month to 95*

2. A web site can successfully increase brand awareness by:

A *making sure every home receives a web tracker*
B *advertising the name of the business*
C *helping to create an identity for the product*
D *sending users free gifts if they visit the web site*

Select **one** answer.

3. Smaller firms may be able to benefit from having a web site because:

A *they can reach a far wider number of potential customers*
B *the market can be shared equally between large firms and small firms*
C *the market reach is more limited*
D *small businesses are better at operating web sites effectively*

Select **one** answer.

## ResultsPlus
### Build Better Answers

A successful e-commerce facility on a web site:

A provides the means for customers to view products easily
B enables customers to be able to put complaints about the web site to the company
C helps to generate sales increases of 20% a year
D is one where the sales generated is equal to or greater than the target set

**Answer D**

Technique guide: Look at all the responses first - it is sometimes worthwhile starting at the bottom and working up to avoid being caught in the trap of always going for the first option.

Think: Which options are obviously wrong and which are plausible answers? Try to recall in your mind at the outset, what e-commerce means. If you can remember that it is the means by which a business provides the opportunity to buy goods or services via a web site this will make it easier to cross out the wrong options.

Then: Go through each option - D is definitely a plausible option but think before jumping in make sure there is nothing else better. An e-commerce facility might be considered successful if it generated sales of 20% but not if the target to increase sales was 60%. C is wrong. There may be a means for customers to offer feedback on a web site but this is not what an e-commerce facility is; B is wrong. The web site allows the customer to view the product not the e-commerce facility so this is also wrong. ■

Choose: Having eliminated A, B and C, the original belief that D is correct can be confirmed. ▲

# examzone

## Know Zone: Topic 4.4
## Communicating via the web

**In this topic you have learned about:** what the Internet is, the role that business websites play in communication with their stakeholders, the fact that not every business will benefit or find a web site useful, the main steps involved in creating a simple business website, the purpose of domain names and hosting, the fact that businesses have various legal obligations in setting up and running web sites and what ways a business might use to measure the success of a web site.

## You should know...

☐ The Internet is a global network of computers that are able to exchange information.

☐ The web is a system of documents that are all linked together which can be viewed at a computer or other device such as a mobile phone or through a browser.

☐ A browser is the software that enables the user to access information and data on the web.

☐ A web server stores web pages and ensures that the page is routed to the correct IP address which is related to individual computers.

☐ Every document on the web has its own specific address called its URL which stands for Universal Resource Locator.

☐ HTML stands for HyperText Markup Language. The language tells the browser exactly what the page should look like.

☐ e-commerce is the selling of goods and service over the Internet.

☐ An online presence means having a web site where anyone, anywhere in the world is able to access and find out about the business.

☐ A web site will be set up for a variety of reasons - not just selling goods or services.

☐ Some businesses have web sites that are really dedicated to giving out information.

☐ A business has to consider who its main users are likely to be and what they will want from the web site.

☐ A website is not appropriate for every business.

☐ Setting up a web site needs consideration of the budget available, the type of content to be presented, the potential users of the site and technical considerations.

☐ Web sites need to be tested before going live to make sure they function and that the links work.

☐ Once the site is launched it is important to maintain it regularly to keep it updated.

☐ A domain name provides the identity for the business and provides customers and other stakeholders with the means of finding and accessing the business quickly and easily.

☐ Having a short and easy to remember domain name means that users will be more likely to be able to remember it.

☐ The domain name has to be registered.

☐ The web site will have to be hosted - hosting means having a server that stores web pages.

☐ In choosing a host the business has to think about price, the range of features provided and the level of customer service provided by the host.

☐ Businesses have to consider their legal obligations which relate to data protection, accessibility, copyright, consumer legislation and privacy.

☐ Meeting legal obligations adds to the cost of setting up and running a web site.

☐ A successful web site has to be measured against the main purpose it was set up for and what the business hoped to achieve as a result of setting up its site.

☐ Success might be judged by increases in brand awareness, sales from e-commerce, increases in market share and how far it meets customer needs.

☐ Different businesses will have different perspectives on the success of their web site.·

## Stretch activity

Choose three different web sites - these can be any which you are familiar with.

Go to the web site of the W3C organisation:

http://validator.w3.org/

Copy and paste the address of the web sites you have chosen into the Validator and select the 'Check' button.

Look at the results that appear on the screen. If the web site meets the basic standards of the W3C you will see a message that says:

**This document was successfully checked as XHTML 1.0 Transitional!**

However, if there are problems with the site the following message will appear:

**Errors found while checking this document as HTML 4.01 Transitional!**

There will be a list of the errors that exist on the site.

After you have checked out the validation of the three sites, go back and look at the web site again. If there are problems with the validation then the web site might not be seen by all users in the same way - some browsers, for example, might not be able to show certain parts of the site.

As a result of your investigation, write a short report on each site and consider the implications for each business of the results of the validation.

(a) Amelia runs a business called Pretty Pictures. She sells highly stylised art work which is noted for its vibrant colours. She decided to set up a web site to show the range of pictures she has through a virtual gallery. She has tried to register a number of domain names but has settled on www.amelias-pretty-pictures.biz

(i) What is meant by the term 'domain name? (1)

(ii) Explain **one** possible problem that Amelia might have with the domain name she has chosen. (3)

Think: What is a domain name? What are the main principles in registering a domain name? Has Amelia stuck to these principles? What problems could arise for users trying to type in her domain name?

| Student answer | Examiner comment | Build a better answer |
|---|---|---|
| (i) A domain name is the address for a business web site. | 🟥 A basic answer which shows some understanding but does not state the key element of a domain name. | 🔺 To really make sure the examiner knows that you understand the term, you must state the fact that a domain name provides the means by which users can identify with the web site. Use an example to illustrate - Pretty Pictures is the name of the business; this is what identifies it. |
| (ii) The domain name she has chosen includes the name of the business and as such customers can find her. The problem is that it is quite long though. | 🟠 A good answer that pin-points the main problem - the length of the name. However, it stops short of giving a little more development to get the full 3 marks. | 🔺 Develop the answer by showing how a long domain name makes it more likely that people will make mistakes typing it in and that the use of hyphens is also adding to the potential for people to get it wrong. A domain name needs to be as simple and short as possible - make this point in relation to Amelia's web site. |

## Support activity

Select three different business web sites. On each, note down the main sections of each web site. State whether each web site is primarily aimed at selling goods or services or providing information.

Prepare a table with headings, as the table on the right.

In the column for each web site give a mark out of 10 for each feature. Write a short summary of your findings and say which web site you think will be the most successful and why.

| Feature | Name of web site 1 | Name of web site 2 | Name of web site 3 |
|---|---|---|---|
| Use of colour | | | |
| Navigation | | | |
| Ease of finding goods | | | |
| Payment methods | | | |
| Information for users | | | |
| Attractiveness of site | | | |

## Practice Exam Questions

Ryan Jones had set up a web site with the intention of selling second hand refurbished games consoles. Ryan had always been good with computers and machines and enjoyed the actual job of cleaning older units and making sure they worked properly to be able to sell them. The success of games consoles was something that was global but Ryan knew that there were people who could not afford to pay full price for new consoles. He sold the units for half the price they were new. His web site was called ryansrefurbished.co.uk

He had negotiated a deal with an international firm of couriers so that he could ship the units to anywhere in the world. The web site displayed all the models that he had available at any one time along with the purchase details and shipping costs and times. After two years Ryan found that he simply could not keep up with the number of e-mails he received through the 'contact' section of the web site asking for particular consoles. He was able to sell all the machines he refurbished but could not handle the demand himself. He was not sure whether he wanted to expand because he enjoyed working on his own and being his own boss. Any bigger and the business would not be the extension of his hobby it originally started out as.

**(a)** Identify **two** possible measures of success that Ryan might best use to judge his web site. (2)

A  Whether people recognised him in the street.
B  The number of sales that he makes.
C  The amount it costs to host the web site.
D  The feedback he gets from customers.
E  Whether the colours he chose were cool.
F  Whether people around the world would be able to see his site.
G  The number of pop-up screens he could include on the site.

**(b)** Describe **one** advantage to Ryan's business of having an online presence. (3)

**(c)** (i) Using the passage, identify **one** possible disadvantage to Ryan of having a web site. (1)
    (ii) For the disadvantage explain the possible effect on Ryan's business. (3)

**(d)** Ryan thought carefully about his domain name before registering ryansrefurbishment.co.uk. In your opinion is this a good domain name? Justify your answer. (6)

# Welcome to examzone

Revising for your exams can sometimes be a scary prospect. In this section of the book we'll take you through the best way of revising for your exams, step-by-step, to help you prepare as well as you can.

## Zone In!

Have you ever had that same feeling in any activity in your life when a challenging task feels easy, and you feel totally absorbed in the task, without worrying about all the other issues in your life? This is a feeling familiar to many athletes and performers, and is one that they strive hard to recreate in order to perform at their very best. It's a feeling of being 'in the zone'.

On the other hand, we all know what it feels like when our brains start running away with us in pressurised situations and can say lots of unhelpful things like 'I've always been bad at exams', or 'I know I am going to forget everything I thought I knew when I look at the exam paper'.

The good news is that 'being in the zone' can be achieved by taking some steps in advance of the exam. Here are our top tips on getting 'into the zone'.

## UNDERSTAND IT

Understand the exam process and what revision you need to do. This will give you confidence but also help you to put things into proportion. These pages are a good place to find some starting pointers for performing well at exams.

## COMPARTMENTALISE

You might not be able to deal with all issues. For example, you may be worried about an ill friend, or just be afraid of the exam. In this case, you can employ a useful technique of putting all of these things into an imagined box in your mind at the start of your revision (or in the exam) and mentally locking it, then opening it again at the end of your revision session.

## DEAL WITH DISTRACTIONS

Think about the issues in your life that may interfere with revision. Write them all down. Then think about how you can deal with each so they don't affect your revision.

## BUILD CONFIDENCE

Use your revision time not just to revise content, but to build your confidence for tackling the examination.

## FRIENDS AND FAMILY

Make sure that they know when you want to revise and even share your revision plan with them. Help them to understand that you must not get distracted. Set aside quality time with them, when you aren't revising and when you aren't worrying about what you should be doing.

## DIET AND EXERCISE

Make sure you eat well and exercise. If your body is not in the right state, how can your mind be?

More on the Active Teach CD

# Planning Zone

The key to success in exams and revision often lies in the right planning. Knowing what you need to do and when you need to do it is your best path to a stress-free experience. Here are some top tips in creating a great personal revision plan.

First of all, know your strengths and weaknesses. Go through each topic making a list of how well you think you know the topic. Use your mock examination results and any further tests that are available to you as a check on your self-assessment. This will help you to plan your personal revision effectively by putting a little more time into your weaker areas. Importantly, make sure you do not just identify strengths and weaknesses in your knowledge of the content but also in terms of exam technique – what aspects of the assessment objectives are you weakest on, for example?

## Next, create your plan!
Use the guidelines across the page to help you.

## Finally, follow the plan!
You can use the sections in the following pages to kick-start your revision and for some great ideas for helping you to revise and remember key points.

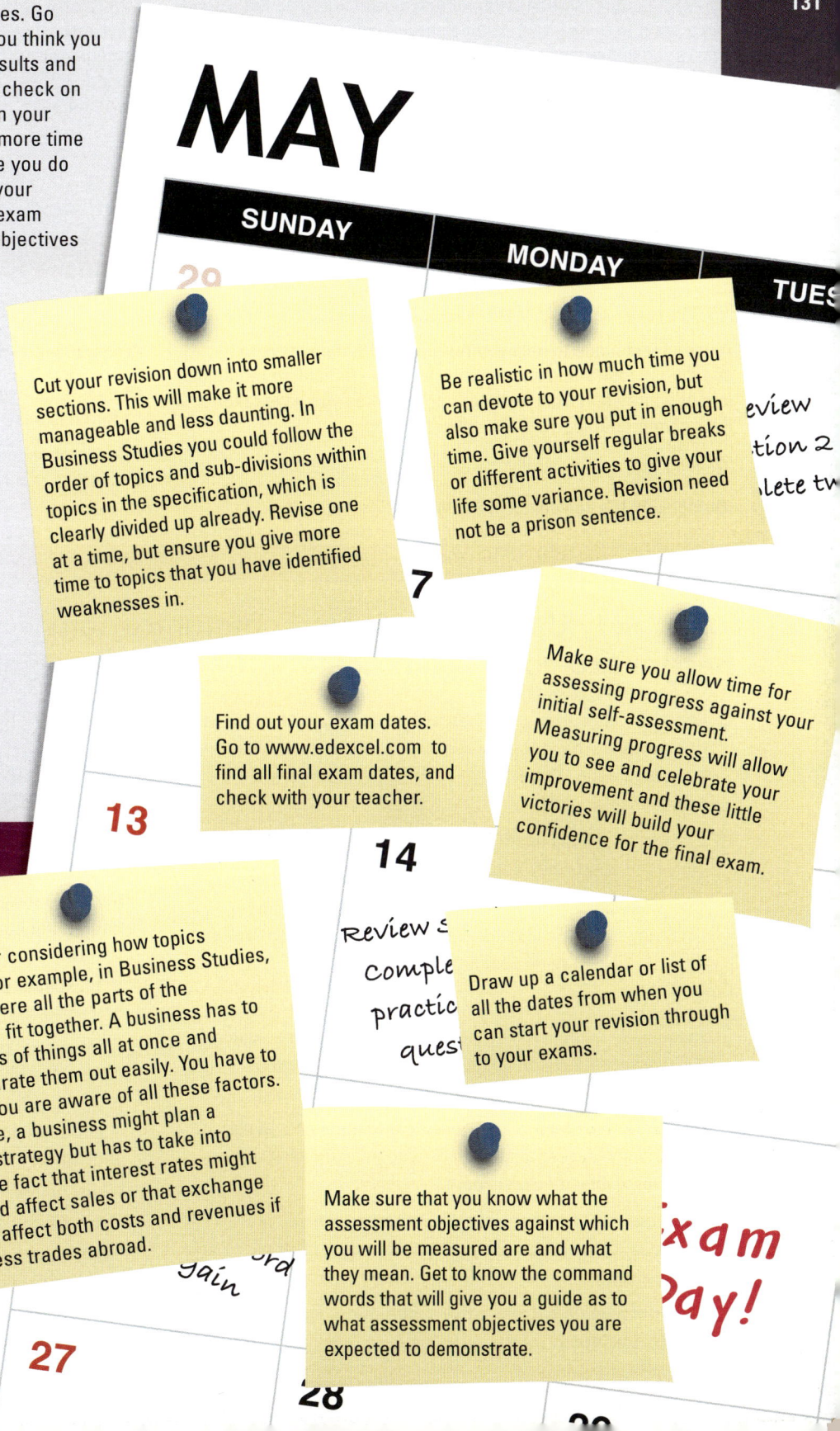

More on the Active Teach CD

# MAY

### SUNDAY

### MONDAY

### TUES

Cut your revision down into smaller sections. This will make it more manageable and less daunting. In Business Studies you could follow the order of topics and sub-divisions within topics in the specification, which is clearly divided up already. Revise one at a time, but ensure you give more time to topics that you have identified weaknesses in.

Be realistic in how much time you can devote to your revision, but also make sure you put in enough time. Give yourself regular breaks or different activities to give your life some variance. Revision need not be a prison sentence.

Find out your exam dates. Go to www.edexcel.com to find all final exam dates, and check with your teacher.

Make sure you allow time for assessing progress against your initial self-assessment. Measuring progress will allow you to see and celebrate your improvement and these little victories will build your confidence for the final exam.

Make time for considering how topics interrelate. For example, in Business Studies, try to see where all the parts of the specification fit together. A business has to deal with lots of things all at once and cannot separate them out easily. You have to show that you are aware of all these factors. For example, a business might plan a marketing strategy but has to take into account the fact that interest rates might change and affect sales or that exchange rates may affect both costs and revenues if the business trades abroad.

Draw up a calendar or list of all the dates from when you can start your revision through to your exams.

Make sure that you know what the assessment objectives against which you will be measured are and what they mean. Get to know the command words that will give you a guide as to what assessment objectives you are expected to demonstrate.

# Know Zone

In this section you'll find some useful suggestions about how to structure your revision for each of the main topics. You might want to skim-read this before starting your revision planning, to help you think about the best way to revise the content. Different people learn in different ways – some remember visually and therefore might want to think about using diagrams and other drawings for their revision. Others remember better through sound or through writing things out. Some people work best alone, whereas others work best when bouncing ideas off friends on the same course. Try to think about what works best for you by trialling a few methods for the first topic.

Remember that each part of the specification could be tested, so revise it all.

## Writing revision plans

A useful technique to help you revise important points is to summarise topics into short points. It can be difficult to remember lots of information from textbooks or the notes you have taken during your course. To make notes on a topic:

● read the topic carefully;

● highlight the key points in the topic;

● identify the important information in each point;

● decide how to summarise each point into a short sentence so that it is easy to remember.

Below is an example of how this could be done for Unit 4 - 'Barriers to good communication' from Topic 4.1.

## Topic 4.1, Unit 4 - Business Communications - Barriers to good communication - revision points

● Communication involves a message being passed from sender to a receiver. The message needs to be understood clearly and acted upon. This may not be the case if barriers to communication exist.

● Barriers to communication are factors that prevent successful communication. They can take many forms.

**Complex language** can hide the message. Senders and receivers must speak the same language, i.e. English, Italian or Arabic, to understand communications.

**Technical details** may not be understood by non-specialists.

**Inadequate feedback** may mean the sender does not know if the message has been understood. A reason for lack of feedback could be that part of the message is missing.

There may be a **lack of understanding of receivers' needs** because the sender does not take into account what the receiver wants, for example.

**Emotions** can distort the sending or understanding of a message if the sender or receiver are angry, upset or under stress.

A lack of **knowledge** may mean a message is incorrectly sent or misunderstood.

Poor **quality of information** can mean that a message is confused or difficult to interpret.

The right **medium** must be chosen to send the message, so that it arrives in the correct format and is understood.

A **lack of trust** of the sender may mean that the receiver does not believe the message is correct or accurate.

**Cultural differences** could mean that the same message is interpreted differently by people of different races or in different countries.

If the sender or receiver does not **listen**, a communication can be misinterpreted.

If the sender has a high **status**, people may take the message more seriously.

● Good communication is important in business for a number of reasons. If messages are not sent and received correctly and understood this can lead to problems such as:

– consumers not receiving the correct orders – they may be angry and the reputation of a business can be harmed

– employees not carrying out tasks efficiently – leading to delays and increased costs;

– employees being confused about what to do – they could become frustrated, angry and demotivated.

## Memory tips

In the examination you will need to remember important facts, information and data that will help you to answer questions. Some of these will simply be a list of terms, such as:

● the types of electronic communication;

● the business documents that can be created using word processing software;

● the stakeholders in a business.

Others might be a list of phrases, such as:

● the advantages and disadvantages of using the Internet;

● the factors influencing the creation of a simple website;

● the ways in which legislation affects web site design.

Different people remember in different ways. You might use some of the following methods to help you.

## Memory tips - Mnemonics

This is a word that is made up from the first letters of the terms you want to remember. Some well-known mnemonics in business studies are:

● PESTLE – the Political, Economic, Social, Technological, Legal and Environmental factors affecting a business;

● SWOT – the Strengths, Weaknesses, Opportunities and Threats facing a business;

● the 4 Ps of the marketing mix – Price, Product, Promotion and Place.

You can make up your own mnemonic for a topic. For example, to remember the types of communication media use the mnemonic SEWFVV – Sound, Electronic, Written, Face-to-face, Verbal and Visual (try to remember it as sew5).

## Memory tips - Visual presentation

Some people remember if the information is a picture or diagram. An example of a diagram that could be used to remember the internal and external shareholders of a business is shown below.

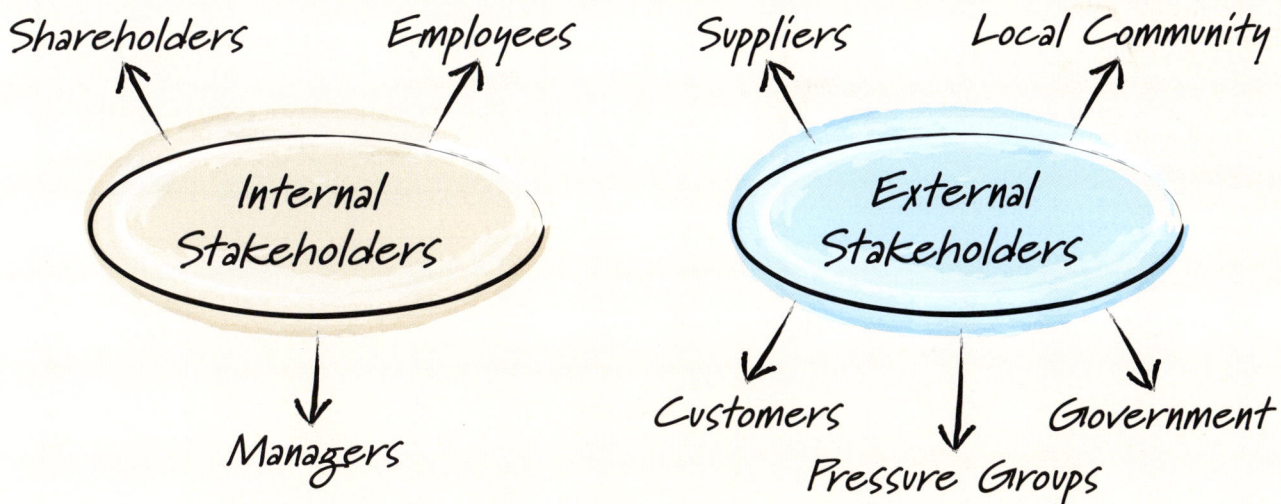

Internal Stakeholders: Shareholders, Employees, Managers

External Stakeholders: Suppliers, Local Community, Customers, Pressure Groups, Government

**More on the Active Teach CD**

# Know Zone

## Memory tips - Mindmaps

A mindmap is a diagram that records words and ideas and shows connections. At the centre of the map, or page, is the main word or idea. Flowing out from this main word or idea is a number of key words and ideas linked to the main word. Mindmaps are used in business. But you can also use a mindmap for your revision. Below is a mindmap outlining different communication media and their advantages and disadvantages.

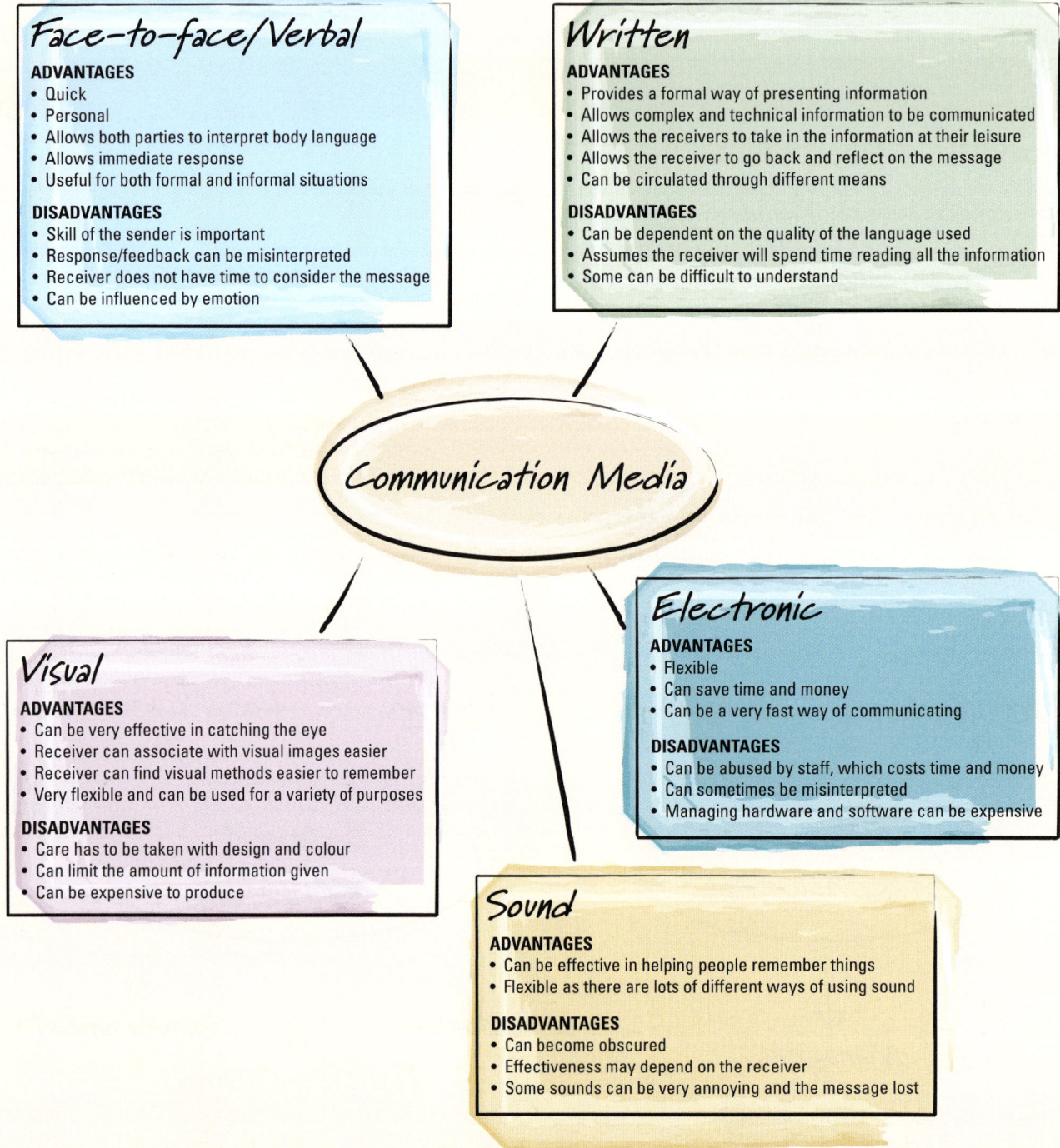

### Face-to-face/Verbal

**ADVANTAGES**
- Quick
- Personal
- Allows both parties to interpret body language
- Allows immediate response
- Useful for both formal and informal situations

**DISADVANTAGES**
- Skill of the sender is important
- Response/feedback can be misinterpreted
- Receiver does not have time to consider the message
- Can be influenced by emotion

### Written

**ADVANTAGES**
- Provides a formal way of presenting information
- Allows complex and technical information to be communicated
- Allows the receivers to take in the information at their leisure
- Allows the receiver to go back and reflect on the message
- Can be circulated through different means

**DISADVANTAGES**
- Can be dependent on the quality of the language used
- Assumes the receiver will spend time reading all the information
- Some can be difficult to understand

**Communication Media**

### Electronic

**ADVANTAGES**
- Flexible
- Can save time and money
- Can be a very fast way of communicating

**DISADVANTAGES**
- Can be abused by staff, which costs time and money
- Can sometimes be misinterpreted
- Managing hardware and software can be expensive

### Visual

**ADVANTAGES**
- Can be very effective in catching the eye
- Receiver can associate with visual images easier
- Receiver can find visual methods easier to remember
- Very flexible and can be used for a variety of purposes

**DISADVANTAGES**
- Care has to be taken with design and colour
- Can limit the amount of information given
- Can be expensive to produce

### Sound

**ADVANTAGES**
- Can be effective in helping people remember things
- Flexible as there are lots of different ways of using sound

**DISADVANTAGES**
- Can become obscured
- Effectiveness may depend on the receiver
- Some sounds can be very annoying and the message lost

# Don't Panic Zone

Once you have completed your revision in your plan, you'll be coming closer and closer to The Big Day. Many students find this the most stressful time and tend to go into panic-mode, either working long hours without really giving their brain a chance to absorb information, or giving up and staring blankly at the wall. Some top tips are shown here.

◗ Test yourself by relating your knowledge to business issues that arise in the news – can you explain what is happening in these issues and why?

◗ Get hold of past papers and the mark schemes for the papers. Look carefully at what the mark schemes are expecting of the candidate in relation to the question.

◗ Get hold of a copy of the Examiner's Report from the previous exam series. It contains lots of useful advice about where candidates performed well and where the main mistakes were. Learn from these. The Examiner's Report and past papers are often available on the awarding body Website – check with your teacher.

◗ Do plenty of practice papers to hone your technique, help manage your time and build confidence in dealing with different questions.

◗ Relax the night before your exam – last minute revision for several hours rarely has much additional benefit. A runner doing a marathon is unlikely to practice the night before by going for a quick 15 mile run. Your brain needs to be rested and relaxed to perform at its best.

◗ Remember the purpose of the exam – it is for you to show the examiner what you have learnt and understood about business. It is not a means of trying to trick you.

## Last minute learning tips for Business Studies

The week before the exam should be spent going through past papers. Look at each question carefully and compare question types. Make sure that you are familiar with the different types of question and you know the style needed to answer each question.

There will be **multi choice** questions or **objective test** questions. These ask you to make a choice from a series of options, such as 'Which **two** of the following are the **most important** in spotting a new business opportunity?' or 'Which of the following is a reason why customer service is so important to the success of a small business? Select **one** answer.'

There will be questions assessing your **knowledge** and **application** skills, such as 'What is meant by the term "stakeholder"?' and 'Identify **two** examples of secondary market research data in the passage.'

Certain questions will test **analysis** and **evaluation** such as 'Explain how a hierarchical structure in a business might make communication more difficult' and 'To what extent can a business be ethically responsible and profitable? Justify your answer.'

Try to devote some time to actually writing out the answers in the time period allowed to refine your skills. You can check your answers against the mark scheme to see how you would have performed. Make sure you understand what the command words are for each question and how they relate to the assessment objectives. For example, an 8 mark question might consist of 2 marks for knowledge, 2 for application and 4 for analysis and evaluation.

Remember that you can get full marks by answering in the space provided on the exam paper - it is not the amount you write but the quality and the extent to which you demonstrate the assessment objectives being targeted.

On the night before the exam, relax, give your brain a rest and try and do something you enjoy. Get to bed at a reasonable hour so that you can get a good night's sleep and be refreshed for the exam.

**More on the Active Teach CD**

# Exam Zone

## What to expect in the exam paper

The assessment for Unit 4 is through an examination which will last for one and a half hours. Students are required to answer all questions. There will be a total of 90 marks. The examination will be divided into three sections which include a variety of questions including:

● multiple choice questions;

● short answer questions;

● extended answer questions.

Sections B and C will consist of questions based on a scenario given in the examination.

## Understanding the language of the exam paper

| | |
|---|---|
| **Which of the following is... Select one answer** | You need to identify the correct response from a selection of options. |
| **Which two of the following are...** | You need to identify the two correct responses from a selection of options. |
| **Which of the following is most likely to...** | The key is 'most likely' – this means that there could be more than one option that is possible; you have to decide which is the most likely. |
| **Which of the following is not...** | This is a question asking you to spot the negative option from a list – read each option carefully. |
| **Fill in the blanks** | This may require you to complete some calculations in a table, for example. |
| **What is meant by...** | This requires you to give a definition of a key term in business studies – an example to help support the definition is usually worth giving also. |
| **Identify...** | This type of question requires only a one word answer or a short phrase or sentence – it is associated with knowledge and understanding and often requires the student to extract information from a context. |
| **State...** | Similar to 'identify' – again usually only requires a one word answer. |
| **Describe...** | Give the main characteristics of a topic or issue. |
| **Explain...** | Describe the issue, term etc, giving reasons or features. |
| **Analyse...** | Break down the topic or issue into manageable parts to help explain what is going on, how something works, what relationships may exist and what assumptions might be made. |
| **Assess...** | Offer a judgement on the importance, significance, relevance and value of something, with reasons why you have made such a judgement. |
| **Do you think...** | Asking you to make a judgement – which requires support and reasons to be given for the judgement. |
| **What is the most important...** | Another question asking you to make a judgement and offer support for the judgement. Explain why one factor is more important than another and why. |
| **To what extent...** | Is the issue very, very important/significant/, quite important/significant, moderately important/significant, not very significant/important at all – and why? |
| **Evaluate...** | Arrive at a judgement – with some support for your reasoning. |
| **Justify...** | Offer support and reasons for the judgement you have made – and why. |
| **Write a report...** | A report might consist of advantages and disadvantages, key features, summaries and judgements about the value of one option against others. |

# Exam Zone

## Meet the exam paper

This diagram shows the front cover of the exam paper. These instructions, information and advice will always appear on the front of the paper. It is worth reading it carefully now. Check you understand it. Now is a good opportunity to ask your teacher about anything you are not sure of here.

Print your surname here, and your initial afterwards and sign the paper. This is an additional safeguard to ensure that the exam board awards the marks to the right candidate.

Here will be the school's centre number.

Ensure that you understand exactly how long the examination will last, and plan your time accordingly.

Make sure you are aware of how many marks are given for each question and write to justify these marks.

Here you fill in your personal exam number. Take care when writing it down because the number is important to the exam board when writing your score.

In this box, the examiner will write the total marks you have achieved in the exam paper.

Make sure you understand what you are allowed to take into the exam and what you are not.

Make sure that you understand exactly which questions you should attempt and the style you should use to answer them.

Write your name here

Surname

Other names

Centre Number

Candidate Number

**Edexcel GCSE**

# Business Communications

Unit 4: Business Communications

Time: 1 hour 30 minutes

Paper Reference
**5BS04/01**

You do not need any other materials.

Total Marks

### Instructions

- Use **black** ink or ball-point pen.
- **Fill in the boxes** at the top of this page with your name, centre number and candidate number.
- Answer **all** questions.
- Answer the questions in the spaces provided
  – there may be more space than you need.

### Information

- The total mark for this paper is 90.
- The marks for **each** question are shown in brackets
  – use this as a guide as to how much time to spend on each question.
- Questions labelled with an **asterisk** (*) are ones where the quality of your written communication will be assessed
  – you should take particular care with your spelling, punctuation and grammar, as well as the clarity of expression, on these questions.

### Advice

- Read each question carefully before you start to answer it.
- Keep an eye on the time.
- Try to answer every question.
- Check your answers if you have time at the end.

*Turn over* ▶

N35642A
©2008 Edexcel Limited.
2/2

Edexcel GCSEs in Business          Sample Assessment Materials          © Edexcel Limited 2008   61

**edexcel**
advancing learning, changing lives

**More on the Active Teach CD**

# Zone Out

This section provides answers to the most common questions students have about what happens after they complete their exams. For much more information, visit www.examzone.co.uk

## About your grades

Whether you've done better than, worse than or just as you expected, your grades are the final measure of your performance on your course and in the exams. On this page we explain some of the information that appears on your results slip and tell you what to do if you think something is wrong. We answer the most popular questions about grades and look at some of the options facing you.

### When will my results be published?

Results for summer examinations are issued on the middle two Thursdays in August, with GCE first and GCSE second.

### Can I get my results online?

Visit www.resultsplusdirect.co.uk, where you will find detailed student results information including the 'Edexcel Gradeometer' which demonstrates how close you were to the nearest grade boundary. Students can only gain their results online if their centre gives them permission to do so.

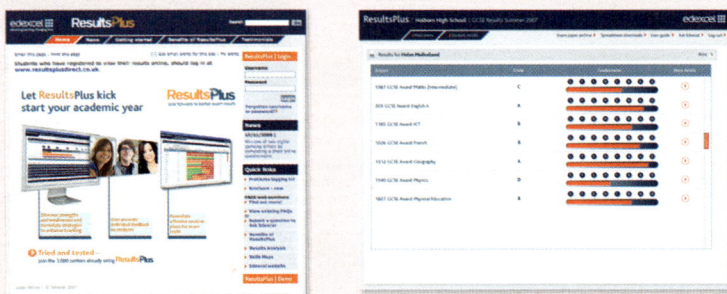

### I haven't done as well as I expected. What can I do now?

First of all, talk to your subject teacher. After all the teaching that you have had, tests and internal examinations, he/she is the person who best knows what grade you are capable of achieving. Take your results slip to your subject teacher, and go through the information on it in detail. If you both think that there is something wrong with the result, the school or college can apply to see your completed examination paper and then, if necessary, ask for a re-mark immediately. The original mark can be confirmed or lowered, as well as raised, as a result of a re-mark.

### How do my grades compare with those of everybody else who sat this exam?

You can compare your results with those of others in the UK who have completed the same examination using the information on our website at: http://www.edexcel.com

### What happens if I was ill over the period of my examinations?

If you become ill before or during the examination period you are eligible for special consideration. This also applies if you have been affected by an accident, bereavement or serious disturbance during an examination.

### If my school has requested special consideration for me, is this shown on my Statement of Results?

If your school has requested special consideration for you, it is not shown on your results slip, but it will be shown on a subject mark report that is sent to your school or college. If you want to know whether special consideration was requested for you, you should ask your Examinations Officer.

### Can I have a re-mark of my examination paper?

Yes, this is possible, but remember that only your school or college can apply for a re-mark, not you or your parents/carers. First of all, you should consider carefully whether or not to ask your school or college to make a request for a re-mark. You should remember that very few re-marks result in a change to a grade - not because Edexcel is embarrassed that a change of marks has been made, but simply because a re-mark request has shown that the original marking was accurate.

Check the closing date for remarking requests with your Examinations Officer.

### When I asked for a re-mark of my paper, my subject grade went down. What can I do?

There is no guarantee that your grades will go up if your papers are remarked. They can also go down or stay the same. After a re-mark, the only way to improve your grade is to take the examination again. Your school or college Examinations Officer can tell you when you can do that.

### Can I resit a unit?

If you are sitting your exams from 2014 onwards, you will be sitting all your exams together at the end of your course. Make sure you know in which order you are sitting the exams, and prepare for each accordingly – check with your teacher if you're not sure. They are likely to be about a week apart, so make sure you allow plenty of revision time for each before your first exam.

For much more information, visit www.examzone.co.uk

**More on the Active Teach CD**

# Index

Page references which appear in colour are defined in the Key Terms sections in each subtopic.